PERFUMED SLEEVES AND TANGLED HAIR

PERFUMED SLEEVES AND TANGLED HAIR

Body, Woman, and Desire in

Medieval Japanese Narratives

Rajyashree Pandey

University of Hawai'i Press

Honolulu

Printed in the United States of America

22 21 20 19 18 17   6 5 4 3 2 1

Library of Congress Cataloging-in-Publication Data
Pandey, Rajyashree, author.
   Perfumed sleeves and tangled hair : body, woman, and desire in medieval Japanese
narratives / Rajyashree Pandey.
      pages cm
   Includes bibliographical references and index.
   ISBN 978-0-8248-5354-9 (cloth : alk. paper)
  1. Japanese literature—To 1600—History and criticism.   2. Human body in literature.
3. Women in literature.   4. Desire in literature.   I. Title.
   PL726.117.B63P36 2016
   895.609'3561—dc23

                                                                                    2015018723

ISBN 978-0-8248-7518-3 (pbk.)

Composition by Westchester Publishing Services

For Sanjay and Nishad

Contents

Acknowledgments

This book has travelled with me across many homes and continents. A happy consequence of having completed it is that I now have the opportunity to thank friends, colleagues, and institutions that have contributed to bringing this project to fruition. Many institutions—Goldsmiths, The School of Oriental and African Studies, the Japan Society of U.K, Tallinn University, Sydney University, University of Queensland, University of California, Irvine, Kyoto University, Osaka City University, Nichibunken, and the conferences of the European Association of Japanese Studies—provided me with opportunities to present my work, and the discussions that ensued have helped in the writing of this book.

Aruna Hardy, Tom Harper, David Martin, Hilary McPhee, Machiko Midorikawa, Robert Morrell, Joshua Mostow, Adrian Pinnington, Miika Pölki, Hitomi Tonomura, Fumiko Umezawa, and Michael Watson read one or more chapters of the book. I am grateful to them for their many constructive comments and criticisms.

Stella Amachree, Chris Berry, Francisco Carballo, Teresa Castelvetere, Francesco Cavallaro, Sudhir Chandra, Novi Djenar, Harriet Evans, Frieda Freiberg, Kiichi Fujiwara, Mike Green, Branwen Gruffydd Jones, Nikhil Hardy, Helen Harris, Beryl Langer, Chris McPherson, Bee Chin Ng, Kaori Okano, Greg Patching, Anita Ray, Rachel Ross, Geetanjali Shree, Chiharu Takenaka, Lidia Tanaka, Ali Ishtiaq, aka Tinku, and many other friends and colleagues offered much-needed encouragement and support. I thank them all.

Work on this project began at the School of Asian Studies at La Trobe University in Melbourne. The university gave me small grants to facilitate research trips to Japan and made available sources not readily accessible in Australia through interlibrary loans.

Life in Melbourne brought many pleasures, providing both a rich intellectual life and the intimacy of friendship. I owe much to the evenings spent with Leela Gandhi and Pauline Nestor; parathas, whiskey, and animated discussions fuelled some of the ideas that have found their way into the book. Michael Dutton and Deborah Kessler gave me a second home both in Melbourne and in London, generously creating a space of happy conviviality and lively discussions over many years. Dipesh Chakrabarty has been a dear friend for a long time. His commitment to staying in touch regardless of the vast distances that have separated us has provided me with a model for friendship. John Hocking and Hilary McPhee's support and encouragement have been invaluable.

The move to London and to Goldsmiths, University of London, opened up new challenges and opportunities to engage with scholars who were not specialists of Japan. I would like to thank Goldsmiths for providing me with a genuinely interdisciplinary environment, and the Politics department for supporting my work through its annual research funds.

The School of Oriental and African Studies gave me a second institutional home by offering me a visiting fellowship with access to its library and seminar series. I thank Steve Dodd, Lucia Dolce, Christine Guth, Robert Khan, Tim Screech, Kristin Surak, and Sarah Teasley for making me part of their fun-filled community of scholars working in London on things Japanese.

London also brought another unexpected pleasure in the form of a visiting professorship at Tallinn University, where I was given the opportunity to develop my ideas among intelligent and erudite teachers and students. My thanks in particular to Rein Raud and his postgraduate students Alari Allik, Aleksi Järvelä, and Miika Pölki for nights of drink and conversation. Raji Steineck generously invited me to give a series of postgraduate seminars at the University of Zurich, which proved to be productive and stimulating.

Needless to say, this book would not have been possible but for the extended support offered to me over many years by institutions, libraries, teachers, and friends in Japan. Rikkyō University, Sophia University, and Waseda University provided institutional affiliation and much-needed academic stimulation and help. A research grant from Kokugakuin University and from the Japan Foundation Endowment Committee made available funding that supported work on the first two chapters of the book. A visiting fellowship at the Graduate School of Asian and African Area Studies at Kyoto University in late 2013 allowed me to finish the final draft of the manuscript.

I would like to thank Konishi Jin'ichi, Mizuhara Hajime, Yamada Shōzen, and Amino Yoshihiko, who, at different points, have guided and inspired my work. It is with some sadness that I acknowledge my debt to them, for they are no longer with us. I learned a great deal about Indian and Japanese Buddhism through my conversations with Nara Yasuaki in the picturesque surrounds of Shantiniketan (Rabindranath Tagore's university). Wakita Haruko has been a long-standing mentor and friend. I would like to thank her for coming to Pondicherry with me and introducing Adhishakti's theater group to the world of Noh.

I am grateful also to Araki Hiroshi for translating some of my earlier articles into Japanese, thereby opening up new connections for me with young scholars in Japan.

Kate Wildman Nakai's rigorous engagement with my work and her constructive suggestions and criticisms, coupled with her generous encouragement, helped me bring the project to completion. Gaye Rowley has been a long-standing intellectual companion. What she has done exceeds the requirements of the closest of friendships. I cannot thank her enough for reading endless iterations of various chapters, offering wise counsel, meticulous comments, and editorial advice. The Matsui family as always has been the solid bedrock that makes extended trips to Japan feel less lonesome. Aki san, Sonoe san, Miki and Kana, I could not have done it without your hospitality and love.

My thanks to Pamela Kelley, my editor at the University of Hawai'i Press, who has been supportive of this project throughout, and to the anonymous readers of the book, who made helpful suggestions and comments. Hank Glassman, Christina Laffin, and Joshua Mostow patiently answered my queries about illustrations and copyright. Aya Hino found herself carrying the unexpected responsibility of helping me with the technicalities of getting the manuscript ready for submission. I thank her for being part of my affective world, and for her patience in the face of my ineptitude.

My extended familial network has offered not only unconditional love but also uncompromising intellectual challenges. My brother-in-law, Friedhelm Hardy, first introduced me to the pleasures of intellectual work. In leaving us all prematurely, he has deprived me of many conversations that remain unfinished. My sister, Aruna Hardy (Didi), has, as always, been a bedrock of unconditional support and love. My niece Monika Green and her boys, Joseph and Sebastian, have been delightful distractions from the solitude of academic work.

The Seth family has played an important part in my intellectual work. Sushil set the standard, making ideas an intrinsic part of family gatherings. Suman has been the younger brother I never had; his affection, to my delight, has often taken the form of wonderful culinary creations! Vanita has been with this book from the very beginning. She was the one who first recognized that I had a question that could eventually become a project; her intellectual curiosity and astuteness, and above all her enthusiasm and energy have been infectious and have infused this project with a sense of fun.

More than anyone, my son, Nishad Pandey, has wanted me to write this book and has encouraged and cajoled me into finishing it. He has also brought new pleasures to my life by including me in his musical world. I cannot thank him enough for his unwavering support and love.

Some debts are hard to express let alone repay. Sanjay Seth has been at the receiving end of my enthusiasms and anxieties about the book on a virtually daily basis. His patience has been unflagging and his generosity boundless. He has read and reread the manuscript in its manifold iterations and brought to it his acute insights and criticisms. This book is for him and Nishad.

Introduction

This book emerges out of a series of questions that began to trouble my reading of medieval Japanese texts. Increasingly, some of the conceptual vocabulary that had long served as my cultural compass began to feel inadequate to the task of guiding me through the world that I encountered in these works. What did it mean to interpret texts that belonged to a time and place far removed from my own through categories such as the body, sexuality, woman, and gender that were either wholly modern inventions or that had, in some way, come to be inflected with significations that belong to our own historical time? What was to be done about the anachronistic readings that sometimes resulted from such a transposition of categories, given that there could be no unmediated access to these distant and unfamiliar worlds? It seemed to me that the dogged empiricism that for the most part has dominated the discipline of medieval Japanese literary studies within which I was schooled left little room for reflecting on these questions.

What follows is a brief excursus into the ways in which my ideas shifted through the course of this intellectual journey; it also serves to explain why this book explicitly thematizes some of these reflections and seeks to revisit well-known texts from a new vantage point. When I first began to think of the centrality of the theme of amorous affairs and their consequences in a work such as the *Tale of Genji* (*Genji monogatari*), I assumed that the body would be at the center of erotic and amorous desire. And yet, rather than enfleshed, corporeal beings, presented in their fullness, what I found instead were vaguely defined, elusive, shadowy figures, which hardly registered as bodies. Recognizing the presence of the body in a work such as the *Genji* required a reexamination of the assumptions that undergird our understanding of it as a category; it meant taking account of the fact that the body that we take to be universal was in fact a product of a particular history that belonged to the post-Renaissance West, and hence necessarily inadequate for making sense of the bodies that appeared in medieval Japanese texts.

Rethinking the body also called for a reconceptualization of the notion of desire. So ingrained was the idea of desire as a subjective, psychological state, possessed by every individual, driven by hormones or the unconscious—take your pick—that it seemed natural, at first, to speak in terms of desiring subjects actively in search of objects.[1] And yet, what struck me as noteworthy in my readings of texts such as the *Genji* was not so much the presence of individuals as active agents, imbued with initiative and will and driven by desire, but rather the existence of a force field of erotic and affective sensations—the disposition of things, to borrow François Jullien's evocative phrase[2]—which created a pleasurable ambience and generated in those who came under its spell a propensity, if you will, to react and respond. The ideal *irogonomi* (one who was fond of and receptive to amorous and erotic play) of medieval texts was best understood, I began to think, not as a Don Juan, in search of objects to satisfy an insatiable innate desire, but rather as one who, by displaying a heightened receptivity to situations, which had an erotic and affective potential, was ideally placed to fashion him/herself as an exemplar of the proper performance of courtly love.

The words *omoi* and *koi,* which appear frequently in Japanese poetry (*waka*) and romance narratives (*monogatari*) to signal the feelings of desire, love, and longing that followed fateful encounters, made no distinction between the physical and emotional aspects of love, for carnal desire and romantic love did not constitute two separate experiences; moreover, what mattered was not the individual as the bearer and generator of feelings but rather the ebbs and flows that shifted the movement of love and desire. Desire in Japanese texts, it seemed to me, needed to be disentangled from modern discourses of sexuality, which assume that it emanates from an individual subject, who is constituted through his/her sexual identity.

Thinking about courtly love in this way led me to reflect on the way in which the notion of desire (Sk. *rajas, kāma;* Jp. *yoku*) was understood in Buddhist discourse, where it was identified as the root cause of all suffering, producing a deluded sense of attachment to a world whose nature is essentially insubstantial and transient. Buddhist canonical texts provide an elaborate taxonomy of the five desires (*goyoku*), which are associated with the five senses (*gokon*), things seen, heard, smelled, tasted, or touched. They often speak of sex as one of the most easily aroused of all desires. It is for this reason that the six sexual attractions (*rokuyoku*) arising from color, form, carriage, voice (or speech), softness (or smoothness), and features are to be especially resisted by those leading a monastic life.

Buddhist understandings of desire, at first glance, seemed closer to our modern conceptions of it in that they seemed to assume some notion of it as a natural predisposition, which makes some people particularly susceptible to its temptations. However, upon closer examination, it became apparent that different forms of desire in Buddhism were understood as products of the stimulation of the senses from without, rather than as the workings of a natural, innate drive. Furthermore, sex, in this schema, far from being privileged as the master drive animating all aspects of human action, was only *one* among many other stimulants such as food, material wealth, sleep, and so on, all of which generated desires that could obstruct the path to enlightenment.

If desire and the body in Japanese texts appeared different from our commonly held conceptions of them, this did not mean that they were different in the same way in all the texts I encountered. A courtly tale of romance such as the *Genji* produced a different conception of love and desire from the one articulated in popular Buddhist tales, which sought to caution against the dangers of desire and deluded attachment. In contrast to courtly texts, where the body barely registered as a physical presence, it took an exaggerated form in the more popular tales of the time, where it became the site of laughter. The extraordinary heterogeneity of meanings that swirled around the body and desire even in works that were composed in the same historical period, and what is more, on occasion, even by the same author, pointed to the inadequacy of a reading practice that treated these terms as transparent reflections or representations of a "reality," which lay outside them.

Konishi Jin'ichi's conceptual framework, which distinguishes between literary texts that are high and refined (*ga*), as opposed to the low, unrefined, and mundane (*zoku*),[3] helped in part to account for the differences in the nature of the bodies and the forms of desire that were produced in medieval texts. Courtly prose narratives and poetry, for example, which were both composed, recited, and read by a small, aristocratic, and self-referential group that prided itself on its refined sensibilities, observed a certain decorum and restraint with regard to the quotidian functions of the body—no descriptions of sex or defecating, for example, appear in a text such as the *Genji*. There is only one scene in the whole tale where women are shown eating. The more popular tales in the *setsuwa* genre, on the other hand, ranged more widely from edifying tales of Buddhist salvation to entertaining and humorous stories about sex, food, and defecation.[4]

Useful as Konishi's framework was for thinking about the ways in which aesthetic sensibilities and conventions came to be established, it did not account for the discernable differences among texts that belonged, say, to the same refined world of *ga*, when they addressed similar themes. Why was the language of love and sex in poetry written in Chinese (*kanbun*), for example, so different from the one found in *waka*, composed in the same period, even when both forms of writing belonged undoubtedly to the world of high culture? A consideration of genres proved to be productive for it allowed for a greater emphasis on formal codes and conventions, which, once established, circumscribed both the kinds of topics that could be thematized as well as the language and style in which this could be done. Generic conventions were a useful way of thinking about the differences between poetry composed in *kanbun* as opposed to that composed in Japanese: while perfectly acceptable to speak about the pleasures attendant on sexual intercourse in the former, it would be unthinkable to do so in the latter.

Needless to say, genres did not function as watertight categories. Often, in many texts from the Japanese repertoire, what stood out more than the difference between genres were the ways in which they overlapped, and the degree to which each genre incorporated, reproduced, and transformed styles and meanings derived from other genres. Indeed, the very application of genre theory to Japanese classical and medieval texts with any rigidity was bound to be problematic, given that the genres that we use as taxonomical devices are, for the most part, nineteenth-century inventions, created in an attempt to find equivalent categories in Japanese writing to those that were supposed to exist in the West.[5] Genres then were useful only as provisional groupings of texts, which bore a family resemblance to one another, but which maintained wide kinship networks with other texts. It was by turning to this dialogic relationship between genres that it became possible to understand how diverse texts were linked with one another, and how a common repertoire of materials and meanings circulated from one discursive sphere to the next.

Notwithstanding the heterogeneous nature of texts that follow different generic conventions, these texts are bound together by a sense of a shared conceptual universe, which is shaped by the Buddhist epistemic framework that dominated the medieval age.[6] The writings that are the focus of this study span the periods from the tenth to the fourteenth centuries. Following William LaFleur's expansive definition of the term "medieval" as signifying "that epoch during which the basic intellectual problems, the most authoritative texts and resources, and the central symbols were all Buddhist,"[7] I have chosen, as a heuristic device, to refer to works belonging to very different historical periods—from the Heian period classic the *Tale of Genji* to tales from the Muromachi age (*otogizōshi*)—as medieval. I do so on the grounds that, for all their differences, what gives these texts produced across different time frames a certain coherence is that none of the questions they raise, the issues they problematize, or the resolutions they offer can be properly understood outside of the Buddhist paradigm that frames the discursive possibilities available to them.

If Buddhism was indeed at the center of medieval hermeneutics, it raised another question about the problem of speaking of Buddhism and literature as if they were two distinct entities. For was there not a certain anachronism in assuming that the "religious" on the one hand and the "secular" on the other were natural ways to separate human activity? The medieval age was one where engaging in worldly writing and following the Buddhist Way had not yet emerged as two entirely disconnected spheres of activity, and where it was perfectly possible for priests to be poets.

This did not mean, of course, that no distinction was made between the two. Often, texts engaged in a self-conscious thematization of the relationship between the two—the problem, for example, of how literary and artistic practices stood in relation to the Buddhist goals of detachment and renunciation was a recurring concern in many works across different generic boundaries. What engaged writers of the medieval period was not the question of whether they were related but rather how they were connected and intertwined, and what forms those connections could take. Irrespective of their particular orientation, medieval texts shared in the view that worldly activities (of which writing was one), far from belonging to an autonomous domain, were in some way integrally connected to the question of religious awakening and enlightenment.

Generic conventions mattered in that they created diverse possibilities for the ways in which these questions, themes, and ideas could be manipulated, but it was always within the parameters of a Buddhist worldview that the playing out of these possibilities occurred. While certain texts may strike us as more literary than others, how we draw the line between a literary and religious work in the context of the medieval period is perforce an exercise in arbitrariness. Scholars of literature (*kokubungakusha*) in Japan, who claim that Kamo no Chōmei was a litterateur par excellence, and Buddhist scholars (*bukkyōgakusha*), who argue the opposite, insisting that he was first and foremost an exemplary Buddhist, often fail to arrive at a common meeting ground precisely because academic disciplines have tended to create a sharp distinction between literature and Buddhism of a kind that would have been unrecognizable to medieval writers like Kamo no Chōmei himself.[8]

Thinking about the body, desire, and Buddhism, it became immediately apparent that it was not possible to consider these terms without addressing the "woman" question. Many of the contemporary debates around the construction of the body, gender, and sexuality have rightly identified "woman" as central to the ways in which these categories have come to be constituted. This is reflected in academic writing on medieval Japan, where there has been a growing interest in the role and status of women in Buddhism and in the ways in which their bodies and sex have contributed to their inferior status and to their denigration in medieval society.

In my own work, reflecting as it did some of these concerns, I saw little need to question or unpack "woman" itself, for the term seemed self-explanatory; medieval texts were self-evidently populated by people who were clearly identifiable as either male or female. While granting that the category "woman" needed to be pluralized given the diverse range of female figures that appeared in medieval texts, that "woman" derived her meaning through her sexual and gendered differentiation from man was a "truth" that occasioned little reflection. And yet, increasingly this reading of "woman," as constituted exclusively through her body and sexuality, came to feel like a distorting and debilitating constriction that foreclosed many of the questions that the rich and multivalent significations afforded to her in medieval texts appeared to raise.

Was sexual difference always the ground upon which the distinction between women and men rested, irrespective of time and place? Was woman necessarily a category produced in terms of a stark opposition and antagonism to man, or could the two be understood correlatively, as more fluid, complementary forces? Was it possible to speak of woman either as agent or victim in medieval texts without questioning what we mean by agency? How did the textual figure of woman, often mistakenly conflated with the "real" woman, function as a topos in classical and medieval texts, and what was the nature of the diverse significations that came to be assigned to her in different contexts? These were some of the questions that I sensed might prove useful for the line of inquiry I sought to follow. What was required, it seemed to me, was a new journey through the familiar terrain of medieval narratives, traversing a different path, which could generate new questions. Along the way, the very category "woman" began to lose its familiar bearings, and "man" and "woman" revealed themselves to be fluid and malleable, and hardly reducible to their biological differences.

While recognizing that categories such as the body, woman, sex, and desire do not necessarily resonate in the same way as they do for us in the texts that are the subject of this study, insofar as these categories form our grid of intelligibility and are born of our own historical conditions, they are, inescapably, the necessary starting point of our hermeneutic endeavors, for how can we find a neutral vantage point from which to gain access to the "true" meaning of texts far removed from our own times? In approaching Japanese medieval texts through concepts that are modern inventions, I hope, in a Gadamerian spirit, to follow a reading practice that stays open to the otherness of these distant texts and to the challenges they pose to the prejudices that inevitably guide the questions I ask of them. In so doing, the categories that inform this book, I suggest, will do double duty, by providing new insights into distant texts far removed from our own worlds, while at the same time pointing to the parochialism that is at the heart of our own thinking.

Chapter One explores the foundations of the categories body, woman, sex, and agency, which have become part of our analytical apparatus today, to demonstrate that these terms were born of a specific history that belongs to Europe, and therefore that they are not amenable to being transposed unquestioningly to other lifeworlds that do not share the same history. I trace the genealogy of these terms to highlight how their meanings, even in the West, far from being fixed, underwent significant changes from the medieval to the post-Renaissance periods. Their status as categories of analysis has now become so thoroughly naturalized within academic discourse that often their historical contingency has tended to be obscured, such that they have universal purchase across the chasms of time and place. It is this claim to universality that I seek to challenge by considering what the body, woman, sex, and agency might mean in the context of medieval Japanese texts that were shaped by religious, philosophical, and medical traditions, whose core assumptions diverged significantly from those that obtained in the West.

The remainder of this book is an attempt to flesh out, through close textual readings, the claims that I make in the opening chapter. The weight of an extraordinary exegetical tradition notwithstanding, I have made so bold, despite being a nonspecialist in this field, as to start with two chapters on the *Tale of Genji.* This is because the *Genji,* it seems to me, is the perfect site for revisiting some of the assumptions about the body, desire, and love that have guided contemporary readings of this text. In the last few decades there has been a widening recognition of the importance of the body for an understanding of the workings of love and desire in the *Genji.* Often thematized under the appellation *shintairon* (debates on the body), this scholarship has contributed significantly to our understanding of how the body and the senses are engaged in the play of eroticism in the text.[9]

However, there has been little interrogation in these academic writings of the term *shintai* itself as a category of analysis. For *shintai,* a modern invention, is not a neutral concept but already carries assumptions about the body that derive from contemporary Western understandings of it. A reorientation whereby we shift our focus from *shintai* to *mi,* the term for body used in medieval texts, allows for an exploration of a radically different form of embodiment, which registers as an unfamiliar and virtually unrecognizable presence in the *Genji.*

If the body in the *Genji* is not given substance through flesh and bones, what are the attributes that endow it with beauty and ugliness, and how does it become the site of desire? What do we make of the centrality of clothes, hair, and calligraphy in the text, and how is the performative body linked to the ebb and flow of love and desire? My central argument in Chapter Two is that the body is most powerfully apprehended, not through a description of its individual attributes but rather through robes and hair, which are metonymically linked to the body and self, and imbued with both the material and psychic qualities that make for personhood. And furthermore, that it is not the body as an object but rather as a phenomenological entity, engaged in performance, that registers most palpably as a presence, and that it is this body that has the power to evoke strong erotic and affective attachments.

Chapter Three explicitly revisits the interplay of the body and eroticism in the *Tale of Genji,* to argue that far from belonging to the realm of a pure aesthetics, untouched by questions of power and politics, the body and its performative modes are always imbricated in the complex hierarchies of gender and social rank, which are central to the text's construction of beauty and love. Erotic and affective intensities in the text are fuelled not by imagining relationships through the grid of equality and similitude but through differences of status and gender. At the same time, as I hope to demonstrate, neither status nor gender works as a stable and immutable category in the *Genji;* it is precisely this fluidity that makes it impossible to isolate either one as a causal explanation for the workings of power in the text. There are constant slippages and it is through an examination of the interplay of gender, social status, and bodily performance within specific erotic configurations that I seek to demonstrate how power works as a productive force both for generating and dampening affect and desire in the text.

Chapter Four turns specifically to the question of how to read "woman" in medieval texts. As I indicated earlier, it has now become almost de rigueur to talk about the fundamental misogyny of Buddhism and to suggest that the body and sexuality became the primary sites for discriminating against women in the medieval period. Focusing on the persona of one important figure, the Heian poet and lady-in-waiting Izumi Shikibu, I explore the creative reimaginings that were effected on the textual body of this famous literary figure in the narratives about her that proliferated in the Kamakura and Muromachi periods.

The object here is not to uncover the real Izumi Shikibu, an impossible task, but to explore the ways in which her life story came to be imagined in later ages to thematize major questions and debates that were central to the medieval age. It is my contention that the many imaginative fictions created around Izumi, and the failings and proscriptions enunciated under her name, served a larger end, namely to illuminate a set of questions regarding the nature of poetry, sexual attachment, and enlightenment, which were deemed to be of the utmost importance by medieval poets, priests, laymen, and nuns—men and women alike. Izumi Shikibu in medieval narratives is made to stand in for much more than solely "woman" and it is her role as a favored topos, incorporating questions to do with poetry, sex, and enlightenment that I seek to explore in this chapter.

The final chapter serves to challenge further the idea that medieval texts produced a unitary vision of women, and that Buddhism sought either to victimize or empower them. I do so by examining discursive formulations around one Buddhist practice, *fujōkan,* or meditating on the foul and impure body. Here I seek to demonstrate how medieval texts weave together widely divergent readings of the topos of *fujō,* and by extension, of the body, woman, and desire. By focusing on the centrality of intertextual exchanges in the production of *fujō* in medieval texts, the chapter problematizes any straightforward distinction between "literary" and "Buddhist" perspectives on this theme.

In the *Genji,* for example, the experience of death and dying leads not to detachment and renunciation but rather, in line with the generic requirements of a romance narrative, a reworking of a Buddhist theme such that it produces instead a heightening of erotic and affective intensities. Two texts in the *setsuwa* genre, *Hosshinshū* (Collection of Tales of Religious Awakening) by Kamo no Chōmei, and *Kankyo no tomo* (Companion in Solitude) by Priest Keisei, which deal explicitly with the theme of *fujō,* at first glance qualify as straightforward "Buddhist" works, which seek to preach, through *fujō,* the truth about the impurity of the body. However, by following the protocols of *waka* and *monogatari,* these texts, I argue, offer readings of *fujō,* which are often at odds with those found in canonical Buddhist texts. By considering at some length how one Buddhist topos is transformed in different texts and contexts, I hope to reveal how the body, woman, attachment, and desire, far from being stable and unchanging, are in fact products of the intermingling of a variety of generic conventions and protocols.

The final short epilogue revisits the questions that are at the center of the book by asking what emendations we need to make to our categories in order to render texts from the medieval period intelligible to us. Drawing upon a small number of anomalous tales, which defy easy categorization, I bring them into conversation with the broader hermeneutical questions that have preoccupied scholars working in other times and cultures in a variety of disciplines. What does it mean, for example, that in many a medieval tale, sex is the preserve not only of humans, but that animals and vegetables too are also accorded a place in sexual intercourse? The alien and unsettling nature of these tales may serve to highlight the impossibility of subsuming the Japanese medieval world within our own.

CHAPTER ONE

Rethinking Body, Woman, Sex, and Agency in Medieval Japanese Narratives

Body

Even in the modern West, the body, far from being a term whose meaning is self-evident, is in fact a hotly contested concept that has become the subject of considerable debate in the last few decades.[1] Nietzsche's invective against Western thinkers on the grounds that "they despised the body; they left it out of the account: more, they treated it as an enemy,"[2] whether true or otherwise, seems to capture succinctly how the body has come to be thematized, a century later, in an entirely new field of research devoted exclusively to it. What we might call the "body question" has spawned a bewilderingly diverse array of scholarly works in the Western academy, much of it a reaction against its own philosophical tradition, which it accuses of neglecting the body, or worse, showering it with abuse.[3]

The argument runs that for all the differences between, say, Greek philosophy and medieval Christian theology, Western thinking has been marked by a profound dualism in which the body has come to be constituted in opposition to the soul/spirit/mind, and that as the unprivileged term in the binary, it has for a long time been subjected to systematic neglect or denigration. That Western thought is dualistic; that the body has always been in a position of subordination to the soul/mind; and that woman, who is identified with the body, has been positioned as inferior to man—these, it would appear, are some of the constitutive features of the Western tradition.

Many scholars have sought to complicate and pluralize this particular account of the Western tradition.[4] They have argued, for instance, that Descartes's writings marked a seminal moment in Western thought when a radical break occurred with medieval conceptions of the body—for the first time, both the body and nature became passive and inert entities, disconnected from the cosmos and divorced from the soul, and the mind became the sole repository of thought and of mental processes.[5] It has also been suggested that new developments in the sciences in the late sixteenth and seventeenth centuries in Europe brought about new ways of imagining the body. The practice of dissection, for example, led to the body being understood as a machine, which could be observed as an object, and analyzed as a discreet anatomical entity, made up of muscle, flesh, bones, viscera, and a skeletal structure.[6] Regardless of the differences between those who believe that the body has been reviled since the dawn of Western civilization and those who argue that it is with Descartes that the body became loaded with negative connotations, what is indisputable is that "body studies" is born of the need to subvert and challenge the discourses on the body produced by that tradition.

Until recently these debates on the body have tended to veer between two poles. On the one hand, there are those who insist that there is an ontological basis to the body prior to social meaning or linguistic signification. In this view the body is first and foremost constituted through biology, which forms the physical substrate upon which different social and cultural meanings come to be inscribed. As Chris Shilling puts it, "we 'all know' that the body consists of such features as flesh, muscles, bones and blood, and contains species-specific capacities which identify us as humans."[7] While granting that the specific features of the body may change over time—bones grow brittle, hair thins, the flesh sags—the body, understood as a biological entity, is in this view universal, regardless of time or place.

On the other hand, the social constructivist approach has sought to move away from an emphasis on the physicality of the body and the attendant dangers of biological reductionism, by focusing instead on the body's symbolic forms, and on the meanings with which it is inscribed in different cultural and historical contexts. This approach makes the idea of the body as a given, with fixed meanings, unsustainable. For, like childhood, death, madness, sex, and so on the body too now has a history, and far from being universal and stable, bodies are seen as particular, contingent, and changing formations that are historically and culturally variable. We recognize, not least because of the work of Michel Foucault, that the "body" is historically constructed and that it varies even in the history of the West.[8]

These contesting claims, for all their differences, have been framed within the mind/body and nature/culture debates, which have haunted Western thought since the eighteenth century.[9] Given that these debates belong to a history that has little to do with the world of medieval Japan, is there a way in which we can speak about the body in medieval Japanese texts, without reproducing some of the core presumptions that have gone into its making as a category? I would suggest that the body/bodies we encounter in these texts begin to acquire some semblance of intelligibility only when they are inserted within the context of the larger epistemic framework of what one might loosely call the East Asian medical, religious, and philosophical traditions within which they are produced.[10]

The medieval Japanese world shared with its European medieval counterparts a conception of the cosmos in which the human and natural order were integrally linked. This was a world in which men, women, animals, and gods inhabited a common cosmological order, often intermingling promiscuously with one another; gods were active agents and nature was a living presence, yet to be reduced to a passive object, to be given meaning by the Man of Reason. The relationship between the body and mind was not the site of troubled debates in the East Asian traditions, in the way that it was in Western thought. The question that preoccupied Daoists and Buddhists alike was not whether the body and mind were connected (for it was assumed that they were); it was rather how the two could work most effectively together as a mind-body complex. The body, in this framework, was not reducible to muscle, flesh, and bone. Nor was it inert and passive matter, divorced from the mind. Mental and affective processes were understood as integral parts of its materiality, and the body was envisaged as a psychosomatic process, "something done, rather than something one has."[11] "Thought" did not function as the other of "feeling" or emotion, nor was form the antithesis of matter. In the medieval Japanese tradition, the word *kokoro* referred to both heart and mind; the verb *omou* encapsulated both feeling and thinking,[12] and the word for love, *koi,* made no distinction between the physical and spiritual aspects of love. Both material and mental/emotional processes were central to the constitution of a meaningful body/self.

In Daoist religious and medical discourses, for example, the body is understood as linked to material and psychical processes alike through psychophysical matter or energy (Ch. *qi;* Jp. *ki*), and the energy arterial pulses (Jp. *myaku*). Together, they constitute the life force of the self. It is as if the distinction between the internal and the external does not apply, for the body presents itself as a perfectly transparent entity in which the viscera and organs are openly displayed. We are far removed here from the Western practice of dissection in which "the viscera are truths buried in and under dense flesh, and fat and bone . . . secrets that have to be uncovered."[13] This has implications for how the body is imagined and visualized in literary and visual texts.

Mark Elvin's observation that "Chinese pictures of the human body, clothed or semi-clothed, are—to Western eyes—meagre, schematic and inadequate,"[14] highlights the limits of the intelligibility of the body when it fails to correspond to the one that was produced in post-Renaissance Europe, and to which we are heirs. As John Hay observes, the literary and pictorial traditions of the premodern period in China have no "image of a body as a whole object, least of all as a solid and well shaped entity whose shapeliness is supported by the structure of the skeleton and defined in the exteriority of swelling muscle and enclosing flesh."[15] It is the principle of linearity underlying the energy arterial pulses, he argues, that "provided the most convincing way of embodying the kind of structures that gave the body both its existence and its life."[16] This insight is highly suggestive for, as I argue in the following chapter, it is precisely through robes and hair, whose linear forms are analogous to the energy arterial pulses through which *qi* flows, that the body is imagined in a text such as the *Genji*.

Invoking the historicity of the body is not to claim that different cultures or periods produce one single, stable body at any given moment. We cannot speak of a "medieval Japanese body," any more than we can of a "Renaissance body" or a "modern body." For there is always a multiplicity of bodies in play in any given historical period, and both how they appear and the significations with which they are imbued are subject to the particular contexts and generic conventions within which they are discursively produced. In a courtly text such as the *Genji*, for example, the aristocratic body is imagined as a phenomenological entity whose presence is felt, not through elaborate descriptions of its physical appearance but rather through its stylized, performative modes. *Setsuwa* tales, by contrast, which speak to a more heterogeneous audience, produce bodies that engage not only in the refined arts of poetry and music but also in the more vulgar activities of everyday life—sex, eating, defecating, and the like. And yet, the heterogeneity of these bodies notwithstanding, it may be possible to identify something that makes them recognizably akin one to the other, an affinity that rests on certain core presumptions that have gone into their making and which are grounded in the epistemic framework within which they are produced.

Let me explain further what I mean. In medieval Japanese pictorial scrolls (*emaki*), the body is made palpable not through the depiction of the body as an enfleshed entity but rather through robes and through what one might call bodily comportment. The twelfth-century *Genji monogatari emaki* (Picture Scroll of the *Tale of Genji*), for instance, seeks to capture the world of the *Genji* through the immobile postures of noblemen and women, whose faces, indistinguishable one from the other, are sketched minimally through the stylized technique of *hikime kagibana* (dashes for eyes and hooks for noses), registering little by way of emotions, thereby conveying the innate grace, self-possession, and nobility that are meant to inhere naturally to those who belong to the upper classes (Figure 1).

It is for this reason that by representing Kumoinokari in an upright position, as she approaches Yūgiri to snatch a letter from him, the scroll is able to suggest that something dramatic and out of the ordinary has occurred—Kumoinokari is in a state of agitation caused by her suspicion that Yūgiri is involved with another woman. The bodies of ordinary men and women in picture scrolls of the twelfth century such as the *Saigyō monogatari emaki* (Picture Scroll of Life of Monk Saigyō) or *Ban Dainagon emaki* (Picture Scroll of the Courtier Ban Dainagon), on the other hand, are marked by movement and action and exaggerated facial

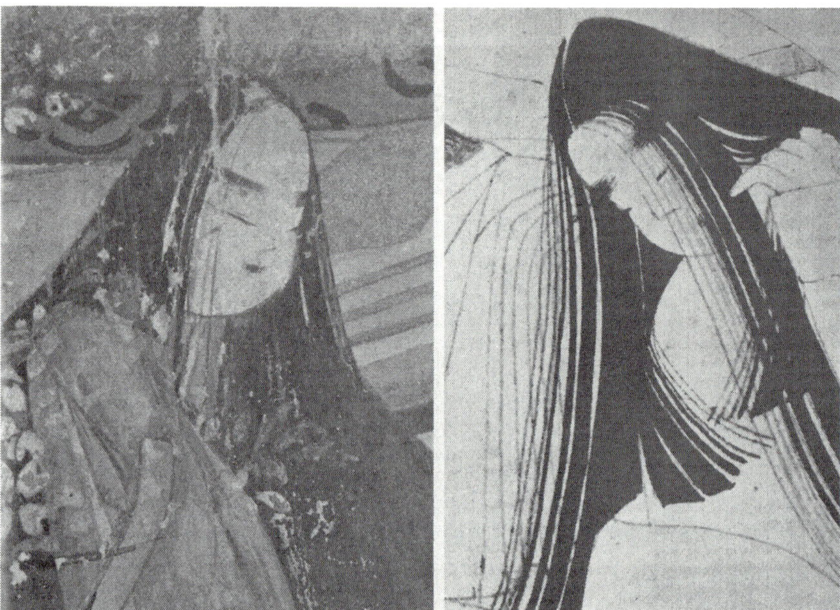

Figure 1. *Genji monogatari emaki* and *Makura no sōshi emaki* (Picture Scroll of the *Tale of Genji* and Picture Scroll of the *Pillow Book*), 12th century, Tokugawa Art Museum, Nagoya.

expressions and gestures, signaling the vast distance that separates them from aristocrats, whose self-contained bodies are manifestations of their supposed mastery of themselves and the world (Figure 2).

The diverse bodies that appear in the Japanese pictorial tradition are only sketchily outlined and are often delineated in a stylized manner. However, regardless of the differences of gender and class, the bodies in *emaki* are repositories not only of the physical but, equally importantly, of the particular mental/social attributes that are believed to characterize different social groups.

The bodies in Buddhist sculpture, which draw on Indian figural traditions, appear to conform to some recognizable principles of physiology and anatomy, that is to say, with conventions with which we are familiar. The guardian figures that flank the gates of temples, protecting the buddhas within, are depicted in a lifelike manner with strong, muscular physiques and bulging veins. Likewise, the statues of Zen masters, like Ikkyū, are cast in a realistic mode: hair, believed to be his own, is implanted on Ikkyū's head, eyebrows, and chin.

At first glance, what distinguishes the bodies in *emaki* as opposed to the figures in Buddhist sculpture is that the latter are depicted realistically. And yet, this

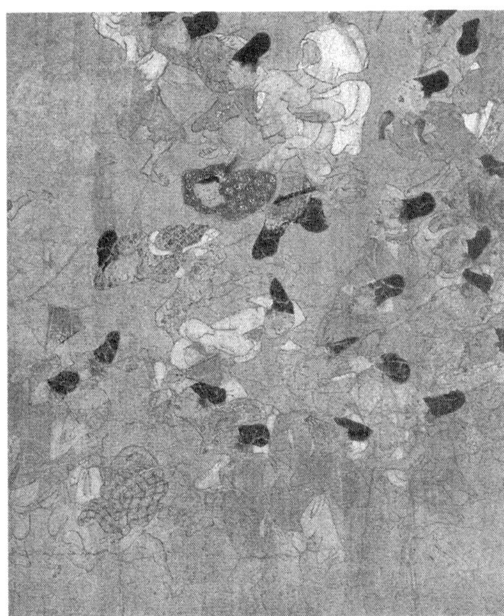

Figure 2. *Ban Dainagon emaki* (Picture Scroll of the Courtier Ban Dainagon), 12th century, Sakai Collection, Tokyo.

lifelike quality is not an attempt at a representation of the human body as an object, whose entirety is captured through the precision and accuracy of its anatomical detail. The statues of the patriarchs and guardians are not symbolic representations of holy figures, for they are not envisaged in a mimetic mode. Rather, they are seen as living embodiments of a life force made manifest in material form (Figure 3). What appears to have interested Japanese sculptors was the best way to capture "the energy and power by which the dharma—invisible, inconceivable, unknowable—mystically projected itself into the everyday world."[17]

The bodies in these lifelike statues are seen as repositories not only of the physical but also the psychic attributes that go into the constitution of personhood. Sculpted statues of illustrious monks often contained their ashes, thereby suffusing them with the presence of these masters.[18] Likewise, in using Ikkyū's own hair to produce his statue the aim was not to create the most perfect likeness of Ikkyū; it was rather to inject the spirit of this holy figure into his statue. When medieval Buddhist tales speak of people going to the temple to pray before the Buddha, it is telling that they do not refer to the "Buddha image" (*butsuzō*), a word, which is a more recent invention.[19] That no distinction was drawn between the image and what we would call the "actual" Buddha tells us something about the way in which the image was seen as making palpably manifest the body-mind of

Figure 3. The Indian Patriarch Mujaku by Unkei, 13th century, Kōfukuji, Nara.

the sacred figure. The eye-opening ceremony (*kaigen*) that accompanied the consecration of a statue or sacred object to formally declare it as being animated by its spirit constituted an institutionalized ritual, which reflected the commonly held understanding that statues, paintings, stupas, mandalas, and the like were all living sacred presences.

What Buddhist statues exemplify is a conception of the body in which the body does not exist separately from the mind; the two are integrated into a kind of mind-body (*shinshin*) complex that functions as a single psychosomatic entity.[20] Life or existence in Buddhist thought is made up of the five elements or aggregates (Sk. *pañca skandhā*) of which the first, *rūpa-skandhā*, is form or matter, related to the six organs of the senses (Jp. *rokkon*), while the other four are associated with mental faculties. The distinctions of form and matter or body and mind have no valence here given that the six sense organs in the Buddhist framework include not only what we would categorize as physical attributes—the eye, the ear, the nose, the tongue, and the body—but also the mind/consciousness.[21] Both the figures drawn in *emaki* and the holy figures that appear in Buddhist sculpture, for all their differences, share in the assumption that the body is not mere matter and that the heart/mind is integral to its very constitution.

Neither materialist arguments nor social constructivist claims are entirely adequate to conceptualizing the body in medieval Japanese texts. The social constructivist move to historicize the body is critical for recognizing that the meanings with which the body is imbued are not universal or constant, and that they are inseparably linked to the social and historical contexts within which they are produced. However, historicization need not lead to a denial of the materiality of the body, as in some extreme versions of culturalism, where the body seems to disappear altogether in a fug of discourse. It is worth taking the corporeality of the body seriously, while acknowledging that what constitutes the body's materiality is itself subject to variability. The body we encounter in the East Asian tradition is not an anatomical entity made up of flesh, bones, and muscles. Furthermore, its materiality already carries within it the psychological dispositions and mental attributes that go into the formation of the body and personhood. Even the physical substrate of the body, which we assume to be universal, is itself historically variable. The choice between the natural versus the social/cultural body that is on offer in these debates is part of a very particular history that belongs to the West, and hence necessarily inadequate to thinking about other traditions of embodiment, in which the body is imagined outside of the well-worn binary of nature and culture. It is this, to us, unfamiliar body that I seek to explore in this book.

Woman/Sex/Gender

It has become part of our common sense to assume that what distinguishes men from women is sexual difference and that this difference is biologically determined. As feminist scholars have long argued, sexual difference has been the basis for justifying the idea that women are innately inferior to men. It is by associating them first and foremost with their reproductive functions and, by extension, with their bodies, that women are seen as being naturally different from and, by implication, lesser than men. The profound somatophobia that characterizes Western thought, feminists argue, has had serious implications for the ways in which women have come to be positioned within this tradition. For if the body has been seen as a danger to the operations of reason, or to the salvation of the soul, then it follows that woman, who is synonymous with the body, and with unreason, is marked as inferior to man and to everything else that is valorized in that moral and ethical system.[22]

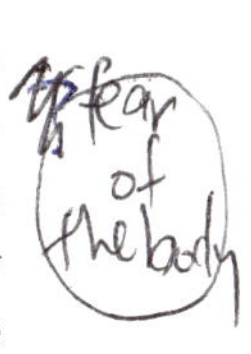

Scholars who have challenged the idea that the body has uniformly been the site of denigration or neglect have had to do so by questioning the assumption that there has been a constant and unchanging alignment, in all of Western thought, between male and soul/mind, on the one hand, and woman and body, on the other. Caroline Bynum, for example, has argued that gender imagery in medieval Europe was marked by an extraordinary degree of fluidity and that "medieval theologians and natural philosophers often mixed and fused the genders, treating not just the body of Christ but all bodies as both male and female."[23] Thomas Laqueur, likewise, has demonstrated how until the seventeenth century, what prevailed was the "one sex model," in which men and women were seen as having essentially the same sexual organs—no linguistic distinction was made between ovaries and testicles, which shared the same name, and what distinguished men from women was merely that men's genitalia lay on the outside while those of women were inverted.[24]

The one-sex model did not presume that men and women were equal: it was taken for granted that the male constituted the normative model of which the female was simply an inferior version. What is significant, however, was that neither the body nor its sexual organs were the privileged sites for the justification of particular social arrangements. To be one's gender, to occupy a particular place within the social order as a man or woman, was itself seen as part of the natural order. Both what we would call "nature" and "culture" were cut of the same cloth, part of the same divine scheme, and there was no need to turn to the body for affirming this preordained hierarchy. Sex did not function as a biological category any more than gender did as a social one.[25]

The epistemological shift from the medieval world that transformed the body into a machine, whose workings were seen as being governed by the laws of nature, and whose constituent elements could be observed and analyzed through the practice of dissection, also brought with it new ways of understanding woman, sex, and gender. By the eighteenth century, men and women came to be seen as radically different, and the isomorphism of their anatomy gave way to new theories about the incommensurability of their sexual organs. Among the many causes for this there is no doubt that political developments loomed large. When hierarchy was taken as given, and seen as part of the natural order of things, there was no specific need to justify the differential and unequal treatment of women. But in an age that began to speak of equality and liberty as being the "natural" state of man, a rationale was needed for why this equality and liberty did not pertain to women (or indeed to those of different "colors" or "races").[26]

The radical difference that was seen to separate men from women now came to be grounded in a biological truth, a fact of nature that could not be challenged or changed.[27] In place of the fluid gender boundaries and a belief in the interchangeable and permeable nature of the sexes that had characterized medieval thinking, sex now became the defining characteristic that marked woman off from man and served as the overarching explanation for differences between men and women tout court. For those who sought to contest this view, the chief argument became that sexual or biological difference did not determine intellectual and other differences. The category "gender" emerged precisely as a way of arguing that social roles were not necessarily bound to sex; gender, it was argued, was "a social category imposed on a sexed body."[28] 

The feminist project of the sixties and seventies assumed the naturalness of sex, while challenging the social roles that were seen as following from "natural" biological differences. It was in this context that what we now call "women's history" emerged; at the heart of the political project of feminism that informed this history was a radical questioning of the androcentric biases of history writing and an attempt to rediscover stories about women, which had been silenced and written out of historical accounts. There emerged in these writings an autonomous women's sphere within which women were active agents, alive, and even rebellious; the task of retrieval meant that women from the past could now be re-presented as the foremothers of and role models for women today.

The project of writing women's histories reverberated across many other disciplines. Religious traditions came to be interrogated by feminist scholars who sought to expose the patriarchal and misogynous assumptions that they saw at the very heart of these traditions. Feminists who were also Christians were the first to undertake a thoroughgoing critique of the scriptural texts and to put forward a radical new exegesis of the Christian tradition from a feminist perspective.

It is not surprising, then, that in many ways the work done on women and Buddhism mirrors some of the same concerns and strategies that were first adopted by feminists working within the Christian tradition.[29] It is within the tradition  of sixties' and seventies' feminism that much of our current work on women in medieval Japanese studies is squarely located. Narratives about nuns, princesses, courtesans, and women poets are now seen as central to the way in which we tell the story of both Buddhism and literature in medieval Japan.[30] Likewise, there has been considerable scholarly activity to discover women and their activities in historical records.[31] Rescuing women who until now were "hidden from history" has undoubtedly helped us rethink the nature of medieval Japanese society, of its religious practices, and of women's place in them.

The project of retrieval, however, has been fraught with problems. Underpinning much of our work is the assumption that "Woman" is a self-evident, transcendental category that subsumes within its fold the diverse multitude of women who appear in medieval texts. We may grant that women in this period did not all belong to the same social class and that there was a vast gap in their material and cultural circumstances. In place of "Woman" we may choose the more encompassing "women" as our category of analysis. And yet, this lowercase, pluralizing amendment still leaves us trapped in an ahistoricism whereby the very processes through which the category came into being is left unexamined. What is at issue here is obviously not the existence of real women, for who would deny that claim? It is rather the assumption that women constitute a self-evident and distinct category, and that women recognize themselves everywhere and at all times as so constituted. Many of the questions and doubts I have raised above have been central to recent debates within feminism itself; it is a measure of our inattentiveness to these ongoing conversations that we continue to speak of women in medieval Japanese texts as if they formed a natural, pregiven identity, in little need of further examination.[32]

What is more, we assume unreflexively that men and women in medieval Japan were merely versions of us moderns, and that for them, like us, the sexed body was the single most important and overarching site of difference between men and women. And yet, what are the grounds for claiming that men and women, regardless of time or place, have always been seen as being constituted through the differences between their sexual organs? Neither the "one-sex" model that prevailed in the West until the seventeenth century nor the sexual dimorphism that informed subsequent understandings of the body are necessarily applicable for interpreting how "male" and "female" came to be constructed in premodern China and Japan. As Charlotte Furth argues, classical Chinese medical texts, which formed the basis of Japanese medical theories, conceived of the feminine (*yin*) and masculine (*yang*) principles as complementary aspects of the body, which were seen to interpenetrate both men and women. The ideal body was the androgynous one, which held together both elements *yin* and *yang* in perfect balance. In Chinese medicine "healthy males and females, when seen as a fertile couple, formed the matching *yin yang* opposites of homologous gender."[33]

In this schema, not unlike the one that obtained in medieval Europe, sex and gender, which are premised upon a division between natural attributes and social roles, had little meaning given that "the categories of male and female were understood as both natural and social, and their bodily powers were given spiritual significance as fitting microcosmic participants in a universal order."[34] It is for this reason that social relations were seen as mirroring the same principles that applied to the body and to the cosmos. "Male" and "female" were understood as complementary rather than mutually opposed, antagonistic forces. This did not imply, of course, that the two were equal: the male principle was the normative one and necessarily superior, but the perfect balance of the two was seen as central to producing harmony in both natural and social relationships.

For all the differences between medico/philosophical texts and literary creations, what marked the textual tradition of the medieval period in Japan was that "man" and "woman" made sense only when imagined in relation to others within the society to which they belonged, rather than as autonomous and transcendental entities, whose meanings were fixed and immutable. It was often as mothers, wives, and daughters, rather than as women qua women, that they were identified in texts. Rather than as individuals, it was their status and position in society at large that determined the manner in which they came to be known. In the *Tale of Genji*, for example, Onna Ichi no Miya, Onna Ni no Miya, and Onna San no Miya are introduced to us in terms of their social status and their relationship to each other as the first, second, and third imperial princesses, respectively. That they are women is not without relevance, but what their names signal is the fact that they are siblings, born of an impeccable lineage.

If we consider the semantic range of the word *onna* (woman) and *otoko* (man), it is clear that it was conceptually fluid, carrying many significations, which were always contingent upon context.[35] It is only within the specific context of amorous encounters that men and women in the *Tale of Genji* appear simply as *otoko* and *onna*, without any reference to their kinship status or rank. Even here, however, what these terms signify is not generic man and woman. Through its use of the terms *otoko* and *onna* the text evokes those suspended moments when intense emotional and erotic possibilities unfold, bringing into play *young* men and women who are still of an age when they can participate in the secular world of amorous sport, before their inevitable withdrawal from a life of worldly pleasures and attachment. For example, Murasaki is referred to as *himegimi* in the Aoi chapter. It is when the text suddenly transforms her into *onnagimi* and Genji into *otokogimi* that it becomes clear that their union has been consummated.[36] Likewise, it is when Yūgiri puts all his energies into trying to convince Ochiba no Miya to give in to his advances that the text transforms him from Taishō (Commandant), the social rank he holds, to simply *otoko*.[37] In the *Genji*, it is in that moment when amorous union takes place that *otoko* and *onna* erase the particularity of the two lovers in question, recasting them as figural sites of love, longing, and amorous desire.

In the world of the *Genji* and *waka* poetry, animals and plants are also metonymically associated with *otoko* and *onna*—morning glory (*asagao*), for example, is the face of a female lover in the morning; the child who is stroked (*nadeshiko*) is at once a flower as well as a girl, who is much loved and raised into womanhood by a man, while *ominaeshi* (maidenflower) functions both as flower and "maiden."[38] Through a thick web of connections the deer is figured as male, while the bush clover, for whom it/he pines, is associatively linked to the female.

What is striking about the flora and fauna, however, is that they are not treated as symbols or representations of real men and women. Everything that exists within nature and the cosmos—animate and inanimate alike—is organized around a set of correspondences, and male and female is one among many ways of imagining relationships that are complementary to one another.

Onna in the medieval lexicon is a world removed from the modern word for woman/women, *josei,* which was coined in the Meiji period and which, as the character *sei* demonstrates, was founded on new biological understandings of men and women as constituted through their sexuality.[39] There is little to suggest that in medieval Japanese texts sex was "natural" while gender was socially learned and "constructed." It is this sense of the term "gender," understood not purely as a social construction, as opposed to the biological truth of sex, that I seek to maintain when I use it as an analytical category in the book. Gender, in this context, I see as a kind of script, and it is the specificity of the gendered performance, that is to say, the particularity of the script that is enacted, that gives substance to the categories "male" and "female" in medieval texts. This is what makes it possible for a male poet to slip seamlessly into the persona of the waiting female, and allows even a monk who has ostensibly renounced the world to enact the role of a woman pining for her lover.[40] While acknowledging that "textual cross-dressing" was less available to women than it was for men in courtly texts, I maintain that what it meant to be a woman in a text such as the *Genji* or the *Pillow Book* (*Makura no sōshi*) was not predetermined by her sex, and that gender as a performative act always left open the possibility of deviating from script, thereby creating polyphonous voices, which can only provisionally be recuperated under the sign "woman."

Women and Buddhism

I have suggested above that in texts such as the *Tale of Genji,* "woman," far from being framed as a transcendental category, is endowed with different meanings, which are always contingent upon context, and that in these texts, being a woman is not a function of her body's sexual attributes but rather something that is tied to the enactment and performance of the protocols that give gender some semblance of stability. But what then of Buddhist canonical texts and popular narratives often used for proselytizing the faith, which identify certain characteristics as intrinsic to women, and sometimes claim that these attributes constitute an impediment to the attainment of enlightenment? For, as we know, women are often seen as being burdened by the five obstructions;[41] they are afflicted by particularly jealous dispositions; and their bodies are marked by impurities connected to menstruation and childbirth, which call for special injunctions prohibiting them from entering sacred places.

Scholars have focused precisely on these negative representations of women to argue that Buddhism is discriminatory toward women, and that the portrayal of women as inferior to men is a structural feature of its beliefs and practices. Indeed, part of the project of reinscribing women into patriarchal historical and religious narratives has entailed not only an investigation of the hidden and unacknowledged role played by women in shaping Buddhist doctrines and practices but also an exposure of the power structures that have been instrumental in their discrimination and exclusion.

Many of the debates regarding Buddhist attitudes to women rest on contending claims that seek either to establish Buddhism's misogyny or else to argue for its inherent egalitarianism. The claim for egalitarianism can take different forms. The fact that women often appear in Buddhist narratives as bodhisattvas and other enlightened beings is offered in support of the argument that Buddhism fundamentally holds women in high regard. Another approach has been to acknowledge Buddhism's decline into misogyny by historicizing the different phases of Buddhism, claiming that Buddhism's origins were pure and unsullied and that it became antiwoman only when it became corrupted by influences that were extraneous and antithetical to the core beliefs of its religious system. These claims, for all their differences, rest on certain shared assumptions that merit closer examination.

Buddhism is often treated as if it were a single, unitary, purposeful, and highly anthropomorphized category (rather than as a heterogeneous set of doctrines and practices) that either consciously or unconsciously seeks to impose its will on women. The fact that Buddhist texts speak of women's impurity and sinfulness, or of their power to arouse men and trap them in the web of deluded attachment, is offered as incontrovertible proof of the fact that Buddhism holds an essentialist view of women as constituted through their sexual organs. In a curious circularity, the critique of Buddhism as a religion that reduces women to their sex is made precisely by invoking the same master code, sexuality, that gives substance and cohesion to the category "woman."[42]

And yet, is there sufficient evidence in the texts themselves to suggest that women formed an identifiable group that cohered around the specificity of their sexual attributes? The word in the Japanese medieval lexicon that corresponds to the term "body," *mi,* like the word *shintai,* which is used today to signify the physical body, refers to the bodies of human beings and animals as well as to the life force that animates these beings. *Mi,* however, makes no distinction between the physical body and what we might call the psychic, social, or cultural body; indeed, *mi* extends beyond the body to signify a self, understood not as an individual subject, or autonomous agent separate from society, but rather as one that is meaningful only as a social entity. It is for this reason that one of the most common usages of the term *mi* is to signify a person's status or standing in the world. We are far removed here from modern conceptions of the individual, as a lone figure, abstracted from society, and often in opposition to it. When medieval texts speak of *onna no mi* they mean more than the physical and sexed body that makes for womanhood; for both her mental and emotional attributes as well as her relationship to others as a social being are involved in the constitution of what we might call the female body/self.

The body in the medieval context was not something set in stone, where the distinction between man and woman was predetermined by their respective sexual characteristics; neither the body nor nature was seen as inert and passive matter with immutable attributes. This was of profound significance with far-reaching consequences, for it meant that medieval bodies were granted transformative powers that rendered the boundaries between gods, humans, and beasts porous and fluid. Both within canonical texts as well as in popular narratives, women and their bodies became shape-shifting forms that defied any consolidation of "woman" as a stable entity.

If the Lotus Sutra made rebirth as a man one of the conditions for attaining enlightenment,[43] the Vimalakirti Sutra argued that viewed from within the Buddhist doctrine of nonduality, neither maleness nor femaleness could be seen as innate or stable characteristics, thereby attesting to the provisional nature of gendered identities.[44] In many Buddhist texts, women who lure men into the trap of attachment are revealed to be bodhisattvas, and beautiful women turn out to be fox spirits or demons, seamlessly crossing the boundaries between the human and nonhuman worlds.[45]

"Woman" in the Buddhist schema was at once singled out by a particularity that marked her as different. She was hindered by the five obstructions; her beauty was dangerous for men who had chosen the path of renunciation; her body was marked by the impurities of childbirth and menstruation. At the same time, woman could never be an unchanging and essentialist category, always fixed in the same way. For all bodies, even those of women, far from being "the flat, horizontal, immovable foundation of physical fact: sex,"[46] were conceptualized as active agents that could defy common expectations and perform miraculous transformations, thereby attesting to the power of the Buddhist faith.

That women were positioned as different from men, and that they were not their equals, is beyond dispute. This does not, however, render Buddhism misogynist, if by that term we mean a conscious and willful hatred of women by men.

In a world that was both naturally and socially (understood not as two separate realms) hierarchically ordered, Buddhists assumed that women were lesser than men, and there was little need to justify this "truth" by making women the objects of sustained attack through polemical treatises and learned disquisitions. While it is true that women's shortcomings and sinful dispositions were often used in Buddhist discourse, what these writings sought to highlight was not women's inferiority to *men* but rather the nature of the profound hurdles that had to be overcome in order to attain salvation. In other words, "woman" served as a kind of placeholder, who made possible the playing out of questions and solutions that were central to the Buddhist project.

Buddhist texts creatively used the topos of "woman" (marked by particular shortcomings and failings, but only provisionally so), as a skillful means, a *hōben*, if you will, to demonstrate the miraculous powers of the Buddhist teachings, which made enlightenment possible for all beings. In the process, what they revealed, through the topos of woman, was the temporary and provisional nature of all that seemed real in the mundane world of *samsāra*. This may be one way of reading the drama that unfolds in the Devadatta chapter of the Lotus Sutra, in which one of the Buddha's disciples, Sāriputra, expresses doubts about the eight-year-old daughter of the dragon king possessing the necessary requisites for attaining Buddhahood on the grounds that the female body was a "filthy" thing, subject to the five obstructions. It is by overturning this narrative and recounting how the dragon girl swiftly transforms herself into a man and eventually achieves Buddhahood that Manjusri demonstrates the shifting boundaries between men, women, dragons, and buddhas. The rhetorical tour de force acquires its particular potency from the use of "woman" as a particularly graphic instance of the ways in which conventional and supposedly unchangeable realities can be overturned and reversed.[47] It is in this sense that the figure of "woman" is structurally central to the soteriological aims of the Lotus Sutra.

Discussions about women in *setsuwa* narratives, while ostensibly about women, also suggest an order of inquiry in which the central point of interest is not women qua women. What might be the best way to make one's way in this world, and ensure one's salvation in the next; how to outsmart one's partner; how to make sense of events that befall one; what might be learned by being attentive to the intricate workings of karma? It is these mundane predicaments, attendant on living in the world of *samsāra*, that often find expression through narratives about women. Their pedagogical value goes beyond proselytizing exclusively to real women, for the textual figure of woman in these tales is a powerful reminder to men and women alike of the miraculous transformations that faith can effect.

Agency

I have argued that imputing egalitarianism or misogyny to Buddhism is based on the assumption that women constitute a self-evident category and that they recognize themselves as such, and hence work in their own interests as *women*. Let me return again to the project of "retrieval," which presumes the existence of a female subjectivity, which is under constant threat by the workings of Buddhism. Once "retrieved," woman presents herself in many guises: she sometimes appears to be able to mobilize her agency heroically and act in ways that challenge the attempts by Buddhism and patriarchy to degrade her as a *woman;* at other times, sadly, as a creature of false consciousness, she is complicit with Buddhism's ideological agenda, or simply a passive victim of it. The project of unveiling women's agency, empowerment, and resistance is always haunted by the doppelganger of women's oppression, victimhood, and, worse, their own collusion with patriarchal values.[48]

How we then judge medieval texts that are seen as offering these conflicting perspectives becomes an exercise in arbitrariness. To sustain the idea of Buddhist misogyny it is imperative to show that women are oppressed. At the same time the emancipatory project, built into feminism, demands that women be seen as agents, actively fighting oppression. If the texts themselves are resistant to either of these interpretations, then extratextual evidence is often mobilized to secure the argument—texts here are often treated as little more than ideological reflections of a reality that lies outside of them. In each case what is left unexamined is the concept of agency itself.

As I have argued earlier, the medieval world was populated by gods, buddhas, men, women, and animals, all of whom consorted together as active agents within a shared cosmological order. Humans had yet to be privileged as the sole bearers of agency, with gods and buddhas explained away as "projections," or manifestations of the human mind.[49] In the medieval universe, gods and buddhas were often the central actors who instigated, inhibited, or mediated the actions taken by human beings. Our privileging of human agency bears the marks of our particular history—modern liberal thought presumes the existence of a subject who has complete political and moral autonomy, and who is naturally predisposed to seek freedom. Liberal notions of freedom presuppose the existence of a free will, which operates independent of social and religious customs and traditions, such that both a challenge to these traditions or complicity with them are to be read as emanating from a woman's own desire or will to be liberated or dominated.[50] Agency is often treated as conceptually interchangeable with the idea of resistance against relations of power and domination. Even when female agency is not expressly articulated, or is hard to locate, the actions of women are read as signs of a "nascent feminist consciousness"[51] that may produce effects that challenge or disrupt the dominant male order.

Underlying modern conceptions of agency is the assumption that behind every act there is the presence of an autonomous individual, who has the innate desire to strike out against the norms of her society. What if we were to let go of this anachronistic assumption, and were to decouple agency from liberal thought?[52] Would it not then open up a space for imagining alternate readings of agency that do not presuppose the validity and universality of conceptions and norms based on modern notions of autonomy and freedom? It is this, from our point of view, limiting notion of agency that is worth reinstating in considering women's actions in medieval Japanese texts.[53]

The tradition of taking the tonsure is a case in point. In medieval times, both men and women, regardless of their status in society, or the circumstances that led to them taking religious vows, shared in the aspiration to become lay nuns or monks at some stage in life, in the hope of retiring from the world of social obligations and preparing for a favorable death. Furthermore, there were many forms that tonsure could take, requiring varying degrees of seclusion from the secular world. The category "nun," for example, incorporated a wide variety of religious practices and living arrangements, ranging from women who continued to live within the household without taking part in sexual activities and procreation to those who lived in complete seclusion.

Scholars have singled out nunhood as one of the sites upon which both Buddhism's misogyny and women's response to it came to be played out in the medieval period. Some have seen the act of tonsure as an act of resistance to patriarchal social arrangements, and in that sense as an illustration of female agency. Fighting against the constraints that society imposes on them, women who take the tonsure are seen as exercising their right to decide and to choose how they want to live. Nunhood, in this reading, becomes the space of freedom.[54] Others, working within the same conceptual framework of agency, have claimed precisely the opposite, arguing that the practice of tonsure was proof of women's oppression and subservience in the face of patriarchal domination and Buddhist misogyny.[55] Or, in another manifestation of their subjection, nuns are seen as traitors who betray their own sisters by subscribing to patriarchal norms. As Bernard Faure puts it, "What if they [nuns] were only the 'spokespersons' of a dominantly male tradition and so complicit in the silencing of female voices?"[56] If we work within the framework of liberation or subjection, the particular reading that we favor becomes little more than an arbitrary choice. No one would deny that a woman taking the tonsure served a variety of ends, ranging from testing the affections of a lover whose attentions had flagged to withdrawing altogether from a relationship that had gone wrong.[57] Becoming a nun may well have been a consequence of unfortunate social circumstances, but to see these acts as manifestations of either empowerment or victimhood reduces medieval players to little more than versions of our own selves. If personhood in medieval Japan is located in the social, and if it is not imagined as an individual and secular identity, then agency in this context would have to be disentangled from nineteenth-century liberalism, which speaks an altogether different language of choice and self-determination.[58]

This would allow us to read women's tonsure as providing a socially available model for escaping from the trials of worldly life as well as engaging in the performance of pious and virtuous deeds that work not against but rather in conformity with the traditions and practices of medieval society. It would also allow us to recognize why tonsure, which bespoke a faith that enabled both men and women to give up what they and the world to which they belonged held most dear, resonated deeply within medieval texts. For tonsure in religious/literary texts, regardless of the circumstances that may have led to the act, elicited both admiration and sadness in equal measure.

Taking the tonsure and leading the life of a nun suggests the expression of a very different modality of action, which lies outside of the category of agency understood as resistance. Often the proper enactment of a pious and ethical life prescribed by that tradition meant "losing" rather than "finding" oneself. It was for this reason that stories about men and women who had performed acts of great self-sacrifice were retold in various forms over many centuries. The many versions of the Karukaya legend, for example, which focus on the religious quest of a father who abandons his family to become a monk at Mount Koya, and his wife and son who set off in search of him, gain their poignancy from the suffering and ultimate death of the wife and the sorrow of her husband, who now turned monk, cannot but be moved by the power of worldly ties.

That such stories, which were often narrated by Kumano *bikuni,* had such extraordinary appeal was in no small measure because they spoke to men and women alike; by dramatizing a tension that was central to becoming a good Buddhist, they brought to life the pain and suffering that were the necessary conditions for breaking the bonds of attachment. The forms that suffering and pain took were undoubtedly gendered and it was the stylized enactment of these conventional roles that had the power to produce affective intensities. However, religious acts for both men and women involved abandoning the self—understood not as an individualized entity but rather as something inextricably tied to clan and kin by bonds of affect and duty—and reconfiguring it through surrender to the ascetic discipline and/or devotion required by Buddhism.

When we seek to reveal the misogynist and patriarchal assumptions undergirding medieval Japanese texts, we are not surprised to find our claims vindicated in works written or promoted by men, for it is assumed that men, for the most part, speak for their sex, in the process maligning or denigrating women, their oppositional other. More puzzling and inexplicable for us are those texts written by women that depict their own kind as passive beings, who lack the ability to shape their own destinies. For passivity implies subjection. Often an explanation for this curious lack of female agency in a woman-authored text is found by turning to the world outside of it: polygamy and other oppressive social arrangements during the Heian period are made, for example, to account for women's helplessness in texts such as the *Genji*. In medieval times, this text came to be associated with the sin of falsehood and had to be defended from the charge of lasciviousness and immorality by arguing that its author was in fact a bodhisattva who wished to alert readers to the dangers of amorous attachment.[59] Today, we no longer take seriously the medieval defense of this text. Modern interpretations of the text are equally products of their times and are often situated in secular assumptions, which revolve around questions of the inequality of social and gender relations. It is not surprising then to find that some of the more extreme denunciations of the sexual politics that the text reveals have come from such secular readings, which argue that Genji was a rapist, and that it was the cruelty of men toward women that Murasaki, the author, sought to lay bare in her work.[60]

We may have distanced ourselves from the more extreme readings of our own times that caricaturize Genji as a rapist,[61] but the ascription of either resistance or passivity to women continues to color our readings of the female characters in the *Genji*. However, as I have argued, agency understood purely in terms of *human* will and consciousness, acting upon the world, independent of gods and buddhas, does not adequately explain why so many of the protagonists of the tale view the circumstances that unfold in their lives less as consequences of their deeds in their present lives, but rather as manifestations of karma from previous existences.

There is also a problem with conflating gender relations in the real world with their textual figurations;[62] in medieval *waka* poetry, *setsuwa*, and *monogatari*, *otoko* and *onna* often function not as literal representations of man and woman as fixed and unified categories but rather as variable performative stances that make possible a diversity of modes through which love and longing can be played out. The man who visits and the woman who pines and waits, rather than serving as instances of men's agency and women's passivity, become more amenable to being read as figures of speech, which make possible the performance of stylized gendered positions, working in consonance with and, on occasion, overturning the prescribed trajectory of romance.

Misogyny, subjection, passivity, complicity, agency, rebellion, and resistance: these terms have now become integral to the repertoire that allows us to formulate the "woman question." Likewise, it is "woman" that has become the axis around which the terms body, sex, eroticism, and gender—the terms I have chosen as the central analytical categories of this book—now revolve. These categories I have sought to argue are modern inventions and have a particular history that is rooted in Western thought. However, to the degree that they have now become part of our common sense, we cannot dispense with them altogether, for the questions we wish to ask of texts that belong to another time and place are inevitably driven by our own preoccupations. In charting how these terms came to be within the history of Western thought, and in suggesting some of the conceptual difficulties that they pose in our reading of medieval Japanese texts, I hope to have signalled what is at stake when we embark on acts of interpretation using concepts that may not have made sense to those who inhabited the texts we seek to illuminate.

CHAPTER TWO

The Erotics of the Body in the Tale of Genji

> . . . she was unusually small and pretty, and gave the impression of
> being nothing but robes (*hito yori ke ni chiisaku utsushige nite, tada
> on zo nomi aru kokochi su*) (Figure 4).

The amorous entanglements of Genji, the eponymous hero of the eleventh-century romance the *Tale of Genji*, the unforeseen consequences of love and attachment, and the workings of desire and longing in all their dimensions—their generation, fulfilment, and ultimate frustration—are at the heart of the thematic structure of this famous text. And yet, of the vast majority of men and women who generate and experience erotic and affective intensities, there are very few whom we can conjure up in their fullness, as people comprised of flesh and bone. For the most part they are fleeting, shadowy, and dispersed forms, which drift in and out of the text, not amenable to a sustained gaze.

We have come to accept as a commonplace that the body's physicality is somehow integral to the generation of erotic desire. Although we would readily grant that different cultures and historical moments privilege certain aspects of the body, be it the ankle, the nape of the neck, or the foot, we are accustomed to assuming that the physical attributes of the body are central to the language of erotics. And yet, we are hard pressed to find in either *monogatari* or *waka* a material body, made manifest through the fullness of the breast, the rosiness of the cheeks, or the shapeliness of the leg.[1] How do we account for this curious "absence" of many of the elements that make the body readily recognizable to us, particularly in a text that has at its very center the workings of love and desire? Some explanations come to mind, all of which, upon reflection, must be rejected.

There is the materialist argument, which would claim that there is nothing surprising about the fact that there are no descriptions of the body in Heian *monogatari* and *waka*, given that aristocratic women at court in that period were swathed in innumerable layers of clothing, and barely visible, as they reclined in dark rooms behind screens of state. Alternately, the absence of descriptions of the body and the sexual act in the *Genji* could be accounted for by the fact that the

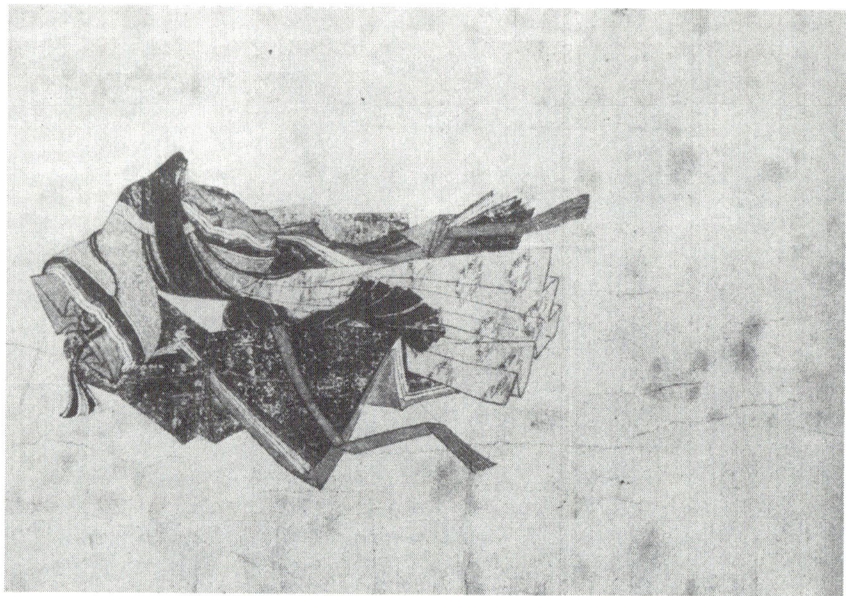

Figure 4. *Sanjūrokkasen emaki* (Picture Scroll of the "Thirty-Six Immortal Poets"), 13th century, Fujiki Collection, Osaka.

Genji is a courtly text that seeks to represent the world of culture, rather than the brute facts of animal nature.

To reduce the erotic simply to a reflection of social reality is to underestimate the degree to which conventions of writing themselves produce certain stylized modes for imagining the play of love and desire. Furthermore, the assumption that the body and sex are always associated with base matter, and hence necessarily antithetical to refined, courtly sensibilities, is to subscribe to a view that the oppositions of nature and culture are universal, and that they are uniformly reproduced in all texts. Courtly texts written in Sanskrit, to take just one example, belong to the realm of "high culture" but operate by a set of literary rules in which the physical body is at the center of erotic pleasures. The *Kāmasutra* provides an elaborate taxonomy of the many stages of the sexual act and the ways in which it is to be performed.[2] The various stages of longing—loss of sleep, physical emaciation, fainting, madness, and death, for example—or the pleasures of sexual foreplay—kissing, scratching, biting, and so forth—elaborated in the *Kāmasutra* travel across into other genres such as Sanskrit poetry and become the acceptable and highly stylized modes for speaking about sexual pleasure and longing. What is at issue here is not the eroticism of "real" bodies but rather the production of a culturally desirable body, in accordance with the rules and prescriptions that govern the genre in question.

There is no doubt that the conventions of *waka* and *monogatari* composition are significantly different from those that shape Sanskrit texts. However, neither the elaborate descriptions of sex found in Sanskrit poetry nor their absence in *waka* and *monogatari* maps on to the discourse of sexuality, produced by modern societies that "dedicated themselves to speaking of it [sex] *ad infinitum,* whilst exploiting it as *the* secret."[3] While it is true that the *Genji,* like many a Victorian novel, does not mention the sexual act, this has little to do with a prudishness that required that ideal relations between respectable men and women be represented as chaste and companionate, and certainly never sexual.

The *Genji* makes no attempt to mask the fact that men *are* interested in possessing women *sexually.* Rather than any direct reference to the act of sex, the text favors an elliptical mode for alluding to the fact that a relationship has been sexually consummated. Ellipsis here constitutes a particular form of decorum, far removed from its use in eighteenth- and nineteenth-century European fiction, when sex became a "public secret," hidden precisely in order to draw attention to itself.[4] The term used for love, *koi,* encapsulates feelings of desire, longing, passion, and affect. There is no distinction between spiritual or platonic love, on the one hand, and sensual and profane love on the other,[5] nor is the body through which physical love is experienced associated with sin or shame.

The explanations for the body's absence, or at any rate for its attenuated presence in the *Genji,* that I have outlined above rest upon a particular preconception about the body, which has its origins in post-Renaissance Europe. This is the body that has acquired the status of the ur-form, of which all others have become mere variants. It is this understanding of the body that I seek to challenge by arguing that the body, far from being absent, bursts through the pages of the *Genji* in the unfamiliar guise of hair, robes, and calligraphy, thereby calling into question the very idea that, at base, the body is a universally recognizable entity, even if it comes cloaked in different cultural garbs.

Hair and robes that form the subject of this chapter constitute radically alternate forms of embodiment, and it is their workings as potent sites for the generation of erotic and affective feelings that I seek to explore here. First, however, a brief excursus into the relationship between the body and clothing, and the distinction between nakedness and nudity in the Western tradition, may help throw into sharper focus the very different assumptions that guide the imagination of the body and robes in the *Genji.*

Nakedness, Nudity, and Clothing

Our commonsense tells us that clothing is what distinguishes us from beasts, and that in most cultures it is a potent marker of status, wealth, and beauty. However, the distinction between the body and clothing is not self-evident, for the body, insofar as it is accessible to us, is not grounded in some objective reality called nature but comes to us already culturally inscribed and coded with meaning. Both the athletic body of the Greek male as well as the tattoos and paint that adorn the naked body of the Maori or the indigenous Australian can be read as forms of clothing.[6] It is hard to tell where the body ends and clothing begins. The line between the two is arbitrary, but where and how it comes to be drawn tells us a great deal about the investments different societies and cultures make in producing the distinctions that fix the relationship between body and clothing.

The Judeo-Christian tradition, from its foundational moment, has accorded the distinction between clothing and the naked body great significance, for the question of innocence and sin is integrally linked to the relationship between the two. Until the Fall Adam and Eve were naked, but that was not a problem for they lived in innocence of it—nakedness had not yet come into being as a category. However, in their postlapsarian state, their naked bodies became a matter of shame and they had to be clothed.[7] Both nakedness and clothing, in the Christian tradition, were born of sin. While nakedness was an ambiguous and double-edged presence, serving as a metaphor for both innocence and its loss, it was nonetheless symbolic of suffering rather than of beauty. Its association with "captives, slaves, prostitutes, the insane, and the dead" made it "the mark of powerlessness and passivity."[8]

The transformation of the naked body, and in particular the female naked body, into an art form, the nude, was a phenomenon that emerged in the post-Renaissance period. In Kenneth Clark's classic formulation, the naked body is no more than the raw material, the "shapeless, pitiful model" as he calls it,[9] which the artist turns into a work of culture. That the distinction between the two rests implicitly on the figure of the female model transformed by the brush of the male artist points to the gendered nature of this distinction in which woman is aligned with nature and man with culture.[10] In fine art, as Ruth Barcan observes, "the nature/culture divide is redoubled within the domain of the undressed body, producing an opposition between 'natural nudity' (i.e. nakedness) and 'cultural nudity.'"[11] François Jullien sees the emergence of the nude as symptomatic of the imperative within Western culture to overcome a dualism that is central to it. The nude, he argues, becomes the favored site for bringing together "through collision and collusion" the binaries of matter and form, of the spiritual and the carnal, of nature and culture, and so on.[12]

If the nude in Western art acquires its aesthetic status by transcending the crude materiality of the naked body, what is its relationship to clothing and what are the connections between eroticism and the body? Pictures of the nude are of course unclothed, but they are often suggestively accompanied by some article of clothing, be it fur or drapery, carelessly cast aside.[13] Mario Perniola argues that it is the movement between the state of being clothed to the state of nudity, the "transit" from the hidden and covered, to the exposed and displayed, that produces the erotic in Western art.[14]

What this suggests is that while clothes are indispensable to the construction of the nude as an aesthetically pleasing and erotic form, their relationship with the body is one in which they are envisaged as being external to and easily detachable from it. It is through the complex operations of the dualisms of nature and culture, and form and matter, that the movement from the clothed to the unclothed, and a further slippage from a state of pitiable nakedness to its aesthetically acceptable transformation into nudity, take place.

It should be immediately apparent that the assumptions that guide the body in the Japanese, and indeed the East Asian tradition more generally, are of an altogether different order. There is no problematization here of the naked body, nor any attempt to transcend it through its reconfiguration as the nude. It is true that the naked body in medieval Japanese visual culture, not unlike its medieval European counterpart, is a sign of abjection, indicating a person's loss of social standing in the world. Often, bodies writhing in pain, as they are tortured in hell, or corpses that have been killed in war are depicted without their clothes, signalling that these bodies/selves have lost their status as social and cultural entities. However, nakedness here does not constitute a lapse into a state of nature. For, in the medieval world of Japan, there is nothing outside of what we would call the cultural body that exists prior to the social meanings with which it is inscribed. Both the body and clothing are integral to the constitution of a meaningful self. In her diary *Murasaki Shikibu Nikki* (The Diary of Murasaki Shikibu), Murasaki Shikibu, upon seeing two ladies-in-waiting whose clothes have been stolen and who are caught with nothing on (*hadakasugata*), observes that their state is both "a little frightening" and "rather amusing." The women in question may well have just lost their outer robes and not been "stark" naked, for a woman was considered naked if her upper torso was bare and she was clad only in her undergarment—the red trousers (*hakama*). In any case, what Murasaki registers is that the loss of clothing is tantamount to being stripped of one's dignity and proper sense of self.[15]

Figure 5. *Yata Jizō engi* (Picture Scroll of Tales of Origin of Jizō of the Yata temple), 14th century, Yatadera, Kyoto.

In the "Night Attack on the Sanjō Palace scroll" of *Heiji monogatari emaki* (Picture Scrolls of the Heiji Tales), for example, the lower-ranking courtiers, who have been attacked and now lie helplessly, are all depicted without their court hats (*eboshi*), which they have lost. The women, who have fallen prey to the attack, lie with their robes in disarray and their breasts exposed. Both the loss of headgear for men and the exposure of women's unclothed bodies signal a disturbance to the natural/social order and convey the state of abjection and suffering into which these men and women have fallen. In this regard, these pictures are not unlike those found in the hell screens where men and women suffer the tortures of hell (Figure 5).

Not unlike medieval Europe, breasts in medieval Japanese texts were not erotic—rather they were symbols of motherhood and nurturance. Indeed, organs that we now associate with the sexual did not necessarily resonate in the same way in medieval times.[16] The suggestion that the depiction of exposed breasts in the Heiji scrolls constitutes "a form of pornography" designed to titillate male viewers[17] misconstrues the relationship between the body, robes, and eroticism in medieval Japan. The ultimate raison d'être of clothes in the game of erotics in Japanese literary and visual texts does not lie in the pleasure they afford in being shed and cast aside. In other words, the erotic charge does not derive from the transit between the clothed and the naked, that is to say, from unveiling the clothed body as in a striptease, thereby reaching the *real* object of desire, the body. Robes, I would argue, are not mere embellishments that adorn, cover, and enhance the beauty of the body: they are part and parcel of embodied being and central to the game of erotics in the *Genji*.

Both the physical and psychic attributes that go into the making of the body often find expression in the robes within which the body is enveloped. After Genji spends the night with Yūgao, he has a chance, the following morning, to observe what she actually looks like. What registers for him is the nature of her attire: it is the soft, pale colored gown that she wears over layers of white inner robes that communicates to him her unassuming and pliant disposition as well as her modesty and grace.[18] In his initial encounter with the young child Murasaki, what he notices first is what she wears. It is her "softly rumpled kerria rose layering over a white gown"[19] that intimates to him that she will grow up to be a great beauty one day. Genji himself, who is the exemplar of beauty and radiance, is a palpable presence in the text not through descriptions of his physical appearance. It is the casual refinement and elegance of his attire that renders him a person of extraordinary beauty.

Descriptions of the body, divorced from clothes, signal a fundamental disturbance to the natural/social/cultural order of things. In a reversal that marks the anomalous nature of Suetsumuhana, we are presented with an extraordinarily detailed account of her physical appearance, which appears before the text turns for confirmation of her unattractiveness through a description of her attire. The text never presents us with instances where the garb is out of kilter with the physical and mental qualities of the one who wears it, for clothes are inseparably aligned with the body and the self.

The Erotics of Attire

In the *Genji* the body and clothing are metonymically linked to one another in a relationship that is marked by contiguity, proximity, and association, each taking on the characteristics of the other. The distinct odors of the body transfer themselves to and mingle with perfumed robes. All the senses—haptic, visual, and olfactory—are involved in experiencing clothes, not as dead objects but rather as living entities, suffused with the essence of the one to whom they belong, and it is this link with the loved one that gives them the power to produce desire and affective intensity.

As the following scene suggests, robes and the body appear to be integral to a sense of embodied being in the same way that the cicada shell is intrinsic to the cicada, even if it always holds the possibility of being shed and discarded. Genji's attempt to renew his seduction of Utsusemi is built around a thick web of associations generated by her robe. When Genji breaks into her room, he finds a sleeping figure that he assumes to be Utsusemi. It turns out to be her stepdaughter Nokiba no Ogi; Genji is not averse to dallying with her partly because she is attractive and partly simply because he can. On his way out he picks up the sheer gown (*kōchiki*) upon which Utsusemi had been lying, and which she has cast aside when she escapes. Later that night, he puts it under his own robe to lie on it.[20] Unable to sleep, he sends her a poem, which alludes to her robe:

> *utsusemi no*   Empty cicada,
> *mi o kaetekeru*   Molting you have left your shell
> *ko no moto ni*   At the foot of the tree;
> *nao hitogara no*   Still I shall recall how sweet
> *natsukashiki kana*   Was the self within the husk.[21]

Genji's erotic and affective attachment to the gown worn by Utsusemi finds expression in the way he treats it, not as an inert object but rather as something that is an extension of her. "He kept the sheer robe, dyed in the fragrance/beauty/allure of the person he longed for, next to his person and sat gazing upon it" (*kano usugoromo wa kōchiki no ito natsukashiki hitoga ni someru o, mi chikaku narashite mi itamaeri*).[22] When Utsusemi reads his poem she thinks of her own robe as analogous with the salty robe left by the Ise fisherman, in that it is suffused with her own bodily fluids. Her anxiety betrays her sense that by allowing Genji to gain access to her *robe,* she has given something of herself to him already. Her own poem, which she sends to Genji, echoes the image of the cicada shell/robe, to which he alludes in his poem:

> *utsusemi no*   Empty cicada—
> *ha ni oku tsuyu no*   On her wings beneath the tree
> *ko gakurete*   Hidden droplets fall;
> *shinobi shinobi ni*   Secretly, oh, secretly
> *nururu sode kana*   These sleeves grow damp with dew.[23]

It is worth noting that nowhere in the poems is Utsusemi's robe likened to a cicada shell. It is through association rather than simile or metaphor that we move back and forth from shell to robe, and from cicada to the body and person of the woman for whom Genji expresses his longing.

In the love poems of the classical Japanese repertoire, robes (*koromo*), sleeves (*sode*), and trouser cords (*shitahimo*) are most closely associated with sexual desire and longing. As the following poems demonstrate, the trouser cord loosening itself of its own accord speaks of a passion that lies outside of the control of the wearer who longs for a lover; turning the sleeves or robes inside out promises a magical meeting of lovers in dreams, and the conceit of sleeves drenched in dew evokes the tears of the grief-stricken lover.

omou to mo	I yearn for you
kou tomo awamu	I long for you
mono nare ya	and yet—we never meet;
yuu te mo tayuku	my fingers weary from tying
tokuru shitahimo	my loosening trouser cord[24]
ito semete	when my longing
koishiki toki wa	grows intolerable
nubatama no	I wear my robes
yoru no koromo o	of the bead-black night
kaeshite zo kiru	turned—inside out[25]

After Yūgao's death, when Genji orders some *hakama* (trousers) to be made as memorial offerings to the temple on her behalf, he expresses his longing for her through the familiar trope of the trouser cord:

naku naku mo	with ceaseless tears
kyō wa waga	her trouser cord
yuu shitahimo o	I tie today;
izure no yo ni ka	in what age to come
tokete miru beki	will I chance to untie it again?[26]

A garment, through its metonymic link with the body, takes on the character of the person who wears it. As a result, it is redolent not only of the smells and tactile pleasures associated with the body but also of the particular qualities that go into the making of a person's character, which is at once unique and individual, while at the same time bearing the marks of his/her status and upbringing. The unprepossessing physical appearance of Suetsumuhana extends metonymically to the embarrassingly old-fashioned clothes she wears and the gauche poems she composes.

Tama **and the Erotics of Keepsake Robes**

The spirit of a person (*tama, tamashii*) was said to reside in his/her garments. *Tama/tamashii* appears as a recurring trope in both *waka* poetry and in the *Genji* to express frustrated longing, which causes the spirit to escape from the body in search of union with the loved one or to destroy those who stand in its way. In the famous poem by Izumi Shikibu, said to have been composed on her way to Kibune shrine to perform rituals to win back the affection of her husband, for example, she expresses the intensity and uncontrollable nature of her longing through the trope of *tama:*

mono omoeba	is it from excess longing
sawa no hotaru mo	that even the firefly in the marshes
waga mi yori	appears to be my spirit
akugare izuru	wandering about, restless and lost
tama ka to zo miru	estranged from my being?[27]

On occasion when driven to extremes of jealousy, the angry spirit (*ikiryō*) could leave the body/clothing/self and attack those who stood in its way. In the *Genji,* when the Rokujō Lady's *tama* escapes, it takes on a life of its own and sets out on its destructive path to kill her rivals Yūgao, Aoi, and eventually Murasaki. When Rokujō's spirit possesses Aoi, she speaks through her to Genji, begging him to help return her *tama* back within her robes, where it properly belongs:

nagekiwabi	with laments and sighs
sora ni midaruru	my spirit wanders
waga tama o	in the skies;
musubitodome yo	tie it down
shitagai no tsuma	by binding the hems of my robe[28]

The *tama* escaping and finding shelter in the sleeves of the loved one is a familiar trope in the *Genji.* When Niou, unwilling to leave Ukifune, delays his departure, the narrator observes that he appears to have lost his spirit in her sleeves. Here the text is alluding to the following poem by Michinoku sent to a woman friend whom he parts with after they have spent time together:

akazari	my spirit must surely
sode no naka ni ya	have entered those sleeves
irinikemu	of which I never tire
waga tamashii no	for I feel as if
naki kokochi suru	it has left me[29]

After Aoi's death, when Tō no Chūjo visits Genji, he finds him so beautiful in his state of grief that he is moved to sensuous thoughts, reflecting that if he himself were a woman, his spirit, after death, would most certainly linger in this world rather than leave Genji (*onna nite misutete naku naramu tamashii kanarazu to-marinamu kashi*).[30]

Tama in the medieval context is not to be understood as soul or spirit in the Christian sense, for it is seen as a power that inheres to all things, animate as well as inanimate: not only humans and animals but also trees, rocks, plants, and so on are said to be imbued with their own *tama*. Moreover, while the spirit may temporarily leave the body, it is only when the two are reunited that the fractured self can be restored to its state of harmony. That *tama,* when it returns, finds its home in robes demonstrates the degree to which robes function as synecdoches of the body/self.

It is perhaps for this reason that keepsake robes (*katami no koromo*) were believed to have the power to connect lovers who were forced to be apart. They functioned as profoundly erotic and affective tropes in classical and medieval texts, bridging the gap between the living and the dead and serving as living repositories of the essence of absent loved ones. Robes that were exchanged as keepsakes were worn against the skin, and it was in that moment where the body of the self and the robe of the other met that temporal, spatial, and emotional boundaries dissolved, and a feeling of intense intimacy was made possible.

Such at any rate is the magic supposedly woven into the fabric of keepsake robes. The Akashi Lady, skeptical of the power of the robe to ensure Genji's fidelity after he returns to the capital, presents him with a hunting cloak that she has sewn herself and to which she appends the following poem:

yoru nami ni	Where the waves roll in
tachikasanetaru	Over and over have I bent
tabigoromo	To sew those clothes,
shiodokeshi to ya	Travel weeds you may find rough,
hito no itowamu	Drenched as they are in brine.

In offering the clothes that she has laboriously sewn for Genji, the Akashi Lady indicates both that she has given herself to him and that she/her robes may not be worthy of his attention.[31] For Genji, *katami,* a well-worn figure of speech, serves as a shorthand for reassuring Akashi of the seriousness of their liaison:

katami ni zo	Keepsakes each to each
kaubekarikeru	Should our inner garments be
au koto no	For that time between,
hikazu hedaten	The estranging web of days
naka no koromo o	Before we join again.[32]

Genji, it is to be noted, wears the robe that the Akashi Lady has made for him in acknowledgment of the kindness and sincerity of her gesture and the effort that has gone into its making. There is no suggestion here that he does so because he cannot bear to be parted from her. He sends her the clothes he has been wearing, which have been in close contact with his body, confident that they, more than anything else, will make for the ideal keepsakes by which she will remember him. The narratorial voice appears to endorse Genji's thoughts by explaining, "How could the fragrance attached to his incomparable robes not transfer itself and dye her thoughts and feelings as well?" (*enaranu onzo ni nioi no utsuritaru o, ikade hito no kokoro ni mo shimezaramu*).[33] The ambiguity of Genji's intentions and plans with regard to the Akashi Lady notwithstanding, the keepsake robes prove to be enchanted, for his encounter with her turns out to be no fleeting affair; she bears him a daughter who marries an emperor, thereby securing his political fortunes.

The body and self are contiguous with clothing and it is this proximity that allows for feelings and desires to flow freely from one to the other: individual identity finds a home in robes. Could this explain why a sexually coercive act against a woman in medieval narratives such as *Konjaku monogatari* (Tales of Times Now Past) is registered not through an account of the violation of her individual "physical body" but through an emphasis on the state of her attire and her loss of social status? A low-ranking officer violates a married woman and makes off with her clothes. The compiler concludes that it is unadvisable for inexperienced women to travel and that the officer's behavior is reprehensible because he steals the woman's clothes.[34] The tale that follows recounts another incident in which a man forces himself sexually upon a woman. In this instance, he is praised for leaving behind the woman's clothes.[35] In Lady Nijō's account in *Towazugatari* (Telling Without Being Asked) of the night when the retired emperor Go-Fukakusa forces himself upon her, what she draws our attention to is not her body but the fact that her thin gown is badly torn. What appears as a curious displacement of violence from the body on to robes in fact suggests an altogether different relationship between the two, pointing to the degree to which metonymic substitutions between the body, clothes, and self had come to be naturalized in the medieval imagination.

Beauty and the Body

Robes and the body in the *Genji,* I have argued, are mutually constitutive such that it is hard to tell where robes end and the body begins. The grace, sensibility, and inner disposition of a person reveal themselves through robes, and it is this appreciation of clothing as part and parcel of embodied being that has the power to arouse strong feelings of desire and affect. This is not to suggest, however, that the face and the physical aspects of the body pass unnoticed in the text. For the most part, however, their beauty is conveyed cursorily in highly stylized terms. The twelfth-century *Genji monogatari emaki* is in tune with the text's mode of depicting the beauty of the face. The plump faces, the thick brows, the small rosebud lips, and the long flowing hair are little more than conventionalized modes for suggesting ideal female courtly beauty, and it is only when something out of the ordinary contravenes these accepted standards that the text draws attention to it.

In the late thirteenth-century picture scroll *Obusumasaburō emaki* (Picture Scroll of Obusumasaburō), for example, the virtuousness, refinement, and beauty of the girl Jihi are conveyed in conventional terms that require little elaboration. Her cousin, on the other hand, daughter of the wicked Obusumasaburō, is depicted in considerably greater detail: her curly hair, large eyes, sharp nose, and tall stature represent the physical characteristics of the ugly woman of the medieval period. It is through her anomalous appearance that we grasp the unattractiveness of her person.[36] Any deviation from acceptable standards of beauty is noteworthy: this is why we have a much clearer sense of what the hapless red-nosed Suetsumuhana looks like compared to the more conventional beauties in the text.[37]

Rather than the beauty of the individual features of the body, what the text draws attention to is the favorable impression, both physical and emotional, that the body/robes/self as a whole communicate. There is a constellation of related terms—*tsuki, sama, arisama, katachi, ge, kehai,* and *keshiki*—which is used frequently in the text to connote the aspect, shape, form, impression, or appearance of the face, the hand, the forehead, the eyes, and so on. The terms *tsuratsuki, hitaitsuki, kashiratsuki,* or *kuchitsuki,* for example, which are often used to suggest the pleasing nature of the face, forehead, head, and mouth, reveal more about the pleasurable impressions and feelings they generate rather than anything specific about their physical proportions, contours, and characteristics.

It is the phenomenological effects that the body produces, rather than its ontological status, that the text highlights in moments charged with erotic and affective possibilities. What registers as the body in the *Genji* is its performative mode rather than an apprehension of it as something with fixed, immutable attributes.[38] When the Akashi Lady is described as being peerless in the beauty of her writing, the term the text uses for pen(wo)manship is *te no sama,* literally, the appearance of her hand.[39] What is at issue here is not the smallness or beauty of her hand but rather its performative potential, its ability to produce an aesthetically pleasing calligraphic style. When Genji gives the young Murasaki a music lesson, the text tells us that what he finds beautiful is her hand (*otetsuki*). *Tetsuki* here conjures up hand not in the purely physical sense but rather its engagement in performance. Given her diminutive size, Murasaki has to stretch her fingers in order to manipulate the *koto* string, and it is this, coupled with the touching quality of one so young striving to play a complex melody, that renders her hand/performance (*otetsuki*) winsomely pretty.[40]

The apprehension of beauty as performance does not occur solely through the ocular but through a wide range of senses, ranging from the haptic to the olfactory. This is reflected in the terms themselves, each of which is subtly suggestive of specific sensory stimulations. *Kehai* is an impression that is conveyed and experienced primarily through the senses of sound, touch, and smell: the rustling of robes, the tenor of the voice, the scent of perfume, and so on, while *keshiki* speaks more to appearance grasped visually.[41] In the "Trefoil Knots" chapter of the *Genji,* when Kaoru enters Ōigimi's room, he catches a glimpse of her in the dim light of the lamp. When he strokes and brushes aside her hair that falls over her face, he finds, just as he had expected, a quality of refined beauty (*ogushi no koborekakaritaru o, kaki yaritsutsu mitamaeba, hito no onkehai omou yō ni kaori okashige nari*).[42] The phrase *hito no on kehai* is ambiguous: it could refer to the general impression created by her face (as Tyler reads it) or by her person in general.[43]

It does not much matter, for this indeterminacy is central to the way in which beauty is apprehended in the text; rather than through the individual features of the face viewed clearly, it is experienced as a pleasurable sensation that is grasped through a multiplicity of senses. That the word *kaori,* which means fragrance or incense, also doubles as a term signifying lustrous beauty indicates the degree to which beauty is a diffuse quality that communicates itself not just visually but through a multiplicity of senses.

The terms *okashi, utsukushi, namamekashi, rōtashi, medetashi, natsukashi,* and so on, which appear frequently in the *Genji,* convey a wide range of nuances, signifying different forms of allure: charming, beautiful, appealing, desirable, refined, youthful, and winsomely appealing are only some of the ways in which these terms have been translated into English. Even when the text points to the beauty of the face, it is associated less with the shape or color of the eyes or mouth than with the feeling and sentiment that they convey. The word *namamekashi* bespeaks a youthful exuberance and grace, while a certain quality of irresistible sweetness, tinged with a sadness that elicits protective feelings, is best captured by the term *rōtashi.*[44]

Few characters are irrevocably defined by only one kind of beauty; rather, the transformation of a person's emotional/physical state produces corresponding changes in the nature of his/her allure, for beauty is always born of context. When we first encounter Aoi in the "Young Murasaki" chapter, she is presented as an intimidating figure who treats Genji coldly. When he attempts to placate her she casts him a sidelong glance, and it is the effect that her gaze produces that the text registers: "her eyes and her deportment suggested a noble beauty that put one to shame" (*mami ito hazukashigeni, ketakō utsukushige naru onkatachi nari*). The phrase *utsukushige naru* suggests the self-confident, noble, and haughty nature of Aoi's beauty.[45]

Later, when Aoi is seriously ill, possessed by the angry spirit of the Rokujō Lady, she is transformed from a proud and unyielding figure to a frail and helpless one. Genji, observing her lying weak and spent, with her long, luxurious hair forming a striking contrast with her white gown, finds *this* configuration far more alluring and endearingly beautiful than her imperious and refined bearing (*kōte koso rōtage ni namamekitaru kata soite okashikarikere to miyu*).[46] This is the first time that the term *rōtage* is used to describe Aoi. When Genji visits Aoi one last time after her childbirth and shortly before her death, the sight of her lying there extremely weakened, appearing as if she were almost not of this world, arouses in him unbearable pain brought on by her piteously beautiful state. The term *rōtage* reappears: (*ito okashigenaru hito no, itō yowari sokonawarete, aru ka naki ka no keshiki nite fushitamaeru sama, ito rōtage ni kokorogurushige nari*).[47]

To conclude, rather than the individual features of the face or the body, what the text highlights are the feelings, sensations, and impressions generated by the body through its performative gestures and modes of comportment; furthermore, these sensations are grasped not only visually but through the engagement of all the senses. Hair, which is described at length in the text and constitutes an important marker of female beauty, is at first glance surely an exception, given that it is a physical feature of the body. However, as I hope to demonstrate in the section that follows, hair is more than simply a material attribute. Like robes, it serves as the privileged repository of both the physical and psychic attributes that go toward the constitution of the female body/self.

The Power of Hair

In the world of the *Genji* hair is analogous to clothes in more ways than one. Hair is both of the body and outside of it, for it has a life of its own that survives even after a person is dead. Like clothes, it has the power to attract the spirits of absent or dead lovers, and together with objects such as combs, and comb boxes associated with it, it functions as a *katami*, or memento of the absent one, for it is here that her spirit (*tama*) is thought to reside.[48] The linearity of form, which it

Figure 6. *Genji monogatari emaki* (Picture Scroll of the *Tale of Genji*), 12th century, Tokugawa Art Museum, Nagoya.

shares with clothes, is not unlike the arterial pulses through which *qi* flows, capturing something of the way in which the body as a living force is experienced in the text.

Conventions of beauty required that women grew their hair extremely long; often the length of their hair exceeded their own height. That the same term, *suso,* is used for the train or hem of robes and for the ends of the hair that trail the ground suggests the degree to which the two share the same conceptual terrain. Hair, like clothing, is the privileged site through which the beauty and eroticism of the body are made manifest.[49] If in the *Genji,* colors, textures, dyes, weaves, and fragrances are the measures for judging the quality of robes, and, by extension, of those who wear them, we find in descriptions of the length, richness, luster, thickness, and texture of hair analogous modes for gauging a woman's beauty and erotic potential. Like clothing, women's hair carries not only the physical but also the psychical attributes to whom it belongs, revealing a great deal about the character, disposition, and caliber of the woman who "wears" it. Hair is not a passive or inert entity that serves as an erotic object of men's desires. It is perhaps best understood as a living force, pregnant with many meanings. Like a text it invites itself to be read. It is through hair that women are able to gauge and express their own feelings, and often what they intuit about themselves through it is at odds with the ways in which men read their hair. Women in the *Genji* may not be voluble but their hair speaks volumes (Figure 6).

The Erotics of Liminality

As with other markers of beauty, hair in the *Genji* is described in highly stylized terms, for it is taken for granted that a woman of distinction is likely to be blessed with long, lustrous hair. It is when hair deviates from the norm, in situations that are unusual or out of the ordinary, as in childbirth, tonsure, or death, that it becomes particularly charged with erotic significance.[50] Murasaki's hair is not the object of elaborate attention when she is at the height of her youth. It is when she is a child, and much later when she is ill and dying, that her hair becomes central to the semiotics of eroticism. When Genji first encounters Murasaki as a ten-year-old girl, he is struck by the fact that she is no ordinary child and that she holds the promise of being a great beauty one day. It is her attire and her hair that signal to Genji both that she is still a young girl, outside the realm of the sexual, but also, and integrally tied to her liminal status, that she will be the source of erotic and affective pleasures in the future.

Hair is a recurring motif in the "Young Murasaki" chapter where the fateful meeting between Genji and the child, Murasaki, occurs. Watching Murasaki as she runs, Genji observes that her hair spreads out and bounces like a fan behind her. After having noticed how attractive her wet nurse is, with her long, flowing hair, his gaze is drawn once again to Murasaki. It is the line of her eyebrows, still unshaven because she has yet to come of age, and the manner in which she sweeps away her hair from her forehead that he finds particularly charming. Later he observes her grandmother stroking her tangled hair and hears her remarking on how beautiful it is despite the child's resistance to having it combed.[51] The imagery of tangled hair being combed or of hair being stroked is a dominant trope for the expression of sexual passion and tender love in both *waka* and *monogatari*. Its association with the erotic, never explicitly stated here, serves nonetheless to suggest the direction in which Genji's thoughts are likely to wander.

Hair has been closely associated with the forces of life, and particularly with sexual energy in many cultures. It is for this reason that severing worldly ties and embracing a life of celibacy have often entailed shaving the head or "taking the tonsure." Given the extraordinary significance attached to long hair in the *Genji*, it is striking that the act of tonsure, a particularly charged and momentous event, marking a withdrawal from worldly concerns, serves not to dampen but rather to fuel even greater erotic and affective intensities.

Earlier, before he encounters Murasaki, Genji has had occasion to spy on her grandmother, whom he finds deeply attractive, even though she is a nun and over forty years of age. It is the affecting sight of the ends of her hair, cut just below her shoulders, in a style appropriate to nuns who continue to live at home,[52] that Genji finds incomparably more stylish and beautiful than long hair (*kami no utsukushige ni sogaretaru sue mo, naka naka nagaki yori mo koyo nau imamekashiki mono kana, to aware ni mitamau*).[53]

It is through hair that the conjunction between the nun and the child is brought home to the reader. It is surely not fortuitous that the *amasogi* style, adopted by many of the women in the text—Murasaki's grandmother, Onna San no Miya, Ukifune, to name but a few—was, "conceptually, intended to resemble the haircut appropriate for a child."[54] Both young girls and nuns were meant to lie outside of the libidinal economy, but it is by focusing on the extraordinary beauty of their hair that the text reinserts them into an erotic framework. Distant echoes of the scene with Murasaki and her grandmother are audible later, in the "Pilgrimage to Sumiyoshi" chapter, when Genji visits the Rokujō Lady, who is seriously ill, and happens to catch a glimpse of both mother and daughter through an opening in the curtain. He is moved to observe the Rokujō Lady reclining on an armrest, looking like a picture drawn in a painting, her hair full of beauty and richness, cut to her shoulders (*ongushi ito okashige ni hanayaka ni sogite yori itamaeru, e no kakitaramu sama shite ito aware nari*).[55]

Her young daughter awakens Genji's interest, despite the explicit warning given by the Rokujō Lady that he desist from lascivious thoughts about her daughter.[56] In this vignette, Genji is drawn both to the Rokujō Lady, whom he finds attractive precisely because of her nun's cut, as well as to her daughter, who is a picture of sweetness and youthful vulnerability, and what is more, not out of bounds as her mother now is.

When Ukifune takes the tonsure, the nun who attends on her connives to expose her to the gaze of a certain captain. Seeing the almost overabundant ends of her hair spread out over her shoulders like a five-ribbed fan (*kami wa itsue no aogi o hirogetaru yō ni kochitaki sue tsuki nari*), the nun is convinced that the captain will not be disappointed. She is right: the captain decides that she is even more attractive and irresistible in her current state as a nun; it is the sight of her hair that strengthens his resolve to establish a relationship with her and to keep her for himself.[57]

As with childhood and tonsure in the form of *amasogi,* hair, when associated with sickness and death, is filled with a particularly urgent erotic and affective charge. When Genji visits Murasaki during her illness, he is particularly struck by the beauty of her long hair, which, having been freshly washed, is spread out around her, without a single strand out of place, its richness and luster producing a striking contrast to the paleness of her skin.[58] In death, her hair shows no sign of being in a disorderly state; on the contrary, it appears incomparably glossy and beautiful (*tsuyu bakari midaretaru keshiki mo nau, tsuya tsuya to utsukushige naru sama zo kagiri naki*). The same is true of Yūgao. After her death, when Koremitsu carries her into the carriage, the beauty of her hair tumbling out of the mat, in which she has been wrapped, reduces Genji to a state of such dizzying sorrow that he does not want to let her out of his sight.[59] Hair in the *Genji* is at its most alluring when it appears in liminal spaces and contexts, where the longing for what cannot be finds its most powerful expression.

Hair as Mirror of the Female Self

In the classical *waka* repertoire, hair figures as a trope through which women articulate feelings of sexual pleasure and longing. In the following poem (*Goshuishū* 755) by Izumi Shikibu (970–1030), sexual pleasure and intimacy are expressed through the image of tangled hair:

kurokami no	as I lay down
midare mo shirazu	oblivious of my black hair
uchifuseba	in a state of wild disarray
mazu kakiyarishi	I longed for him who earlier,
hito zo koishiki	had stroked it smooth.[60]

In the *Genji* women rarely associate their hair with an experience of a love that is mutually shared. It is through an apprehension of its erotic possibilities that women come to an understanding not of the pleasures but rather of the anxieties generated by amorous relationships with men; more often than not, these entanglements serve as reminders of the fundamentally unstable nature of human ties, marked as they are by change and uncertainty. Hair, which thins, turns grey, and loses its luster, becomes emblematic of the short-lived nature of female beauty and of the inconstancy of men's affections.

As we shall see, it is by cutting their hair and taking the tonsure that some of the central female figures in the text, such as Fujitsubo, Murasaki, Onna San no Miya, and Ukifune, seek to withdraw from the world of amorous engagement and affirm their commitment to the Buddhist Path. Tonsure here is not a subversive act, in the sense of an assertion of individual will and agency. It is perhaps better understood as a communally shared and culturally available model for men and women alike to register both disillusionment with worldly life and the illusionary bonds of amorous attachment, and, equally importantly, to participate in practices that hold out the promise of salvation in one of Amida's paradises.

Hair figures as a particularly dominant trope in the scenes involving Ochiba no Miya, who, like many of the female protagonists in the text, seeks to escape from her amorous predicament by cutting her hair and severing her worldly ties. After the death of her husband, Kashiwagi, when she finds herself the object of Yūgiri's attentions, she resists him stubbornly, knowing that for someone of her exalted status, a second marriage, following an unsuccessful relationship with Kashiwagi, is likely to bring further humiliation to both herself and her family. Her mother, who is seriously ill, makes it clear that a liaison with Yūgiri would be disastrous for her daughter's reputation, and this adds in no small measure to Ochiba no Miya's resentment of him, for she also holds him responsible for precipitating her mother's death.

After the period of mourning is over, her ladies-in-waiting coax her to receive Yūgiri and to change into more colorful robes. It is through her hair that she recognizes the complete disjuncture between her own feelings and those expressed by her attendants. As she allows herself, against her will, to be dressed in brighter colors, she draws back her hair, which she has longed above all else to cut and cast away. She notices that it is six feet long (an impressive length) but that it has thinned a little. She recalls how those around her see it as entirely lacking in any imperfection, but in her own heart she cannot help but feel that it has deteriorated and that it is in no condition to be shown to others.[61]

Hair for Ochiba no Miya serves as a poignant reminder of the transience of youth and beauty; moreover, the fact that her hair has thinned a little presages for her the inevitable loss of interest and commitment from any man with whom she is likely to be involved. Her thoughts and feelings reveal a willful misreading of the semiotics of her hair—a misreading that flies in the face of the evidence she herself provides when she notes that it is six feet long and that her attendants do not see in it any imperfection. It is by rejecting the beauty of her own hair and refusing to recognize it as worthy of attention that she begins to entertain the possibility of taking the tonsure. Her hopes remain unrealized, for her ladies-in-waiting make sure not to leave any scissors around just in case she takes this drastic step.

Unable to contain Yūgiri's relentless ardor, she hides away from him, pulling her single layered robe over her hair and head, thereby rendering herself obstinately unerotic under his gaze.[62] Yūgiri is confounded by her extraordinary implacability. He recognizes that there are conventions that demand that she not give in too quickly, but she has taken matters too far, showing no signs of softening her stance even when things have gone beyond the point of no return. In the end, the text tells us, he pulls off the gown under which she has buried her head and, "brushing aside her badly tangled hair, he briefly sees her" (*ito utate midaretaru ogushi kakiyari nado shite hono mitatematsuri tamau*).[63] *Miru*, in this context, is to be read as a sign that in this scene Yūgiri comes to know Ochiba no Miya sexually.

When Yūgiri marvels at her unwavering resistance "less yielding than rocks and trees,"[64] he wonders whether it is the weakness of their karmic bond from past lives that accounts for her unequivocal rejection of him. After their sexual encounter, however, the narrator registers a change. Ochiba no Miya is transformed simply into *onna,* who now exudes an extremely refined and feminine beauty (*ito ate ni onna shu, namameitaru kehai shitamaeri*), and he, likewise, becomes simply *otoko,* who seems incomparably more alluring when he comports with her with intimacy, as opposed to when he adopted a more formal stance (*otoko no onsama wa, uruwashidachi tamaeru toki yori mo, uchitokete mono shitamau wa, kagiri mo nau kiyoge nari*).[65] The moment of intimacy is marked by a suspension of their particular identities and the fraught conditions under which their encounter takes place. They are returned, briefly, to the world of *waka,* a decontextualized space in which lovers meet or lament the absence of the other.

The moment of intimacy passes, and Ochiba no Miya remains inconsolable, for she cannot believe that Yūgiri's interest in her is anything but short-lived, given the degree to which, in her eyes, her looks have deteriorated. There is little sense here that Ochiba no Miya's rejection of Yūgiri has anything to do with her assessment of him as an individual. Rather, it is driven by a more depersonalized apprehension of a larger truth, namely that love and constancy are chimerical, and that those who believe otherwise are bound to be hurt and disappointed. It is through her hair that Ochiba no Miya is granted this insight into the true nature of amorous relationships.[66]

The trope of hair in disarray being stroked by the lover, central to the pleasure associated with sexual encounters, takes on a different meaning in the *Genji.* Hair being caressed or cared for is reassuring to women not when it is associated with the world of men but rather when it conjures up the lost world of maternal love and security.[67] After failing to cut her hair and to become a nun, Ochiba no Miya is forced to return to her home in the capital where Yūgiri has installed himself, in anticipation of winning her over. As she enters her carriage, her eyes cloud over with tears. She recalls another occasion when, upon arriving in Ono, her mother had caressed her hair and put it in order before helping her out of the carriage, despite her own state of ill health.[68]

Like Ochiba no Miya before her, Ukifune's feelings, after she resolves to become a nun, are articulated through an appraisal of her own hair and through the memories of maternal love that hair evokes. In preparation for taking the tonsure she loosens her hair a little, incapable of doing more, given its extraordinary length and thickness. She thinks of the nun who has looked after her as a surrogate mother, remembering how she has allowed no one other than her to comb it for her. Although she has, of her own accord, decided to take the step of becoming a nun, she is deeply saddened at the thought that her own mother will never see her long hair again (*oya ni ima hitotabi kō nagara no sama o miezu narinamu koso, hito yari narazu ito kanashikere*). She herself assumes that her hair has thinned a little because of her long illness, but the text tells us that it has not suffered at all and that it is as thick as ever, and still strikingly beautiful, six feet in length, down to the tips, each individual hair finely textured and full of allure.[69]

This long description of her hair tells us a great deal about the magnitude of Ukifune's decision, and about what is at stake in taking the tonsure at the height of youth and beauty. Her regret at having to leave the world of affective and erotic pleasures and her sorrow at having failed to live up to her mother's ambitions for her take shape through the image of her mother caressing her hair, which she expresses in the form of a single line "that I might be thus" (*kakare to te shimo*)."[70] She is alluding here to the following poem from the *Gosenshū* (124) by the Priest Henjō:

tarachime wa	surely my mother
kakare to te shimo	did not caress
mubatama no	my bead-black
waga kurokami o	dark hair
nadezu ya arikemu	that I might be thus

Tonsure in the *Genji* is a trope of ambivalence, associated both with a sense of release from the pain of attachment as well as with feelings of regret at having to leave the world of love and intimacy. Women in the *Genji* speak through their hair. It is the locus of anxiety, for its thinning and graying presages the inevitable loss of youth and the inconstancy of amorous ties. Tonsure is at once a way of withdrawing from the world of *samsāra* and its illusionary bonds as well as opening oneself to the more heartening promise of salvation in the world beyond. It is the tension between the pain occasioned by amorous involvement and the sense of loss following withdrawal from the world of affective engagement that the text communicates—not through descriptions of women's inner psychological states but rather through their altered relationship with their hair.

Men "Reading" Women's Hair

Women's hair is the repository of both the physical and psychic elements that go into the constitution of the body and self. Rather than an inert and passive attribute of the body it is a powerful site of signification, providing women with privileged access to their own thoughts and feelings. Woman's hair is open to multiple interpretations, and often when men attempt to read women's hair they reveal more about their own emotional states and erotic responses than they do about the women themselves. "The Warbler's First Song" chapter is striking in that Genji's feelings for the women in his entourage are captured through his response to their deportment, their clothing, and, above all, their hair.[71] His first visit is to Hanachirusato: the text tells us that the passage of time has removed all distance between them and that theirs is a relationship marked by genuine feeling and affection. The fact that he does not force her to engage in (sexual) intimacy (*ima anagachi ni chikayaka naru onarisama mo motenashi kikoetamawazarikeri*) is admirable, but his observations about her clothes and her hair soon reveal that what lies at the heart of his lack of interest is the fact that she has lost all erotic appeal. Genji notes that "her hair had seen better days and that she would be better off wearing a wig."[72] He congratulates himself for sticking with her, given that others in his position would find the prospect distasteful.

His next visit is to see Tamakazura, who has only recently been ensconced in the west wing, not far from Hanachirusato. Tamakazura's youthful beauty serves as a direct counterpoint to the lack of appeal of her aging neighbor. In contrast to the subdued appearance of Hanachirusato in her sky-blue robe, Tamakazura, as befits her age, looks dazzling in her kerria rose-patterned gown. If Hanachirusato's thinning hair confirms, for Genji, her lack of erotic appeal, Tamakatsura's hair, whose ends, we are told, have thinned a little, "perhaps because she is consumed with sad longing" (*mono omoi ni shizumitamaeru hodo no shiwaza ni ya, kami no suso sukoshi hosorite . . .*),[73] far from rendering her unattractive, serves instead as confirmation of the fact that someone of her winsome beauty needs Genji's protection. As the narrator observes, under the circumstances it is only to be expected that Genji cannot countenance losing her.[74]

His next stop is at the residence of the Akashi Lady. In her case, the sheer discretion and grace with which she conducts herself and the self-effacing beauty of her penwomanship make Genji realize how completely out of the ordinary she is. It is, above all, through her hair that Genji recognizes Akashi's unusual qualities. "The clear lines of her hair, thinning slightly at the ends, juxtaposed against her white robe, produced an effect of understated beauty, which added all the more to her charm. The sight filled him with such fond memories of the past that he spent the night with her" (*kezayaka naru kami no kakari no, sukoshi suwuruku naru hodo ni usuraginikeru mo, itodo namamekashisa soite natsukashikereba . . . konata ni tomaritamainu*).[75] That Genji finds her like no other (*nao hito yori wa koto nari to obosu*)[76] is because her quiet, unassuming grace has now come to be intimately connected with her exalted status as the mother of a future empress; her thinning hair bespeaks her forbearance and self-sacrifice, for she has forsaken the prerogative of bringing up her own child to ensure her daughter's and, by extension, Genji's advancement in the world.[77]

Genji's reaction to Suetsumuhana serves as a comical counterpoint to the finely wrought emotions provoked by the other women/hair in his entourage. Genji notes that the splendidly rich and long hair of her youth—her one redeeming feature—has now lost its former beauty. To indicate that it has turned white we are told that her hair, viewed in profile, would put even a pool of water below a waterfall to shame. Genji finds the sight so painfully sad that he is forced to look away (*inishie sakari to mieshi onwakagami mo, toshigoro ni otoroiyuki, mashite taki no yodomi hazukashige naru onkatawara me nado o ito oshi to oboseba, maho ni mo mukai tamawazu*).[78] Her hair, which extends metonymically to her person, can be no more than an object of pity.

Hair, like robes, far from being simply one of the body's many attributes, constitutes a form of embodiment, for it is seen to be the repository of the physical, mental, and emotional dispositions that make up the body/self. It is through the semiotics of hair that we gain an understanding of the thoughts and feelings of the shadowy figures that inhabit the *Genji*. When we speak of the novel in the West we associate it with characters, who are presented to us as unique individuals, imbued with interiority and a particular form of expressivity, which allows their psychological state to be communicated to the reader through their utterances or inner thoughts. Such is the mode through which Jane Austen's Elizabeth, for example, speaks to us in *Pride and Prejudice*. Compared with her, Murasaki's inner life seems more elusive, less accessible.

If we turn elsewhere, not only to what the narratorial voices and characters in the *Genji* think and say but to the language of clothes and hair, we hear, through a different register, how the protagonists of the text experience their world and express their thoughts and emotions. The extraordinary attention to clothes and hair in the *Genji* may strike a modern reader as excessive and pointless detail. These linear forms, however, suggest other styles, albeit unfamiliar ones, of figuring the body, not only as a physical entity but also as the privileged site for both the apprehension and expression of thought, feelings, and affect.

CHAPTER THREE

The Erotics of Power in the Tale of Genji

He felt for them all, each according to her station (*izure o mo, hodo hodo ni tsukete aware to oboshitari*).

The body in the *Genji*, I have argued, is imagined and experienced not as an anatomical entity made up of flesh, bones, and blood but rather through its metonymic links with robes and hair; it is seen as the repository not only of the material but also of the psychological and mental attributes that constitute the self; furthermore, conceptions of beauty, refinement, and sensitivity in the text are tied not to the physical aspects of the body but to robes, hair, and forms of bodily comportment and performance. My exploration of the connections between the beauty of the body and the generation of affective and erotic desire could well be construed as a return to a reading of the *Genji* as an unsullied space of pure aesthetics, untouched by the outside world, in which men and women composed love poetry, played music, and engaged in amorous affairs.

Given the many scholarly works that have convincingly challenged this way of reading the text,[1] there would be little justification now for resuscitating the ghost of aesthetics as a separate domain, and celebrating the work as an exemplification of the "rule of taste," untouched by politics.[2] The *Genji* requires neither extratextual evidence nor a deeply convoluted reading to excavate the workings of power and politics, for the text openly displays an acute understanding of the degree to which hierarchies and asymmetries of gender and social status are central to the play of erotics and to the constitution of amorous relationships. Hair, as we have observed, is clearly a gendered marker of beauty. The erotic and affective feelings it generates in different contexts cannot be deciphered outside of considerations of gender and class. Implicit in my reading in Chapter 2 of the body's beauty and its connections with eroticism was the assumption that far from belonging to a rarefied and exclusive domain called aesthetics, both were profoundly imbricated in the operations of power. This chapter seeks to thematize more explicitly, through a series of close textual readings, the connections between gender, social status, the body, and eroticism, and to demonstrate the centrality of power to the very constitution of romance in the text.

However, in arguing that literary texts such as the *Genji* are political, I do not treat culture as a discreet domain, separate from politics; for to do so would be to assume that poetry, music, and other artistic accomplishments are little more than mere façades that obfuscate what really lie behind the refined world of the text, namely the ugly operations of politics and power.[3] This chapter works from an altogether different presumption, arguing that the text's literariness is inextricably tied to its politics and that it is not possible to reach at this politics without taking seriously the centrality that the text accords to robes and hair as well as the arts of poetry, calligraphy, music, and so on.

Within the dense social world of the *Genji,* gender, status, and a highly aestheticized form of erotics often crisscross, sometimes working in tandem and at other times pulling in different directions, always creating a multitude of possibilities. In each instance, what these artistic practices and ideals of beauty mean cannot be deciphered without taking into account the workings of power within which they are embedded. At the same time, power itself does not exist separately from the aesthetic forms—poetry, incense, calligraphy, robes, hair—through which it works.

I use the term "power" here in the Foucauldian sense, as something diffuse and pervasive, "something which circulates . . . in the form of a chain,"[4] rather than as a weapon that is wielded by individuals, or groups, through acts of domination and coercion. Far from being simply negative, repressive, or coercive, it is often a productive force in which individuals "are not only its inert or consenting target; they are always also the elements of its articulation."[5] If we take our cue from Foucault, seeing how power operates in the *Genji* then becomes a matter not of establishing how men in the text dominate women or how those of the higher classes oppress those of the lower ranks. Rather, it is to recognize that power suffuses all relationships, and that romance itself is constituted through the play of power such that, in the *Genji,* the asymmetries of rank and gender, far from being antithetical to love and desire, are in fact the very conditions of possibility for their generation.[6]

While the text registers powerfully the suffering of those who are entangled in amorous relationships and displays a profound awareness of how the asymmetries of gender and status work, the *Genji* cannot be read through our modern lenses as a tale of human injustice. For the unforeseen consequences of love are seen less as a result of individual agency than as the unfolding of a pattern discernable in all human and natural phenomena, namely the inconstancy and changing nature of existence. It is perhaps not fortuitous that women such as

Yūgao, Tamakazura, Murasaki, and Ukifune are at the center of romance in the text, for their indeterminate social status is metonymically linked to one of the central themes of the text, namely, the uncertain and ephemeral nature of amorous affairs, with their unexpected twists and turns.

To say that gender and class/status intersect is of course true, but it can have (at least) two different meanings. In one, gender is fixed or static, and variations in it are due to class—a serving woman has fewer privileges but perhaps also greater freedom because of her class. In this reading, her "womanness" is fixed, but how it plays out in social terms is determined by class. The categories are stable, and one could more or less represent the range of possibilities in a graph, where the vertical line is gender and the horizontal line class; where they intersect gives us a reading/representation of what it was like to be a serving woman, an aristocratic woman of the middling ranks, a woman belonging to the uppermost echelons of court nobility, and so on. In the second reading, and one that informs what follows, gender is performative, not fixed and given, and thus how it is performed—what constitutes being a woman—is itself shaped by class, which again, far from being stable, functions as a dynamic and fluid category.

If, as I have argued, gender in the *Genji* functions as a kind of script, and that it is the specificity of the gendered performance, that is to say, the particularity of the script that is enacted, rather than the sexual attributes and reproductive functions of the body that gives substance to the categories "male" and "female,"[7] then the performance of gender can never be uniform. The performance of gender as a script always holds the possibility of its own undoing.[8] It is the possibilities offered by different ways of "doing" gender that the text explores through the many romantic encounters that constitute the tale. Focusing on scenes within the text, which foreground robes and bodily comportment, I hope to demonstrate how the interplay of gender, social status, the body, and its performative modes is never entirely predictable, and that it produces a kaleidoscopic effect, reflecting the ever-changing configurations of the politics of love.

The Significance of Déshabillé: Genji as an Erotic Figure

Of all the characters in the text, Genji is perhaps the one whose beauty and radiance is most celebrated and commented upon by the narrating figures, the serving women, and the men who observe him. The significance accorded to robes, and to informal garb in particular, for creating an image of Genji as irresistibly erotic is of particular interest here, particularly when juxtaposed against the scenes of Genji secretly watching Utsusemi and Nokiba no Ogi playing *go*, or of Kaoru spying on Ōigimi and Nakanokimi, and on the First Princess. In each instance, robes intersect in different ways with status and gender to generate or dampen erotic and affective desires, demonstrating the inseparability of conceptions of beauty and refinement from the workings of power.

In "The Green Branch" chapter, when Tō no Chūjō gives a banquet in which one of his sons sings the *saibara* folk song "Takasago," Genji, who is deeply moved and impressed, takes off one of his robes and drapes it over the boy's shoulder. The beauty of his face, revealing to an unusual degree his excited state, is described as being without compare, and his skin, glowing through the summer robes, is so beautiful that the elderly scholars watching him cannot but shed tears.[9] There is no doubt that the scene in question is a highly erotic one in which the sight of Genji arouses passion in even the most arid and ancient of scholars.

The question is: How is eroticism constituted in this scene? What the text draws attention to is the fact that Genji's face exudes a special kind of beauty, caused by his unusually excited state. The word *midare* (*rei yori wa uchimidare tamaeru onkao no nioi*), used in this context, suggests an abandonment of self-control and restraint, an unusual display of emotion, which would normally be kept well concealed, but which is now available as a public spectacle. Genji is excited by the beauty of the young boy and by the song he sings, which is about passionate love.[10]

Given the body's metonymic connections with clothing, the fact that Genji takes off his own robe and drapes it over the boy's shoulder signals both a claim to intimacy as well as proof of the degree to which he is both moved and aroused by the boy. It is at the moment when Genji sheds his own robe that the beauty of his skin is revealed. Rather than the physical attributes of his body that are revealed through his thin inner robe, it is the nature of the scene in which the performative body is seen in action, and when robes are transferred from one body to another, that produces erotic reverberations all around, touching Genji, the elderly spectators, and the readers/auditors of the text alike.[11]

What is striking is the degree to which Genji's beauty is constituted through his apparel and his bodily comportment rather than through his physical features. Early in the text, in the "Rainy Night Discussion," the figure of Genji lying down, dressed casually in soft white gowns covered with only a summer cloak (*nōshi*), with the cord cast aside, we are told, cuts such a delightful figure in the lamplight that those around him wish that he were a woman.[12] It may well be that the contours of his body are more clearly visible in his casual dress than they would normally be, but what the text draws attention to is not his body but the informality of his attire. As Tyler points out, Genji appears not to be wearing the gathered trousers (*sashi-nuki*) that would normally go with this outfit.[13] The undone cord (*himo*), likewise, accompanied by the casual and languorous pose, call to mind the intimate setting of lovers. The *shitahimo* or trouser cord was, of course, a potent sexual metaphor in Heian poetry: the loosening or removal of the cord is metonymically linked to amorous desire, longing, and love's fulfillment.[14] The *himo* in question here belongs to Genji's robe, but it is the sight of it casually cast aside that plays a part in turning this into a scene with strong erotic overtones.

A very similar reading suggests itself in a scene in the Aoi chapter, when Tō no Chūjō arrives to see Genji after the death of Aoi. He encounters Genji leaning on the railing by the door: cupping his chin in his hand, in a gesture reflecting his melancholy mood, Genji sheds tears, "as if competing with the rain" that falls outside, and recites a poem. Tō no Chūjō, who finds himself stirred into an amorous mood (*iromekashiki kokochi*), observes that if he himself were a woman, his spirit (*tama*) would stay with Genji even after his death instead of leaving.[15] Unlike Tō no Chūjō, Genji is dressed in a carelessly informal and casual manner (*shidokenaku uchi midareru sama*). He wears a summer cloak (*nōshi*) over a plain crimson robe, and the cord of his outer robe is clearly undone, for he reties it when Tō no Chūjō sits down beside him. Genji's refined beauty finds expression not through his physical attributes or the body revealed through his thin robes but rather through the informality of his attire and the performative mode that he adopts—his lovelorn pose, his weeping, and his poetic recital. It is the overall mood created by this scene that produces a diffuse sense of erotic and aesthetic pleasure.

In descriptions of Genji's clothing, we often find the presence of words such as *shidokenaku, uchimidaru, azaretaru, uchitoketaru,* and *yatsureru*.[16] All these terms convey a sense of casualness, careless ease, languor, and informality of attire. Indeed, a conspicuous feature of the text is that there are very few descriptions of Genji in formal attire. He is often described as presenting his *uchiki sugata*, which is to say, his appearance in undergarments worn under the formal *nōshi* or *karaginu*. Informality of attire may well reveal something of the body, but that in itself is accorded little significance in the text. Equally, casual garb does not always produce erotic desire. As we shall see, it is the context within which casual garb appears, and the particular configurations of gender and status within which it is embedded, that give it the power either to generate or dampen amorous interest.

In depictions of Genji as an erotic figure the text draws attention to the fact that the men observing Genji see him either as they would a woman or wish that they *were* themselves women.[17] Some scholars have read these scenes as homoerotic moments in the text and have described Genji's beauty as androgynous or bisexual, and hence appealing to both men as well as women.[18] The term "bisexual" in this context is somewhat anachronistic and therefore misleading. For it was not until the nineteenth century, when new discourses on sexuality brought disparate elements of Japan's premodern erotic and libidinal economies under a coherent regime, that the normative category heterosexuality emerged along with its other, homosexuality, with bisexuality understood as a combination of the two.[19] Neither Genji's body nor his robes are marked by his sex/gender, further attesting to the fact that "male" and "female" were not constituted through conceptions of innate bodily difference or through distinctions in attire.[20] The fact that the text does not specify whether it is the viewer who wishes to be a woman or whether he or she wishes to see Genji as a woman points to the fluid and interchangeable nature of "male" and "female" here. The scenes in which the men around Genji express their erotic feelings are perhaps best read not as manifestations of homosexual desire but rather as culturally available performative stances in which the tropes of *otoko* and *onna,* so central to the unfolding of amorous affairs in *waka* and *monogatari,* could be playfully manipulated by the male protagonists of the text, irrespective of the nature of their physical sexual attributes. To argue for the fluidity of gender in the *Genji* is not to suggest that there is no difference between male and female gendered positions. After all, the possibilities of play afforded by crossing gender boundaries appear far more limited for women in the *Genji,* particularly when they belong to the highest rungs of the aristocracy. However, each particular context determines how gender will play out; far from being fixed in the same way, it is through its interaction with other modalities of power that it reveals its variability.

The Closed versus Open Body

A striking feature of the many scenes where men observe and evaluate women's erotic potential is that they do so covertly. The well-known topos of *kaimami* (peeping) has been the subject of considerable research, for it is unarguably an invaluable site for a consideration of how gender, the male gaze, and female subjectivity are constructed in the *Genji.* A variety of methodological approaches— psychoanalysis, with its focus on desire and the unconscious;[21] reception theory, which deals with the role of the reader in re-creating texts; and feminism, which foregrounds questions of female agency and subjectivity[22]—have been brought to bear on the *Genji,* to offer complex readings of the significance of *kaimami* for reading gender relations in the text.

In line with the overarching themes and concerns of the book, I am principally interested in exploring not only the possibilities but also the limits of the category gender as the foundational site for reading how men and women are positioned in the erotics of *kaimami.* Each voyeuristic scene in the text, as I hope to demonstrate, echoes past acts of peeping, and it is through this mode of repetition with difference that the complex configurations of power, not reducible to a single origin or cause such as gender, are best revealed. The body's performative modes are central to the generation of erotic and affective longing, but how they are apprehended and appraised are always imbricated in the complex and shifting dynamics of power that inflect who sees and what is seen. It is this aspect of *kaimami* that is the focus of what follows.

Let us begin with the scene in which, unbeknownst to them, Genji is able to get a clear view of Utsusemi and her stepdaughter, Nokiba no Ogi. He first observes one of the women whom he assumes, rightly, to be Utsusemi. What strike him most are her attire and her bodily comportment. The shape of her head and her slender build, he notes, are hardly noteworthy (*monoge naki sugata zo shitaru*), but what is remarkable about her is the way in which she takes the trouble to hide her face from the woman facing her. Indeed, she goes so far as to make sure that her thin hands are hidden from view. His gaze now shifts to her partner, who sits facing him, thereby affording him an unobstructed view. The fulsomeness of the description that follows matches the leisurely nature of his gaze. She is attired in thin white robes covered with a gown worn carelessly, exposing her breasts all the way down to her scarlet trouser cord, exhibiting a certain coarseness of behavior (*hōzoku motenashi nari*). He then moves to an appraisal of her physical appearance: tall, fair skinned, and plump, she is strikingly good-looking, leaving nothing to be desired.[23]

Genji's eyes shift to Utsusemi again, but he is unable to see her fully because she keeps her mouth carefully covered with her sleeve. The text unambiguously contrasts Nokiba no Ogi's youthful and full-bodied good looks with Utsusemi's rather undistinguished appearance. If the former cuts a flamboyantly lively and attractive figure (*hanayaka naru katachi nari*), Utsusemi, by contrast, has little that is sparkingly beautiful about her (*niowashiki tokoro mo miezu*). Indeed, she has slightly swollen eyes and her rather ill-defined nose tends to makes her look past her prime. Genji even goes so far as to observe that if one were to put it bluntly, she comes close to being simply plain (*iitatsureba waroki ni yoreru katachi*).

And yet it is to Utsusemi that his heart is drawn, for compared to the one who is superior to her in looks, he cannot but help discern in her a greater depth that is more compelling.[24] Genji's appraisal of Utsusemi, on the one hand, and of Nokiba no Ogi, on the other, is symptomatic of a tension that runs through the text, between the contending claims of women who conform to the prescribed code of decorum by performing restraint, implacability, or vulnerability as the occasion demands, and those whose comportment is lively, unguarded, and more responsive to male attention. In the many passages in which Genji forms his judgments about the two women, we see him at once drawn to the un-self-conscious and exuberantly open disposition of women like Nokiba no Ogi, while at the same time experiencing a certain unease and a curious dampening of his attraction brought on precisely by those very qualities.

Genji considers Nokiba no Ogi frivolous and shallow (*awatsukeshi*), but he admits that he is fickle enough not to pass up the chance of sleeping with someone as obviously pretty as her. Her lively outbursts during the *go* game lead him to conclude that she is somewhat lacking in class and breeding (*sukoshi shina oku-retari*). He wishes, for example, that her beauty could be accompanied by a corresponding composure and self-restraint (*kokochi nao shizuka naru ke o soebaya to futo miyuru*). At the same time he recognizes that most women with whom he has been intimate only reveal a well-composed profile that gives nothing away. It is for this reason that he feels that this rare opportunity to look on, unnoticed, at someone who disports herself in such an uninhibited manner is not to be missed, and he longs to continue with his transgressive peeping. Later that night, in pursuit of Utsusemi, he ends up sleeping with Nokiba no Ogi, who, "though not unlikeable, also gave little cause for a more long term attachment" (*nikushi to wa nakeredo onkokoro tomarubeki yue mo naki kokochi shite*). He continues to be preoccupied with the implacable Utsusemi instead.

Nokiba no Ogi fails to match up to Utsusemi because she does not contain herself or her body at all times. The text is at pains to draw a sharp contrast between Nokiba no Ogi's careless exposure of herself and Utsusemi's meticulous concern to cover every part of her body, such that her face and even her hands are barely visible even to her own stepdaughter. Likewise, Nokiba no Ogi's voluble outburst during their game of *go* contrasts with the measured and self-controlled words uttered by Utsusemi. The latter's contained and closed body—the way she has it completely covered even to the point where her hands are unexposed—is metonymic of her inaccessibility. The manner in which she guards against any encroachments, even visual ones, on her body is what makes her desirable.

The reason Genji disapproves of Nokiba no Ogi's exposure of her breasts is not because they are erotic and hence best kept modestly hidden.[25] It is the informality of Nokiba no Ogi's attire that is a problem, because it bespeaks a certain lack of class and refinement. Furthermore, her careless exposure of herself renders her vulnerable to male advances. In a world in which being seen (*mirareru*) was often tantamount to being physically possessed (and this is indeed what happens to Nokiba no Ogi), it is her lack of vigilance and the carelessness of her comportment that arouses Genji's short-term interest, without earning her his long-lasting affection.[26]

Genji's reading of the bodily comportments of Nokiba no Ogi and Utsusemi is replayed later in the "Under the Cherry Blossoms" chapter, where he contrasts Oborozukiyo's careless exposure of herself with the admirable modesty and restraint shown by Fujitsubo.[27] As with Nokiba no Ogi, Genji is delighted with Oborozukiyo and is not beyond taking advantage of her easygoing ways, but as the ambiguous last line of the chapter, "it was very pleasing and yet" (*itou ureshiki mono kara*), suggests, although he is delighted by her response to his poem, there is something there that is not entirely to his taste.[28]

It is probably not too far-fetched to suggest, as some Japanese annotators have done, that Genji's ambivalence stems from a certain disappointment at discovering how readily accessible Oborozukiyo is and how easily she matches his own expressions of love and desire with poems that reveal her own receptivity to his advances. In Genji's various reflections on women, one senses a profound ambivalence toward the contending attractions of the closed versus the open body and the charms of an exuberant presence projecting itself outward versus a more restrained and fragile figure, which keeps itself hidden from view. In the case of Nokiba no Ogi and Oborozukiyo, Genji is disappointed that they do not show greater restraint and decorum; in the case of Yūgao, a lady of the middle ranks with whom he establishes a deep bond, however, his reflections on what makes her beautiful are followed by a certain reservation about her lack of self-assertiveness and artfulness (*kokorobamitaru kata o sukoshi soetaraba to mitamainagara*).[29] While restraint is clearly desirable in women in as much as it displays good breeding, neither extreme reticence nor un-self-conscious openness turns out to be entirely satisfying. The pleasure of *kaimami* lies precisely in observing the kinds of bodily comportment that women are likely to adopt, for it is through the performative modes of the body that a surprisingly diverse array of natures and dispositions are revealed, opening up unexpected possibilities for men who are particularly sensitive to the pleasures of amorous play (*irogonomi*). *Kaimami* functions as the stage upon which someone like Genji learns to read (albeit imperfectly) the significations attached to particular forms of bodily comportment, and it is precisely his creative misreadings that propel the amorous adventures that unfold in the text.

The scene of Kaoru spying on Ōigimi and Nakanokimi after the death of their father echoes some of the same motifs that appear in the Utsusemi chapter when Genji peeps in on Utsusemi and Nokiba no Ogi playing *go*.[30] Kaoru first catches a glimpse of the younger sister—although she is dressed in mourning for her father, her robes nonetheless exude a certain brightness, which tells Kaoru something about her temperament. Likewise, the observation that her shoulder cords (*kakeobi*) are casually tied (*obi hakanage ni shinashite*) is intended to reveal more than simply her sartorial style. Her height and posture, as well as her hair and profile, are redolent of such beauty and grace that he cannot help but think of the First Princess whom he has seen only fleetingly in the past. Like Nokiba no Ogi, Nakanokimi suggests a lively and unrestrained disposition: she first steps into view because she watches, from behind a standing curtain, as Kaoru's men wander about outside. At the end of the scene, she sits facing the opening of the sliding panel and, for some reason (*nani goto ni ka aramu*), inadvertently allows herself to be seen fully as she smiles in Kaoru's direction.[31] He, we are told, finds her quite fetching.

If Nakanomi shows a thoughtless disregard for concealing herself, her sister Ōigimi displays an almost obsessive vigilance, guarding against any possibility that she and her sister might be exposing themselves to view. She is in the same mourning robes as her sister, but her appearance is more endearingly charming and evokes in Kaoru feelings of sympathy and pain for her loss. Her hair, which has thinned a little, speaks of her sadness occasioned by the death of her father. Her hands, likewise, are more slender than her sister's and appear to have become very thin (*kare yori mo hososa masarite yase yase narubeshi*).

Like Genji in his response to Nokiba no Ogi, Kaoru is not immune to the fulsome beauty of Nakanokimi, but it is the more austere and dignified figure of Ōigimi that he finds more appealing. Physical appearance and inner dispositions are interdependent in the *Genji*: the frail and emaciated body of Ōigimi is at once a sign of her physical state as well as a mark of her suffering, while the lively figure of Nakanokimi is an expression of an extroverted and exuberant disposition that, while deeply attractive, fails to be as profoundly affecting.

I have juxtaposed these disparate scenes from the *Genji* in order to foreground some of the assumptions that appear to me to be implicit in the text's figuration of the erotic. Genji is presented at his most alluring when he is in a state of déshabillé. Nokiba no Ogi's casual appearance, on the other hand, while not dissimilar to Genji's, is judged to be slovenly and somewhat coarse (*hōzoku nari*). This asymmetry could no doubt be readily explained by the fact that Nokiba no Ogi is a woman, and that it is the foundational difference of gender that accounts for the very different resonances produced by the same modes of bodily comportment.

And yet, to privilege gender alone would be to oversimplify; for Genji's assessment of Nokiba no Ogi is not reducible to the fact that she is a woman and therefore necessarily inferior to him. Her failure to match her stepmother, Utsusemi, is a result of the fact that she makes no effort to emulate the comportment of highborn ladies and thereby merely confirms the insignificance of her own social stature. Here, status is of greater significance than gender.

Oborozukiyo too displays a rather carefree and forward disposition in the way she invites Genji's attentions. And yet, his dalliance with her takes on an altogether different meaning in light of the fact that she is the daughter of the Minister of the Right, and that she has been promised to Genji's half brother, the Crown Prince Suzaku. The affair with Oborozukiyo, which is the immediate cause of Genji's self-imposed exile, is intended to draw attention to the far greater transgression committed by Genji when he sleeps with Fujitsubo, who belongs to his father. Gender alone is an inadequate guide for reading the asymmetries that are constitutive of all relationships in the text. For it is perfectly possible, in other contexts, for a noblewoman to evoke feelings of tenderness and desire even if she is dressed, like Genji, in informal garb.

As we shall see in the following section, Kaoru's intense longing for the First Princess is awakened upon being treated, unexpectedly, to the pleasure of seeing someone of an exalted rank in thin summer robes. However, status too is far from being a stable criterion for gauging the workings of the politics of desire. After all, not all princesses, however highborn, necessarily live up to men's amorous and erotic expectations. The Third Princess (Onna San no Miya) proves to be a great disappointment to Genji despite her impeccable lineage. Kaoru's intense attraction to the First Princess is tied not only to her own noble lineage but also to his intense awareness of his own relatively inferior status. The shifting contexts within which amorous encounters take place are always imbricated in a variety of asymmetries and hierarchies, which sometimes work together and at other times pull in different directions, thereby attesting to the inadequacy of treating either gender or class in isolation, outside of the setting or stage (*bamen*) upon which they are brought into play.

The Erotics of Anxiety

The fact of Kaoru's commoner status haunts the "Ivy" chapter in which we are constantly reminded of the dissonance between Kaoru's standing, determined by his birth, and the extraordinary heights to which he rises, favored as he is by the emperor.[32] Much to the astonishment and disapproval of many at court, the emperor decides to marry his daughter the Second Princess to him. The narrator points out how unbearably sad it is to see a daughter so beloved by her father, being given away to a mere commoner (*tadabito no gu shi tatematsuri tamau zo, nao akazu kokorogurushiku miyuru*).[33] At a party thrown by the emperor, attended by the most senior noblemen, Kaoru receives the unusual honor, given his position as a commoner, of partaking of a cup of wine presented by the emperor. Protocol requires that after drinking the cup, the recipient return to his seat. In

Kaoru's case this draws attention to the ignominy of having to take the humble seat that marks his place within the hierarchy. The narrator draws our attention to this by commenting that the sight of him returning to his lower seat was almost painful to behold (*kudaritaru za ni kaeri tsukitamaeru hodo, kokoro gurushiki made zo miekeru*).[34]

Kaoru makes a highly advantageous marriage and there is nothing about the Second Princess that is cause for disappointment. Kaoru knows how lucky he is to have her, but he remains preoccupied with thoughts of Ōigimi, whose death leaves him restless and in search of substitutes who might take her place. It is in this context that his thoughts turn to the First Princess, who is the daughter of the emperor and the Akashi Empress, and therefore the more highly ranked half sister of his own wife. His marriage to the lesser of the two princesses serves to reinforce further his feelings of inadequacy about his commoner status (the word *tadabito* recurs throughout the chapter) and to create a sense of hopeless longing for the First Princess, who is out of his reach. A striking episode in which he spies on her on a hot summer's day reveals the finely wrought connections between the body, erotic desire, and social standing.

He first glimpses three women and a young girl breaking up blocks of ice. They are all dressed so casually that he cannot imagine a lady as exalted as the First Princess being in their midst. And yet, much to his surprise, he sees her "dressed in a white gossamer gown, holding a piece of ice, watching her women playfully squabbling, with an indescribably beautiful smile on her face."[35] It strikes him that although he has been intimate with many highborn, beautiful women, there has not been one among them who even comes close to her (*kokora yoki hito o miatsumuredo, nirubeku mo arazarikeri to oboyu*). It is telling that the word the text uses for beauty here is not *namamekashi, utsukushi,* or *rōtashi* but rather *yoki,* which means both noble and beautiful. A *yoki hito,* in courtly society, is expected to be beautiful because s/he is of high rank and well placed in the world—beauty and status are meant to be mutually constitutive—but what the text reveals is precisely the failure of the two necessarily to map onto one another.

Kaoru, who is particularly sensitive to the privileges attendant on the accident of birth, recognizes beauty as something that inheres in the highest born. Noteworthy too is the fact that, for Kaoru, the First Princess's light, transparent gown does not bespeak frivolity or carelessness—in someone of such exalted status, the sight of her in informal garb provides an erotic charge both because of the beauty of her form, revealed through her transparent clothes, and perhaps more significantly because he, a commoner, has been treated to the rare sight of a princess of the highest stature exposed to his gaze.

The next morning he wonders how his own wife might compare with her half sister and whether she is in fact inferior to the other who seems so unlike her. Not content with these musings, he orders his gentlewomen to have a gossamer robe made up for her, under the pretext that it would be appropriate for the hot weather. In a finely ironic moment, the serving women, misunderstanding his motives, are delighted with his suggestion, for they assume that his desire to see her in this unusual attire (*rei naranu mono*) stems from an appreciation of her beauty, which they note is at its height. The relentless Kaoru, finding that his wife has not put on the gown once it is ready, reprimands her and proceeds to dress her himself. Although her trousers are no different from those worn by her sister and her hair is as beautifully long, the two sisters fail to resemble one another. Unwilling to give up his experiment, Kaoru orders some ice to be brought in so that he can more accurately reproduce the scene of the previous day.[36]

While we are told that he experiences a certain secret pleasure in giving the Second Princess a piece of ice, in the end, the text is silent about what it is he sees that fails to please. His disappointment finds expression in the sigh he lets out as his thoughts wander once again to the First Princess. He proceeds to inquire whether his wife has been writing regularly to her sister, and then attributes the lack of communication between the two to the fact that the First Princess no longer cares to write to her sister because she has become a commoner through marriage (*tadabito ni narase tamainitari*). He decides to complain to the empress, and when his uncomprehending wife protests, he reiterates his view that the First Princess has stopped writing because she looks down on her sister, who has fallen in status (*gesu ni narinitari*).[37]

Kaoru's obsessive reference to his commoner status plainly reveals what lies at the heart of his erotic and amorous longing for the First Princess. What Kaoru finds irresistibly appealing is the secret view of a lady who is of such high standing that she must necessarily remain out of his reach. His re-creation, with his wife, of the erotic scene with the First Princess, is doomed to fail, because for him his wife's beauty and allure are commensurate with her social position, and therefore bound to fall short of her sister's. Kaoru's own position, which renders him a *tadabito*, despite being the son of a highborn princess (Onna San no Miya), makes him particularly sensitive to questions of status, and this is not without consequence in his treatment not only of his wife but also of Ukifune, whom he seeks to fashion as a substitute for her higher-born half sister Ōigimi, who has passed away.

It is in the nature of substitutes to invite comparison. In a procedure that we are familiar with throughout the text, Ukifune, the lesser figure, is always haunted by the presence of the idealized other. The image of Ukifune hiding her face charmingly behind a fan reminds Kaoru of Ōigimi, but this is quickly followed by the realization that "there seemed to be something wanting in her overly meek and submissive manner (*oirakani amari ohodokisugitaru zo, kokoromoto naka-meru*); "the other, also had a childlike manner, but she displayed gravitas . . ." (*ito itau komeitaru monokara yōi no asakarazu . . .*).[38] Kaoru then proceeds to appraise Ukifune's attire. She wears layered robes, with some thought given to the color combination, but Kaoru's discerning eye detects something in this getup that he finds a little rustic and unrefined (*sukoshi inakabitaru koto mo uchimajirite zo*), leading him to remember the refined beauty of Ōigimi (*ate ni namamekashikari-shi nomi omoiiderarete*).

From an assessment of her appearance and clothes he moves to an evaluation of her musical and poetic accomplishments. The test confirms what Kaoru already suspects: Ukifune's rustic upbringing has deprived her of musical training and of the art of words, manifested in her inability to respond suitably to his amusing anecdotes. However, to his relief, she is not, he decides, irremediably beyond hope. For, "if she had the vulgarly ostentatious manner of rustic boors, or was lacking in any refinement and talked in a rapid fire fashion, she would be of no use to him as a substitute" (*inakabitaru saregokoro motetsukete, shinajina shikarazu hayarika naramashikaba katashiro fuyō naramashi to omoinaoshi tamau*).[39] Kaoru's scheme to tutor Ukifune so that she can be a credible replacement for Ōigimi, which is a tawdry repetition of Genji's own project earlier in the text to educate a child, Murasaki, to take the place of the unattainable Fujitsubo, serves as a reminder that all erotic and affective undertakings, no matter how heartfelt, cannot be disentangled from questions of power and politics.

After Ukifune's "death" the grief-stricken Kaoru thinks of how he would have liked to have her as a charming companion with whom he could interact informally and with ease, unlike the more burdensome responsibilities demanded of a relationship with a woman who is highborn (*omorika naru kata narade, tada kokoro yasuku rōtaki kataraibito ni te arasemu . . .*).[40] This reflection on the pleasures of an easygoing intimacy with women of insignificant social status is at odds with his amorous fantasies about the First Princess, who is desirable precisely because of her exalted status, which stands in contrast to both his wife's relatively inferior rank and his own commoner status. For Kaoru, the game of erotics is always haunted by the specter of dissonance, born of the divisions of status and rank. It is his friend and rival Niou, who, secure in the knowledge that he is an imperial prince of the highest stature, is best able to enjoy the erotic pleasures afforded by crossing the boundaries of class.

Niou first happens to spy on Ukifune at Nijōin, where she is temporarily in residence to visit her half sister Nakanokimi. Struck by her beauty, he notes that for a recently appointed serving woman (for that is what he assumes she is), she leaves nothing to be desired. On this occasion, Niou is unable to possess her sexually; his curiosity whetted by his twilight encounter with a woman whose origins and whereabouts are unknown, he reflects on her social standing and concludes that she does not appear to be anyone of great consequence in terms of her birth and status (*koto kotoshiki hodo ni wa arumajige narishi*);[41] at the same time, he reckons that she is certainly pretty enough to warrant intimacy.

When Kaoru moves Ukifune to Uji, Niou tracks her down and, passing himself off as Kaoru, he enters her quarters, where he is treated to another chance to observe her as she lies in her room surrounded by the women who wait on her. Unsure of her identity, Niou is struck by how much she resembles his own wife, Nakanokimi. Wondering at their extraordinary resemblance, upon further observation, he cannot but note that the one before him lacks the nobility and distinction of the other.[42] Even if it is quite likely that he will find things in her that are wanting, his curiosity has been raised to such a pitch that all he wants is to take possession of her.

Good breeding, which comes with social status, is never absent as a consideration even in the most rashly romantic of undertakings. Niou cannot but compare Ukifune unfavorably to Nakanokimi, whom she resembles. At the same time, he is less inclined than Kaoru to test her cultural accomplishments or to seek to discover her family connections. More than Niou's admiration of women as flesh,[43] it would seem that it is the power to manipulate the boundaries that mark status and rank that transports the purely carnal into the realm of the erotic. For Niou, Ukifune's uncertain origins make possible forms of cross-dressing, which break the boundaries of both status and gender, and this constitutes the frisson that he seeks in amorous adventures with unknown women.

During his first encounter with Ukifune, for example, Niou offers her the washbasin first rather than have her wait on him. It is precisely the pleasure afforded by transgressing the boundaries of gender and status that Niou finds so seductive, for even as he acknowledges that she is the equal of neither Nakanokimi nor Rokunokimi, it is the possibility of disporting with her in a carefree manner—unimaginable with a highborn lady—that renders theirs a genuinely intense and passionate entanglement. During the day and a half that he spends with her, he finds ways to amuse her with drawings and writing practice. So fine are the pictures he draws for her that, as the narratorial voice tells us, her youthful feelings must have found themselves shifting (from Kaoru to Niou) (*wakaki kokochi ni wa, omoi mo utsurinubeshi*).[44]

On his next visit, he carries her off to a secluded house on the other side of the river, away from prying eyes. Niou himself is dressed in light, humble clothing, in view of the fact that he wishes to travel incognito. The simplicity of his garb notwithstanding, he exudes a certain refinement entirely commensurate with his exalted rank. It is through robes that the political nature of their erotic encounter is revealed. Niou gets Ukifune to take off her outer robe so that her slender form is revealed in all its beauty. Niou finds that she looks much more alluring in her five soft gowns than she would if she were wearing layered robes. Again, it is not primarily what is revealed through the thin robes but rather what the informality of her attire signifies that renders her deeply novel and charming in his eyes, for as he notes, he is not accustomed to seeing even the ladies he is intimate with in this kind of attire.

Ukifune is embarrassed to appear exposed in this way in front of so exalted a personage as Niou. Her humiliation is intensified in the knowledge that *even* Jijū, her young and impressionable attendant, who is enjoying the escapade enormously, is privy to seeing her in this state (*kore sae kakaru o nokorinau miru yo to nyōgimi wa imiji to omou*). What Ukifune finds humiliating is not that her body is visible but rather that she presents a *full* view of herself in a compromised position (*nokorinau*) even to someone like Jijū, who is of a lower rank than herself.[45]

Niou playfully borrows Jijū's "rude and rustic apron" (*ayashiki shibira*) and makes Ukifune put it on when she serves him water for his ablutions. Niou indulges in the erotic pleasure of refashioning Ukifune, such that she takes on the role of Jijū, a serving woman. Despite the disapproval of onlookers, he also insists upon carrying her to and from the house that he has chosen for their tryst. Niou's inversions of the accepted protocols of status are central to the erotics that animate their relationship. Ukifune is sufficiently seduced by Niou's playful transgressions to spend the next two days with him, where they "play and cavort"[46] in a manner that the narrator deems to be "unsightly." This is as explicit as the text ever gets about carnal pleasure: Ukifune's tangled hair, a common trope in classical poetry, indicating female passion, is testament to the mutually shared nature of their erotic pleasures.

Neither the playful adventures of Niou nor the solemn undertakings of Kaoru, while imbricated in questions of power, are reducible to an exercise of it. Regardless of differences of gender or status, for both men and women the asymmetries that are integral to amorous relationships are so part of the natural order that Niou's inventive games of love are appealing not only to him but in equal measure to Ukifune as well. Likewise, when Nakanokimi appraises Ukifune's worth, her criteria for judging her half sister are remarkably consonant with those applied by Kaoru himself. While struck by her beauty and her extraordinary resemblance to her older sister Ōigimi, Nakanokimi, like Kaoru, cannot but compare Ukifune to her deceased sister and conclude that she lacks the same degree of refinement and allure.[47] The fact that she attributes Ukifune's inferiority to her youth and diffidence, and that she thinks that the cultivation of greater depth would make her a person of substance, not unworthy as a companion to Kaoru, certainly speaks to her sisterly affection. It is also accompanied, however, by her profound awareness of Ukifune's rustic upbringing and uncertain social status, which necessarily render her lesser than Ōigimi.

Serving Women as *Irogonomi*

Women of the serving classes, who belong ostensibly to the lowest rungs of the court hierarchy, are no more homogeneous than the women they serve. While there are some who serve mistresses who belong to the middling ranks of the aristocracy, there are others who are so valued for their refinement and cultural accomplishments that they are chosen to serve no less than emperors, empresses, and imperial concubines. Ranging from young impressionable girls to older experienced women, they are also highly stratified in terms of age.

A crucial element of their function within the text is the way in which they act as important erotic counterpoints to their mistresses, who, following the codes appropriate to their status, are expected not to give in too readily to men's overtures, and instead, register their understanding of the rules of erotic play by appearing at once noncompliant and vulnerable.[48] It is significant, in this context, to note that the term *irogonomi* is used to speak about women who are professionally employed but never or rarely about ladies of the middle or high ranks who stay at home. In this, women of the serving classes are not unlike men who are also often designated as *irogonomi* in the text. That they are marked off as different from their mistresses does not mean, however, that what it means to be an *irogonomi* is the same for women as it is for men. That gender and status intersect in the text is undoubtedly true, but how the two come to be aligned does not map onto a stable grid for what it means to inhabit a particular gender, and to occupy a particular status within society is itself unstable and subject to change. Page girls, nurses, ladies-in-waiting, and so on all belong to the serving classes, but their status within courtly society varies greatly. Their performance of gender, likewise, is by no means uniform, producing a multiplicity of ways of being "woman."

Much has been written about the indispensability of the figure of the serving woman to the structure of the *Genji*. She propels the narrative forward by performing a crucial role as mediator between her reticent mistress and the men who seek amorous liaisons with her, and provides another point of view from which to observe the unfolding of amorous affairs.[49] She serves as a confidante, messenger, and advisor; she adjudicates on matters both emotional and artistic for the lady she serves, occasionally composing poetry on her behalf and encouraging or thwarting the amorous advances her mistress receives.

The noblewoman, who is expected to cultivate and perform a kind of refined receptivity, must meet amorous advances with judicious silence or with no more than the mot juste. She has to respond to her suitor's poems with her own refined compositions, using the conventional tropes that are appropriate to her position, expressing the inevitable waning of the man's desire, his eventual neglect of the lady he professes to love, and her declaration of her own unworthiness in the face of his interest.

In certain instances when a lady was incapable of crafting even the most basic response to a man's overtures, the women in her entourage were required to step in. This is what happens in the case of the tongue-tied Suetsumuhana. The daughter of her wet nurse, who is described as being a rather indiscreet young thing (*hayarika na wakabito*), responds to Genji's poem, pretending to be the highborn lady herself. Her poem, rather too responsive and enthusiastic in its tenor, leaves Genji speechless because he cannot understand how someone of Suetsumuhana's station could possibly allow herself to sound so familiar and intimate (*hodo yori wa amaete*) in response to his overtures.[50]

The figure of the serving woman often functions as the perfect counterpoint to her mistress, for she is authorized to alter the prescribed performance of gender that her mistress is expected to follow. Her responses point to the possibility of another mode of engagement in which the stylizations so central to amorous play can take a different form, opening up a space for the exchange of suggestive poems, lively banter, and the possibility of striking up sexual relations with men freely—often even with the noblemen who court her own mistress. Her performance of gender, so markedly different from that of her mistress, points to the inadequacy of treating "woman" as a stable category whose meanings are fixed regardless of differences of status and class.

A remarkable feature of the women who are employed to serve, as we have observed, is that they are often characterized as being fond of amorous and erotic play (*irogonomi*). Terms such as *iromekashi, iromeitaru, iro o konomu,* and so on all carry different nuances depending on context. Variously translated as amorous, forward, impetuous, wanton, giddy, romantic, coquettish, frivolous, lascivious, and so on, these terms are not reducible to a single meaning; at their core they do, however, signify a certain disposition that is particularly responsive to erotic situations and to certain forms of behavior and comportment that propel amorous play. This receptivity to the erotic or sexual possibilities inherent in amorous encounters often goes hand in hand with a knowledge of poetry, music, and other arts that is considered a prerequisite for the true connoisseur of the art of love. The term *suki* and related compounds such as *sukimono, sukigokoro, sukiwaza, sukizukishi,* and so on are often used interchangeably in the *Genji* with *irogonomi* and its variants.

Being a person given to amorous sport, as well as acting on those impulses, makes for an *irogonomi,* but rather than constituting a fixed ideal of courtly love, how the text evaluates such dispositions and actions is entirely contingent upon context. When Genji's father sees him flirting with one of his own middle-aged ladies-in-waiting, Gen no Naishi, he smiles indulgently and remarks to Naishi that while there are those who lament that Genji seems to lack an amorous disposition, he has certainly not let her pass by him (*sukigokoro nashi to tsune ni motenayamumeru o, sa wa iedo, sugusazarikeru*).[51] If his father is amused in this instance, knowing that this lighthearted liaison is unlikely to have any dangerous consequences, he is less sanguine when it comes to Genji's dealings with the Rokujō Lady, whose exalted social stature requires an altogether different approach.

The emperor points out to Genji how regrettable it is that he should treat her lightly, as if she were someone of no (social) consequence. He warns him that if he were to carry on with his wanton ways, doing as his heart pleased, he would most certainly earn the opprobrium of society (*kokoro no susabi ni makasete kaku sukiwaza suru wa ito yo no modoki oinubeki koto nari*). His final words on the matter are that Genji must not behave in a manner that brings shame to such women and that each one must be treated gently so that he does not earn her resentment.[52] Here the text prefigures the catastrophic deaths of Aoi and Yūgao at the hands of the Rokujō Lady, brought on by Genji's failure to heed his father's words.

For both men and women, being an *irogonomi* comes with certain entailments: men's romantic adventures can have serious consequences for the women with whom they form amorous liaisons. It is when Genji marries the Third Princess that Murasaki, bitterly wounded by his infidelity, begins to think of him as an *irogonomi.* When her gentlewomen read out *monogatari* to her she realizes that Genji is not unlike the inconstant (*ada naru otoko*), womanizing (*irogonomi*), and duplicitous (*futagokoro aru hito*) men in these tales. The only difference, she notes sadly, is that even these philanderers eventually settle down and visit only one woman; her own fate, she fears, does not hold out hope for such a change in Genji.[53]

How the receptivity of women of the serving classes to erotic situations is judged, and whether it is treated with benign indulgence, is contingent on many factors: their age, status, and the nature of their gendered performance. Youth is for the most part a privileged space in the text: there are many instances of young women who abandon themselves to the giddy pleasures of girlish infatuation, unrestrained by the protocols that govern the behavior of their own mistresses.

When Ukifune, after a failed attempt at taking her own life, imagines that she will be safe with the nuns who have undertaken to care for her, she finds herself being pursued by a young captain, related by marriage to one of the nuns; wishing to escape from his unwanted attentions she seeks the help of her page girl Komoki, but soon realizes that the girl cannot be relied upon for "so smitten is she by the arresting presence of this rare gentleman that she does not stay with her mistress" (*iromekite kono mezurashiki otoko no endachi itaru kata ni kaeri inikeri*).[54] Here, Komoki's infatuation with a dashing captain, and her inattentiveness to her mistress's needs, is of little consequence, and only to be expected of a young and impressionable working girl.

Earlier in the text, when Niou visits Ukifune and removes her to a villa across the river, he is accompanied on the expedition by his retainer Tokikata and Ukifune's gentlewoman Jijū.[55] Jijū, we are told, was "a young woman of an amorous disposition who found the situation vastly delightful, and spent the hours locked in intimacy with Tokikata" (*Jijū, iromekashiki wakōdo no kokochi ni, ito okashi to omoite, kono taifu to zo monogatari shite kurashikeru*).[56] What is striking here is the ease with which Jijū takes up with Tokikata and the unabashed pleasure she derives from the affair. In this, she serves as a perfect foil to her mistress, Ukifune, who, while more overtly receptive to the charms of her lover than many a heroine in the *Genji,* is unable, nonetheless, to give herself up wholly to her affair with Niou, troubled as she is by anxious thoughts of the potentially disastrous consequences of her romantic escapade.

Young gentlewomen of good lineage, who are accomplished in the arts, are often portrayed as being completely au fait with the ways of love (*iro o konomu*); they are voluble interlocutors and friends with the noblemen who woo their mistresses. The exchanges between Genji and Taifu no Myōbu, a gentlewoman who serves at court, demonstrate the centrality of ostensibly minor figures to the politics of eroticism that animates the text. Taifu is first introduced in the text as the daughter of one of Genji's nurses and the Commissioner of War, who is of imperial lineage. She is described as a young woman who is extremely fond of and adept in the ways of love (*iro konomeru wakōdo*) and therefore someone upon whom Genji relies from time to time.[57]

Keenly aware of Genji's weakness for amorous escapades, and of his interest in discovering a hidden beauty, in the manner of old romantic tales, she tells him about the daughter of a prince, who is forced to live in straightened circumstances after the death of her father. Encouraging him into a liaison with the hidden princess, she displays remarkable connoisseurship of the aesthetic conventions that govern courtly erotics. She first mentions the princess's musical talents, knowing that this is bound to arouse Genji's interest. She then installs him in her own rooms, not far from the main house, and urges the lady to play on the *kin*. Being a person of wit and discernment (*kado aru mono*), she makes sure that the lady plays just long enough to pique Genji's interest and that she stops well before Genji has a chance to be disappointed.

Having let Genji have a foretaste of the delights he might expect from such a liaison, she teases him about the casualness of his attire, which is intended to serve as a disguise during his nightly forays in search of amorous adventures. She observes that his father's concern that he might be far too serious (*mamemameshi*) is surely misplaced, given what his clothes reveal of his intentions. That Taifu here is able to tease him about his amorous ways, and about the emperor's innocent assumption of his son's earnestness, suggests the degree to which inversions of gender and status are possible in a space where performing the role of *irogonomi* is paramount.

Their banter continues. Genji retorts that she is hardly in a position to blame him, and that if his behavior is to be considered wanton (*ada adashiki furumai*) then it would put her in an even more compromising position. We are told that Taifu strikes Genji as being a person greatly enamored of love's games (*amari iro-meitari*), and this is what prompts him to tease her from time to time.[58] Genji has the last word in this exchange, but the nature of their interaction is playful and suggests the kind of camaraderie that also marks Genji's friendship with men such as Tō no Chūjō, and which is in stark contrast to the amorous relationships he establishes with women such as Yūgao, Akashi, or Murasaki. By encouraging him with the hidden princess, Taifu is his confidante and partner in crime, revelling in the erotic possibilities that might unfold, while the noblewoman herself is kept in the dark.

The exchanges between Genji and Taifu point to the centrality of her role not only in orchestrating the encounter but also in providing another point of view from which to assess Genji's motives and actions in this amorous escapade. When the lady refuses to respond to Genji's letters, he complains earnestly to Taifu (*mam-eyaka ni katarai tamau*) that he has been misunderstood and that undoubtedly the lady considers him a frivolous philanderer (*sukizukishiki kata ni utagai yose-tamau ni koso arame*), when in fact his feelings are anything but inconstant and short-lived.[59] Genji's self-defence is ostensibly directed to the unresponsive lady he pursues, but when one considers this incident in the light of the earlier conversation between him and Taifu, in which she laughs at the idea that the emperor takes him to be an overly serious young man (indeed the term she uses is *mam-emameshi,* which is echoed in his response to her), one cannot but read this exchange as Genji's attempt to seek the approval not of the noblewoman but rather of Taifu, a tough and discerning critic in matters of love.

Taifu is aware that she has set in train events that may bring humiliation to the one she has somewhat disingenuously promoted as a hidden princess with extraordinary charms and talents. She tries, unsuccessfully, to stop Genji from going any further and is clearly distressed when he breaks into the lady's quarters and sleeps with her. When Genji, disappointed with the sexual encounter, fails to visit her, Taifu is humiliated on her behalf and complains tearfully to Genji that he has caused great pain not only to the lady but also to all those around her. Genji, we are told, is horrified that Taifu might consider him heartless.

However, from contrition he quickly moves to a different register, as he smiles and explains to her that he has neglected the princess for her own good, in order to teach someone as inexperienced as she something about the feelings of melancholy longing (*mono omoi*) that are attendant on the experience of love. Taifu, who had been tearful a moment earlier when she pleaded her lady's case, now returns his smile indulgently, thinking that it is after all the prerogative of youth and of beauty such as his to be thoughtless and to seek pleasure even in the face of resentment from the woman concerned.[60]

Genji sets out to find a hitherto undiscovered princess; instead of being a hidden gem she turns out to be a gauche and awkward figure, an embarrassing mistake. Earning the cruel sobriquet Suetsumuhana, which suggests both the safflower and the unfortunate red nose with which she is endowed, her unprepossessing looks call into question the assumed connections between beauty and class. In the end, both Taifu's complicity in Genji's schemes and his own miscalculations point to a larger truth about the absurdity of the amorous escapades in which *irogonomi* get embroiled.

The wanton cruelty of these amorous games is explored to its limits in an episode that involves Gen no Naishi, who serves as a caricature of the figure of the *irogonomi*. As her title Dame of Staff (*naishi no suke*) suggests, Gen no Naishi is a high-ranking female official who works in the *Naishi no Tsukasa* (Palace Attendants Bureau). A woman appointed to this post could, if favored by the emperor, find herself elevated to the position of an imperial consort. Gen no Naishi is therefore not unlike Oborozukiyo, who also began her courtly duties as a *naishi*, serving the emperor, attending to his personal needs, and being available to him sexually.[61]

There is nothing then, on the face of it, about Gen no Naishi's status that should render her a laughable figure. Indeed, we are told that she comes from a distinguished family and that she is highly accomplished and well regarded because of her accomplishments. She is clearly favored by the emperor to whose needs she attends personally. She is, however, of an extremely wanton disposition (*imijū adameitaru kokorozama ni te*): this too is not, as we have seen, unusual for gentlewomen in the *Genji*. What makes Gen no Naishi's sexual appetite ridiculous is that she is not a young serving woman who can be forgiven such frivolity. Genji cannot understand how a woman of her advanced age (fifty-seven or fifty-eight) can possibly be so wild in her ways (*nado sashimo midaruramu to ibukashiku oboetamaikereba*).

The incongruity of Gen no Naishi's lascivious disposition (she is repeatedly described as an *irogonomi*), given her age, is captured through descriptions of her clothes, her physical appearance, and her poems, which point to the inappropriateness of her sexual desire. On one occasion when Genji finds himself alone with her, he notices that she is alluringly turned out and decked in bright robes, in an attempt to appear young and attractive, which strikes him as quite distasteful. When she looks at Genji from behind a heavily decorated fan, he sees that the skin around her eyes is dark and sunken and heavily wrinkled.[62] Genji, finding the fan she holds out of keeping with someone of her age, presents her with his own. Her fan, which is inscribed with the line "The grass beneath the trees has turned old"[63] refers to the following poem:

Ōraki no	the grass
mori no shita kusa	beneath the trees at Ōraki
oinureba	has turned old;
koma mo susamezu	no colt grazes there
karu hito mo nashi	no one comes to cut it

It is a barely veiled complaint by Gen no Naishi that men no longer display sexual interest in her in the way that they once did. This is followed by risqué exchanges between Gen no Naishi and Genji in which the sexual metaphor suggested by the colt and the cutting of the grass is exploited even more blatantly.

The affair with Gen no Naishi becomes broad farce when Genji's friend Tō no Chūjō discovers his friend's escapade and takes up with Naishi himself. When he breaks into her quarters pretending to be the jealous lover, Genji is caught out and engages in a tussle with his friend. Their mock outbursts of jealousy and their youthful exuberance are in stark contrast with Naishi's abject cries of horror. Naishi fails to recognize that being an *irogonomi* is a prerogative reserved for the young. As the narrator observes, "her outward appearance of attractive youthfulness notwithstanding, the sight of a fifty seven/eight year old woman creating a commotion without showing the slightest restraint, and cowering in fear in the presence of two peerless youths of twenty was highly inappropriate."[64] By creating a comedy of the absurd, the episode reveals what is often hidden in amorous encounters, namely that the asymmetries that are central to the generation of erotic intensities, when misaligned, can produce deep humiliation and loss of face.

I have suggested that how an *irogonomi* is judged in the *Genji*—whether admiringly or censoriously—is not dependent on either gender or class, understood as two separate categories. The two are always intertwined, configured differently in each context and situation, thereby producing a more fluid and unstable figuration of what it means to be an *irogonomi*. There is always a multitude of ways in which asymmetries and hierarchies come to be aligned. The text points to a certain tension between the freedom that serving women enjoy in giving voice to their amorous inclinations—a freedom that is denied their mistresses—and the possibility that expressing themselves and performing as *irogonomi* may be read as signs of impropriety.

This tension is best captured by Sei Shōnagon and Murasaki Shikibu, both of whom were ladies-in-waiting at the rival courts of Empress Teishi and Empress Shoshi, respectively. In her *Pillow Book* (*Makura no sōshi*), for example, Sei Shōnagon offers a scathing critique of so-called respectable ladies who lead cloistered lives at home as wives, showing very little understanding of the ways of the world. For she feels that women such as herself are often compared unfavorably with the stay-at-homes. As she claims, she "cannot bear men who consider women who work at court as frivolous and unseemly."[65]

Murasaki Shikibu, author of the *Genji*, like her contemporary Sei Shōnagon, is also acutely aware of the critical gaze of men directed at women such as herself. However, for her, the ideal lady-in-waiting is not one who claims to be refined by flaunting her knowledge of the ways of the world and participating brazenly in the games that *irogonomi* play. Women such as Gen no Naishi are the ones who give gentlewomen who work at court a bad name. The exemplary lady-in-waiting by contrast is one who cultivates modesty and quick wit, and uses her connoisseurship of love's games to handle men's advances and adroitly reject those who are unwanted.

Hers is an acutely self-conscious gaze directed not only at men but, more significantly, at herself and at other women who are liable to be subjected to serious scrutiny. In her diary *Murasaki Shikibu nikki,* she describes an interesting encounter between herself and her patron Fujiwara no Michinaga. When he comes upon a copy of the *Genji,* he makes his usual bantering comments and then writes a poem on a piece of paper that holds some plums:

sukimono to	it has made its name
na ni shi tatereba	as a sour fruit,
miru hito no	I doubt that there is anyone

> *orade suguru wa*   who upon seeing it
> *araji to zo omou*   would pass by without having a pluck

The word *suki* here of course means both sour and amorous. Michinaga's poem therefore can also be rendered thus:

> as you are renowned
> for your amorous ways,
> I am sure there are none
> who go by without
> having a taste

Murasaki has no difficulty in grasping the innuendo implied in Michinaga's poem and to skillfully manipulate the same pun to suggest that since she has not allowed herself to be approached by Michinaga, he is surely in no position to spread the word that she is a woman who offers herself to every man who comes along:

> *hito ni mada*   a fruit that has yet
> *orarenu mono o*   to be plucked
> *tare ka kono*   who then can smack his lips
> *sukimono zo to wa*   to claim
> *kuchinarashikemu*   its sourness?[66]

If we read this episode in her diary in conjunction with her portrayal of gentlewomen, who are in the service of women of the finest pedigree, we can see how she reconciles the demands of being a good *irogonomi*—quick-witted, accomplished in the art of poetry, and keenly attuned to the protocols of the game of love—with the qualities of discernment, grace, and modest dignity, which may protect her from the charge that she is frivolous and indiscriminately open to erotic adventures.

Early in the Yūgao chapter, when Genji leaves after a night spent with the Rokujō Lady, her gentlewoman Chūjō accompanies him to the gallery. Her beauty and grace, conveyed by the way in which she ties the train of her thin, gauze inner robe to her waist and the choice of a layered aster (*shion*) robe, which captures perfectly the color of the season,[67] inspires Genji to draw her to his side and recite the following verse:

> *saku hana ni*   though I would hesitate to be known
> *utsuru chō*   as one who flits

na wa tsutsumedomo	from flower to flower,
orade sugiuki	it would be sad indeed not to pick
kesa no asagao	the bluebell that flowers this morning

As in Murasaki's diary, the image of plucking is suggestive. Genji wants Chūjō to know that he does not wish to let the opportunity of dallying with her pass him by. As he takes her hand and asks how they should proceed, Chūjō adroitly recites a poem that turns his poem to one that refers not to herself but rather to her mistress, the Rokujō Lady:

asagiri no	that you would leave
harema mo matanu	without even waiting
keshiki ni te	for the morning mists to clear
hana ni kokoro o	clearly shows that your heart
tomenu to zo miru	cares not for its flower[68]

It is women of the uppermost echelons of the serving classes who come closest to meeting noblemen on their own terms, engaging playfully in amorous dalliance, but also using their skill as *irogonomi* to withdraw, when desirable, from men's erotic overtures. In this regard, gentlewomen, particularly those who work for empresses and imperial concubines, are less precariously placed than aristocratic women of uncertain rank who are more dependent on men for their well-being. The gentlewoman Kozaishō in the *Genji*, who serves the First Princess, the daughter of the Akashi empress, is a minor fictional character. The seemingly insignificant vignette about her, which appears late in the tale, after we have been privy to the tragic fate of the Uji sisters, consolidates all that we have learned in the text both about the constraints and the possibilities afforded to different classes of aristocratic women in the politics of erotics.

Kozaishō is on intimate terms with Kaoru: after the "death" of Ukifune she sends Kaoru a poem, sensitively responding to his loss but also suggesting that had it been she who had passed away, he would not have lamented her death in the same manner. Kaoru is so moved by the delicacy with which she has gauged his melancholy state that, quite out of keeping with the protocols demanded in such amorous affairs, he decides to visit her in her own quarters. She is embarrassed by the cramped nature of her room, so unfit for a gentleman of his stature. At the same time, she does not present herself to him as an abject figure. The text points to the fact that although she finds the situation awkward and embarrassing, she is by no means too self-deprecatory and humble (*amari hige shite mo arade*) and that she is able to engage in dignified conversation with him. Deeply impressed, he cannot help thinking that she appears to have far greater depth than the lady with whom he had been involved (*mishi hito yori mo kore wa kokoro ni-kugige soite mo aru ka na*). He wonders why she has gone into court service, for he would so like to have seen her ensconced somewhere suitable, where he would have access to her.[69] We are told that she is pursued by Niou as well, but that she sees no reason to give in to him as others have done. Later in the chapter, her behavior is endorsed by no less than the empress herself, who praises her for being so discerning a judge of Niou's character.[70]

There is a great deal here that is left unsaid, but it hovers, unmistakably, over the surface of the text. Kozaishō's poem is redolent of a grace, sensitivity, and modesty that would rival that displayed by the most desirable of noblewomen. The irony here is unmistakable even if it eludes Kaoru: her dignity, poise, and self-confidence, the very qualities that Kaoru finds particularly impressive and admirable, are enabled precisely by the freedom afforded her as a gentlewoman who serves the empress, a freedom she would lose if she were reliant solely on a husband or lover. Time and time again in the *Genji,* men who court women are disappointed, for they find them either too withdrawn or too forward. The figure of Kozaishō appears to hold the two in perfect balance. Perhaps she can be read as the text's provisional answer to how one might negotiate the fraught space of libidinal politics in the *Genji.*

Murasaki Shikibu and her contemporaries Sei Shōnagon and Izumi Shikibu, all illustrious women writers and poets of the Heian period, occupied positions at court that were not unlike the one held by Kozaishō. That little was known about their lives and status even during the prime of their lives, and that they fell into obscurity in old age, made them the stuff of myth, providing the ideal ground for imaginative reconfigurations of both their personae and their literary activities in the centuries that followed. The many avatars of one great luminary of the Heian period, Izumi Shikibu, and the creative reimaginings that were effected in the medieval period on the textual body of this famous literary figure are the subjects of the chapter that follows.

CHAPTER FOUR

Woman, Love, Poetry, and Enlightenment

Izumi Shikibu as Topos

The poet Izumi Shikibu was much discussed both in her own lifetime as well as in the centuries that followed her death. And yet, the "facts" that would allow us to construct a coherent biographical account of her life are flimsy at best and tell us little about the actual events and conditions that shaped it. Not unlike other eminent Heian women writers and poets, we know nothing about her later years and the circumstances under which she died. It is through her poetic compositions, a diary *Izumi Shikibu nikki* attributed (not without contention) to her, and the accounts of her contemporaries and near contemporaries in which she briefly makes an appearance that scholars have tried to create a picture of the "real" Izumi Shikibu. Her poems, especially those in which she speaks of passion, love, and longing, have been read as true accounts of her own love affairs and as authentic expressions of her bold and passionate temperament.[1] The assumption guiding these readings is that it is because of her amorous nature, and the many amorous liaisons into which she is supposed to have entered, that she wrote passionate love poetry. In a curious circularity, at the same time, it is the poetry itself, which in part allows for the construction of this image of Izumi as a passionate lover with a colorful past.[2]

In the absence of any real facts that might help to flesh out the lives of many of the poets of that age, the headnotes (*kotobagaki*), which provide a prose preamble and a context for the composition of individual poems or a series of poetic exchanges, have acquired a particularly privileged status as reliable sources for illuminating the real life experiences of poets. While headnotes certainly provide a plausible context within which a particular poem might have been composed, they are not recordings of facts and cannot be granted the status of historical footnotes. For, not unlike the poems they seek to contextualize, headnotes never stray outside the bounds of what is acceptable within the poetic tradition.

We know from the headnotes to the poems in Akazome Emon's anthology *Akazome Emon shū,* for example, that she composed some love poems on behalf of her son Ōe no Takachika, at his request. To speculate about her relationship with her son on the basis of the headnotes and poems, as some scholars have done, and to conclude that her compositions are a mark of her concern and love for him, and therefore proof that she was a good mother, is to burden the "evidence" with far more weight than it can bear.[3] Regardless of the veracity or fictive nature of the information provided to the reader, the function of the headnotes here allows for the creation of a context and pretext for Akazome to write in a male persona and thereby display her expertise and knowledge of the conventions and protocols of writing love poems in different voices and registers.

Another problem with treating either the poems or their headnotes as unmediated reflections of a poet's personal experience is that the same poems can appear with variant headnotes in different poetic anthologies or poem-tales (*uta monogatari*), thereby providing an alternate "biographical" point of reference from which to read the poem. This altered context destabilizes any sense of an author with a proper name and happens most notably when the poet is transformed simply into "man" (*otoko*), "woman" (*onna*), or "person" (*hito*). The way in which Izumi's amorous liaison with Prince Atsumichi comes to be thematized in *Izumi Shikibu nikki* is a case in point. The diary, popularly attributed to Izumi Shikibu, but whose authorship still remains unclear,[4] is written entirely in the third person, and the female protagonist is never named as Izumi but appears simply as *onna* or woman. Rather than bringing to bear extratextual evidence from Izumi's "real life" to explain why the identity of the female protagonist must remain hidden—and here, the argument would be that the affair was of too scandalous a nature for her to speak about it openly—it is worth considering what function the figure of *onna* performs in the text.

The fact that the male protagonist is identified as a prince, and that the text speaks of another prince who has recently died, allows us to read *onna* in two registers—the reader cannot but call to mind the historical Izumi Shikibu, who is said to have had affairs with two princes, Prince Tametaka and Prince Atsumichi; however, that she appears not as a proper name but simply as *onna* renders possible another layer of signification: in keeping with an established tradition within *waka* and *uta monogatari* (of which *Ise monogatari* is an exemplar), *onna* or "woman" in the diary can function as a figure of speech, unmarked by name or hierarchy; she becomes a conventional trope, which makes possible the stylized performance of waiting for the lover who may or may not visit and of communicating through the language of poetry.

It is through a series of poetic exchanges—which are always performed in consonance with the protocols of love poetry, but which stretch the possibilities of the genre to their limits—that *onna* is able to demonstrate her mastery of the rhetoric of romantic discourse, thereby turning the affair to her own advantage.[5] The male figure is marked as an imperial personage, but also, more importantly in the context of the romance, as one who must rise to the high standards set by *onna* and display connoisseurship of both the way of love and the way of poetry, thereby making him worthy of his designated status as one who visits and pursues. In other words, *onna* here can be read as referring to the historical Izumi and/or as a prescribed performative stance that is central to the enactment of the rites of pursuing and being pursued, and thus central to romance.[6]

It is hard then to distill from *waka* poetry any authoritative information on the personal experiences of individual poets, even if these experiences informed their compositions, given that what counted as experience was itself shaped by the language and tropes through which it could be expressed. *Waka* was not a lyrical expression of an "authentic" and individuated self; rather, it was the articulation of a shared sensibility that was created through a sense of belonging to an ongoing conversation, in which a poem stood not alone but as a response to another or others, and with the passage of time, as part of an elaborate dialogue with the tradition itself.[7]

It is striking that contemporary scholarship on classical and medieval texts, particularly that which is produced in Japan, seems, for the most part, to be curiously untouched by the many debates about author and text that were unleashed when Roland Barthes famously proclaimed the "Death of the Author" and argued that a text "does not consist of a line of words, releasing a single 'theological' meaning (the 'message' of the Author-God), but is a space of many dimensions, in which are wedded and contested various kinds of writing, no one of which is original: the text is a tissue of citations, resulting from the thousand sources of culture."[8] Scholarship on medieval Japanese texts continues to be driven by the imperative to search for "facts" about an author's life and to find a correspondence between the author's personal experiences and the text s/he produced. This is further compounded by the fact that it is in fact hard to establish with any certainty the authorship of many of the works that have acquired canonical status today.

Could the persistence of such an approach in part be accounted for by the fact that this way of looking at a text is perceived as being in consonance with a native exegetical tradition that extends back to the very period when these texts were being produced? For it is certainly true that for medieval writers, proselytizers, and commentators in Japan, the "facts" and "events" that surrounded an author's life were not insignificant and were indeed seen as inextricably enmeshed in the texts that s/he was said to have produced. However, what was deemed significant by medieval exegetes was not Izumi's authentic voice but rather the series of improvisations that her life and texts afforded to those who followed in her wake. Historical facts as we understand them had little meaning in a world in which myths and legends intermingled with real events: that the late medieval text

Koshikibu could create a narrative in which Murasaki Shikibu, Izumi Shikibu, and Koshikibu no Naishi were brought together under the sign "mother," "daughter," and "grandchild" was testament to the creative uses to which the past could be put.

There was also no investment here, as we shall see in our discussions of the stories that proliferated around Izumi Shikibu, in the idea of authenticity and ownership, for the author was not reified as the exclusive creator of a text. Izumi's biography was not there in order to be put into the service of illuminating the meanings hidden in her writings. On the contrary, both her biography and her poems were fluid and malleable entities that fed off each other, blurring the boundaries between fact and fiction and opening up endless possibilities of riffing on familiar notes to produce different melodies. Izumi Shikibu was already available to medieval writers and proselytizers as nothing more than a textual fiction. For when they looked back what they found was not a person whose life had been fleshed out in all its richness but rather a persona, a textual effect, created out of the accounts of her contemporaries or near contemporaries and out of her own poetic repertoire.[9]

Contemporary scholarship on Izumi today often draws on methodological protocols that are in fact far removed from medieval modes of reading/listening to texts. Driven by a strong empiricism, there is an imperative here to search for historical "facts" about Izumi Shikibu's life, which can then be used to construct an authentic picture (if such a thing were even possible) of Izumi, against which fictional narratives about her can be juxtaposed. Even if such hard evidence were available to us, surely the point about literary/Buddhist texts is that they are fictional, and therefore not reducible either to being transparent reflections of the real or flagrant misrepresentations of it.[10] What I hope to demonstrate through close readings of some of the tales that proliferated around the figure of Izumi Shikibu in medieval Japan is that Izumi functioned not as a representation of a real historical person but rather as a particularly apposite trope, which allowed medieval writers to engage with a wide range of questions and anxieties that were of the deepest interest to their age.

One way of demonstrating how Izumi works as a trope, standing in for far more than woman, understood as an essentialist category, is by paying closer attention to the broader textual context within which the vignettes about Izumi are situated. For reading each story about Izumi in isolation, decontextualized from the wider narrative framework within which she appears, can easily lead to the production of a composite picture of Izumi, understood as a real woman, who is mis/represented in different ways in medieval narratives. Regardless of the different motives and intentions attributed to them, the authors and/or proselytizers of these texts can then be seen as working together to promote an overarching ideological agenda, driven by Buddhism, patriarchy, or the like, to distort the truth of her lived reality. What is never questioned in such a reading practice is the existence of a stable and constant figure, Izumi, who comes to be manipulated in different ways to suit particular ideological positions.[11]

A very different picture emerges if one reads the tales in which Izumi Shikibu makes an appearance in conjunction with the cluster of tales within which they are located and with similar tales in other works. Rather than revealing the workings of a coherent ideological discourse, what these tales engage in is a dialogic process, in which a series of interesting conversations take place, raising questions that are never entirely resolved, and where inconsistencies and contradictions abound; moreover, this complex web of inter- and intratextuality produces a polyphony of voices, divesting the author of any one text of the power to be the sole producer of meaning. And most importantly for our purposes, what this mode of reading reveals is that the stories about Izumi, rather than being principally concerned with woman qua woman, or about Izumi as a historical person, find in her persona the perfect vehicle for exploring both the possibilities and limitations of the worldly practices of poetry and sex for the attainment of salvation.

It is of course not fortuitous that poetry and sex came to coalesce around the figure of Izumi. As we have observed, it was around these two features of her life, her acknowledged status as a significant poet of her times, and her reputation as someone who was known for her numerous and, on occasion, transgressive affairs that the construction of Izumi's persona occurred both during and not long after her own lifetime. The earliest account that brings together these two aspects of her life is Murasaki Shikibu's diary, *Murasaki Shikibu nikki,* in which she acknowledges that Izumi certainly composed poems that were delightful; however, in her judgement, in the final analysis, Izumi cannot be counted on as a poet of the highest distinction.[12] In speaking of Izumi's ability to carry on a "fascinating correspondence," Murasaki mentions in passing that she had "a rather unsavory side to her character" (*keshikaranu*).[13] This elliptical comment, read in the context of Murasaki's grudging praise of her ability to write interesting letters, could be a reference to the impropriety of the sentiments expressed in the private letters and poems that Izumi exchanged with her many lovers.[14] Izumi's affairs with two members of the imperial family, Prince Tametaka (977–1002), and his half brother Prince Atsumichi (981–1007), which caused something of a scandal, also came to be documented in the "historical" narratives *Eiga monogatari* (Tales of Flowering Fortunes) and in *Ōkagami* (The Great Mirror), respectively.[15]

Izumi's association with both poetry and amorous love, however, does not in itself account for the extraordinary proliferation of stories about her that occurred in the centuries after her death. It is precisely because poetry and love/sex mattered in Buddhist thought and practice, functioning as key sites for arguing about the nature and status of worldly practices vis-à-vis the path of enlightenment, that these narratives found in woman/Izumi a way of bringing the two together under a common sign, thereby infusing new life into what had become well-worn debates. The association of women with sex in medieval tales has generally been read as a sign that women were stigmatized because of their bodies and their sexuality. While it is true that in Buddhist discourse woman in certain contexts was associated with her body and with sex, there was no natural, biological connection that could be drawn between woman and poetry. The introduction of this third term, poetry, within Buddhist debates fundamentally destabilized the categories poetry, sex, and woman and altered what each of these terms meant. The significations attached to them could not be constant and unchanging, given that each term was contingent on the others and on the context within which it appeared.

Reading a small corpus of writings about Izumi, I attempt here to place it within the context of the broader intra- and intertextual conversations that were taking place in medieval texts, to demonstrate that these tales fail to yield a single meaning or purpose, and that rather than as a real woman, Izumi here functions as the figural site par excellence for staging conversations about the nature of attachment and enlightenment, all of which centered on three significant topoi: poetry, love/sex, and woman.[16] Before engaging with the texts, however, a brief examination is required of what was at stake for Buddhist exegetical practice in making poetry and amorous love pivotal to their conversations about the nature of attachment and salvation.

The Way of Poetry as the Way of the Buddha

That *waka* was one of the main axes around which most medieval narratives about Izumi Shikibu revolve is testament not only to Izumi's reputation as a poet of great renown; it points also to the degree to which poetry, by the twelfth century, had acquired a new significance in the cultural imaginary of the courtly life of Japan. The age in which Izumi Shikibu and other poets had lived was one in which *waka* was the mode par excellence through which lovers were expected to express their feelings of longing and desire. Poetry was a central feature of private communication, and often these exchanges found their way into the private anthologies of individual poets. At the same time, *waka* had become an indispensable feature of the public life of the court, where poets were called upon to perform in poetry contests, banquets, and the like. The compilation of the first imperial anthology of Japanese poetry, the *Kokinshū*, confirmed the high status that had come to be accorded to *waka* by the tenth century.

The centuries that followed marked a change, one whereby *waka* no longer remained one among many elegant and refined pastimes through which aristocrats fashioned themselves as men and women of culture. Increasingly, poetry was transformed into a serious vocation that required rigorous training within a particular school, and one that had to be pursued with single-minded dedication.[17] Striking features of this new orientation were the growing interpenetration of literary and Buddhist practices and a new imperative to incorporate poetry within a broader religious framework. Poetry in the age of *Kokinshū*, for example, had not sought to thematize its relationship with Buddhist ideas by creating a separate category of poems that explicitly articulated the connection between the two. The *Goshūishū* (Later Collection of Gleanings, 1086) was the first anthology that included a group of poems under the heading of *shakkyōka* (poems on the teachings of the Buddha Sakyamuni), suggesting the increasing importance of integrating Buddhist themes within a poetic framework.[18]

The ideal of *michi* (the Way) was fundamental in shaping new perceptions about the connections between poetry and Buddhism. Central to the ideal of *michi* was the belief that total dedication to a particular pursuit would lead to the intuitive understanding of a larger Truth. This was as true of the most trivial and insignificant pursuits as it was of the more respected disciplines. The dedicated pursuit of any discipline, no matter how insignificant, could now be seen as being none other than the truth inherent in the Buddhist Dharma.[19]

Emulating the methods of transmission developed by the esoteric Buddhist sects, knowledge of a particular artistic practice could now be passed down only from teacher to pupil, and this knowledge became the monopoly of the chosen few. By the twelfth century, poets such as Minamoto no Shunrai (d. 1129) and Fujiwara no Mototoshi (1055–1138), neither of whom held high rank, became leading figures in *waka* circles and were invited to poetry gatherings held by high-ranking aristocrats. By the end of the twelfth century, *waka* schools came to be established. The Rokujō branch of the Fujiwara was shaped into a school of *waka* by Fujiwara no Arisuke (1090–1156) and his sons Kiyosuke (1104–1177), Shigeie (1161–1207), and Suetsune (1131–1221). Fujiwara no Shunzei (1114–1204), who became a pupil of Fujiwara no Mototoshi, formed the Mikohidari school and, together with his son Fujiwara Teika, dominated the world of poetry in the medieval age.

The Tendai doctrine of the threefold truth—the truth of the void (*kū*), the truth of the provisional (*ke*), and the truth of the mean (*chū*)—and the idea that these three truths penetrate one another and are found perfectly harmonized and united played a significant role in the ways in which *michi* came to be understood. Major poets of this period sought with greater urgency to define poetic goals and practices in Buddhist terms. The concern with poetry as a worldly pursuit, embroiled in matters to do with love and desire, and hence potentially antithetical to the Buddhist Path, led to attempts to justify it on Buddhist grounds even before the twelfth century.[20] However, it was only in the age of poets such as Shunzei that there was a consistent attempt to produce theories in which the Buddhist doctrine itself was creatively used in order to argue that poetry was in no way antithetical to the Buddhist Way. Many poets/priests drew upon the Buddhist doctrine of expedient means (*hōben*) and radical nonduality (*funi*) to argue that the composition of poetry and the performance of Buddhist practice were not mutually contradictory and that the two activities were indeed identical (*waka no michi to hotoke no michi futatsu arazu*).[21] Shunzei, in his poetic treatise *Korai fūteishō* (Notes on poetic style throughout the ages) composed in 1201, drew, for example, on the *Lotus Sutra* to argue that delusion and enlightenment were identical and that "the profound way of poetry could be likened to the three aspects of truth, namely *kū, ke,* and *chū.*"[22]

This shift from *waka* as a nonprofessional activity to a serious practice with strong religious overtones did not mean that the themes and conventions that had dominated poetic anthologies such as *Kokinshū* came to be overturned or radically transformed. On the contrary, the renowned imperial anthology *Shin kokinshū* (ca. 1205), as attested to by its name, *New Collection of Ancient and Modern Poems* or New *Kokinshū,* was a conscious attempt to emulate and follow in the venerable tradition of the first imperial anthology. Poems on the seasons (six books) and on love (five books) dominated the anthology, even as it added two themes not found in *Kokinshū,* Buddhism and Shinto, which were accorded a book each within the compilation. The collection included several poems by women from an earlier age that had been excluded from *Kokinshū.*

That twenty-five poems by Izumi Shikibu were selected as opposed to ten by Kamo no Chōmei, one of the compilers of *Shin kokinshū,* suggests the degree to which her poems were held in high esteem in the centuries following her death. Their inclusion also attests to the fact that the status of love poetry, one of the central topics within *waka* anthologies, continued to flourish in the age of *Shin kokinshū,* hand in hand with the thematization of Buddhism that occurred in the form of poems that dealt explicitly with Buddhist themes—*shakkyōka.* As we shall see later, it was Izumi Shikibu's association with love poetry, as well as with *shakkyōka,* that made her an ideal vehicle for debating the nature and role of poetry within Buddhist discourse.

Izumi Shikibu in Poetic Treatises

The increasing domination of poetry houses by male poets by the twelfth century was accompanied by a sense that the age when women had been dominant as poets was passing.[23] It was in this context that the poetry of famous female poets such as Izumi Shikibu, who had belonged to an earlier time, came to be discussed and reassessed in the many texts on *waka* poetics (*karon*) that proliferated from the twelfth century. These texts ranged widely from poetic theory to stories and anecdotes about famous poets and poetic place names as well as the miraculous powers of poetry. *Shunrai zuinō* (Shunrai's Poetic Essentials, 1115)[24] is the earliest of these poetic treatises in which we are presented with an assessment of Izumi's verses. In a discussion between Lord Sadayori and his father Fujiwara Kintō, the latter is asked to evaluate the relative merits of Izumi Shikibu and Akazome Emon's poetry. While claiming that it would be impossible to offer a judgement in one word, Kintō declares that Izumi was the one who composed the poem "*hima koso nakere ashi no yaebuki,*"[25] and that she was an outstanding poet. His son, intrigued by his father's response, points out that it was her poem "*haruka ni terase yama no ha no tsuki*"[26] that people singled out as her great poem. To this Kintō responds by saying that this simply demonstrates people's ignorance, for the phrase "*kuraki yori kuraki michi ni zo*" was taken from the *Lotus Sutra,* and hence not one that Izumi had hit upon herself; it would be a simple matter to compose the latter part of the poem, as a natural progression from the first. On the other hand, to compose the lines "*koya to mo hito o*" and follow them with the lines "*hima koso nakere*" was amazing and beyond what ordinary, ignorant folk could possibly imagine.[27]

The same narrative is repeated almost verbatim in another collection of poetic lore and criticism, *Fukurozōshi* (A Sack of Notes, ca. 1150s), compiled by Fujiwara Kiyosuke (1104–1177).[28] Kamo no Chōmei continues in the same exegetical vein in his poetic treatise *Mumyōshō* (Nameless Notes, ca. 1211), beginning with an account of Fujiwara Kintō's judgement on the two poems by Izumi quoted earlier. Chōmei is particularly interested in the assessments of poets and their compositions offered by his predecessors and his contemporaries for what they tell him about the contingent nature of all such judgments. He notes that it was Akazome's poetry that was singled out for praise in past records of the formal poetry contests held at court, rather than the verses composed by Izumi Shikibu. He is mystified by Kintō's dismissal of Izumi's "*haruka ni terase*" poem, whose quality he rates very highly.

Chōmei concedes that Izumi's reputation, in his own time, was beyond dispute, higher than Akazome's, but among her own contemporaries, he observes, her poetic skills were of less importance than her character. Quoting extensively from Murasaki Shikibu's diary, he highlights the fact that Murasaki, who found Izumi's behavior reprehensible, rated Akazome as the superior poet of the two. He concludes by noting that despite the fact that Izumi's reputation suffered during her own lifetime, she came to be recognized later as a great poet, who produced a number of excellent poems, and that this accounted for the fact that many of her poems were included in poetic anthologies.[29]

It is worth keeping in mind that Chōmei is less interested here in the truth or otherwise of Izumi's reputation as someone whose behavior was, on occasion, somewhat questionable, than he is in the fact that, as he says, what counts as good and bad (in poetry) is subject to change depending on the age when these judgments are made. He makes the same point in reference to the poet Sone no Yoshitada, who, he points out, was not taken very seriously during his own lifetime and was even referred to as a bit of a fool, but who came to be held in very high esteem in Chōmei's own time. When Shunrai, Kiyosuke, and Chōmei offer evaluations of different poets, they do not compare male with female poets. At the same time, it is not women's innate nature that becomes the basis of their judgments. Speaking of his contemporaries, Tayū[30] and Kojijū,[31] for example, Chōmei compares their relative merits as poets, arguing that while the former was more learned, the latter was unsurpassed in the art of composing apposite verses as the occasion demanded. He quotes Shun'e, who is credited with having said that there was no one who could match Kojijū in the way that she grasped the essence of a poem and composed the perfect verse in response. Turning next to the daughter of Toshinari (Shunrai)[32] and Lady Kunaikyō,[33] what Chōmei focuses on is not the fact that they are women but rather the very different methods they employ in working on their compositions; what he finds noteworthy is their extreme dedication to the way of poetry and their extraordinary mastery of it, which in his view makes them the equals of the great masters of old.[34] Chōmei's treatise highlights the degree to which women were taken seriously in the world of poetry even after the age that had produced the likes of Izumi Shikibu and Ono no Komachi had long passed.[35]

Poetry and the Problem of Love and Sexual Desire

The privileged status accorded to poetry by the aristocracy in the twelfth century did not mean that its assimilation into the Buddhist project of enlightenment was achieved seamlessly, without generating debate. What was striking was precisely the ubiquity of both learned arguments and illustrative tales that sought to establish that *waka* was central to Buddhist practice. Love poetry, however, which was integral to the *waka* tradition, was not so easily reconciled with the religious path, for amorous activities, seen as the source of this poetry, in the Buddhist view produced deluded attachment and hindered progress along the path to enlightenment. It was through a complex series of negotiations that the problem of love came to be overcome, one reflection of which was the new significations that now came to be attached to the terms *irogonomi* and *suki.*

In the Heian period, the term *irogonomi* had been understood as encapsulating both a keen receptivity to erotic encounters as well as a connoisseurship of music, poetry, and other artistic pastimes. The skill and sensitivity with which men and women composed poetry were seen as inextricably linked to the accomplished performance of the game of love. To be a good poet had been a prerequisite for being an *irogonomi.* The term was frequently used synonymously with *suki,* and, as we observed in the *Genji,* it often signified a heightened receptivity to amorous adventures and to artistic practices, both of which were central to the generation of erotic and affective desire. However, by the twelfth century, the playful banter, amorous escapades, and exchange of clever poems that had constituted the world of the *sukimono* and the *irogonomi* underwent significant changes.

The term *suki* gradually came to be divorced from the amorous connotations embodied in the character 好 and came to be written with the substitute characters (*ateji*) 数寄. The *sukimono* was now more specifically associated with a male practitioner who was single-mindedly devoted to a particular art, which he cultivated as a Buddhist practice. *Irogonomi,* perhaps because of the presence of the word *iro* (sex, love) within it, came to be associated not only with poetry and the arts but also with sexual activity and a propensity for amorous play. It is worth noting in this context that the character for *iro* 色 is read as *shiki* or form (Sk. *rūpa*) in Buddhist canonical texts. It often appears in phrases such as *shiki soku ze kū* (色即是空) to mean "form is emptiness," thereby asserting the truth of nonduality, that human experience is simultaneously empty (*kū*) of permanent self or substance and also at the same time phenomenal (*shiki*). It is in this sense that *shiki* can signify "carnal love" but only insofar as "carnal love" is as extension and manifestation of attachment to the phenomenal world.[36]

The term *iro,* when used in the context of women such as Izumi Shikibu and Ono no Komachi, captures both senses of the term *shiki.* Women are identified with beauty and temptation, for it is the female form that produces deluded attachment in men. However, it is through them that the distinction between the provisional and the ultimate, and between Emptiness and Permanent Self or Substance comes to be thematized, and on occasion, dissolved. It is for this reason that women are central to medieval narratives. In what follows I read a number of anecdotes that appear in *setsuwa* collections to explore how the nexus of woman, love, poetry, delusion, and enlightenment came to coalesce around the figure of Izumi, and how the particular configurations in which these terms appear in different contexts give shape to the myriad forms Izumi takes in medieval narratives.

Izumi Shikibu in *Shasekishū*

Shasekishū (A Collection of Sand and Pebbles),[37] by the Tendai monk Mujū Ichien, is a heterogeneous assembly of tales, which range from weighty doctrinal debates to amusing vignettes about defecating and farting. A significant portion of the text is devoted to a justification of poetry as a religious practice. Drawing on Buddhist doctrine, Mujū seeks to demonstrate the value of poetry as a particularly efficacious means of entering the Buddhist Path. He also recounts anecdotes about poets in order to illustrate the skill, sensitivity, and dedication with which they compose poetry and, above all, the miraculous power of poetry to bring both spiritual and material advancement to those who are devoted to it.

Mujū's defense of *waka* poetry is part of a larger argument about the possibility of reconciling writing, a worldly pursuit, with a commitment to the Buddhist Way. Designating his own collection of stories as nothing other than "wild words and specious phrases" (*kyōgen kigo*), he argues that it can, nonetheless, be used as an expedient means (*hōben*) to illustrate the Buddhist teachings. In keeping with medieval exegetical practices, he uses the concept of *honji suijaku* (true nature-manifest traces) to argue that gods were manifestations of the Buddha and that if the first poem in the native language was composed by the god Susa-no-o-mikoto, then it followed that *waka* constituted nothing less than the words of the Buddha himself. Extending this argument with an ingenuity that was shared by other medieval exegetes, he claims that *waka* poems were in fact mystical verses or *dhārāni*.[38]

A recurring anxiety within Buddhist *setsuwa* writings, which also finds a voice in Mujū's *Shasekishū*, was the problem of reconciling the claim that *waka* was the ideal vehicle for realizing the Buddhist Way with the fact that love poems, which produced sexual and affective ties, and therefore generated feelings of attachment to the phenomenal world, were at the heart of *waka* composition. Mujū acknowledges that *waka* are often included in all that constitutes "wild words and specious phrases" because they are steeped in human emotions (*aijō*) and in sex (*iro*). He counters this negative judgement of poetry by arguing:

> If by looking at the leaves falling in the wind, one forgets one's attachment to fame and wealth, and one comprehends the worthlessness of human

existence, and if by reciting poems on the snow and the moon one's heart is awakened into comprehending the unblemished ultimate truth, then *waka* can serve as a go-between for entering the Buddhist path, and serve as a means for intuiting the Buddha's Dharma. It is for this reason that those who engaged in Buddhist practices in the past by no means abandoned the Way of Poetry.[39]

Mujū's strategy for recuperating poetry, and one which he shares with other writers of Buddhist *setsuwa,* as we shall see in Chapter 5, is to sideline the question of love and to focus instead on the ability of such poems to produce a keener awareness of worldly transience, and in this way remain true to the Buddhist teachings. To establish that poetry is most admirably suited to producing the deepest apprehension of the ephemerality of the world, Mujū narrates the story of the conversion of the famous priest Eshin to the Way of Poetry. Eshin, we are told, devoted himself single-mindedly to studying Buddhist texts and despised the pointless activity of engaging in "wild words and specious phrases." Among his disciples there was a young page (*chigo*)[40] who spent all his time reciting poetry. Deciding that he was a bad influence on the other boys, Eshin decided to send him back home. The page, unaware of his master's plan, stood on the veranda, watching the moon. Cupping his hands as if to scoop up some water, he recited a poem,[41] which Eshin found so deeply moving that he himself came to love poetry, and many of his own poems came to be included in anthologies composed over several generations.

The conversion of eminent monks, who were particularly single-minded in their Buddhist devotions to the Way of Poetry, is a recurring theme in medieval narratives. Saigyō is credited with having taught many a venerable priest the true significance of *waka*. In *Togano o Myōe shōnin denki* (Biography of Priest Myōe), Saigyō convinces Myōe of the centrality of *waka* as a religious practice by claiming that "*waka* is the true form of the Buddha. Reciting one line of *waka* is equivalent to carving a statue of the Buddha. Likewise continuing to meditate on one verse of *waka* is like reciting the sacred esoteric texts of *shingon*. It is through poetry that I have mastered the Buddha's Dharma."[42]

Saigyō appears in *Shasekishū* as a recluse who has had the innermost meaning of the Tendai mantras (*shingon*) transmitted to him. When asked by the abbot Jien to communicate these teachings to him, Saigyō is said to have replied, "to begin with, become adept at poetry. If you do not grasp the essence of *waka* you will not understand what is at the heart of the sacred mantras." Mujū concludes by noting that it was only after Jien had mastered *waka* that Saigyō transmitted the esoteric teachings to him.[43] It is with the view to illustrating his claim that poetry constitutes a particularly efficacious practice that Mujū devotes several sections of *Shasekishū* to tales about *waka,* and it is within these sections of the text that the stories about Izumi Shikibu are situated.

The Miraculous Power of Poetry

The first story about Izumi Shikibu appears under the heading "stories of the ways in which people are deeply moved by poetry." Izumi makes a secret visit to the Inari Shrine. On her way, when she is close to the Tanaka Myōjin Shrine, light rain begins to fall. At this point, just when she wonders what she is going to do, she borrows a rough outer garment (*ao*) from a young boy, who is engaged in harvesting crops. On her way back she returns the garment to him. A few days later the boy arrives and presents her with the following poem:

shigure suru	the autumn leaves
inari no yama no	upon which the rain falls
momiji ba wa	in Mount Inari
aokarishi yori	ever since they were green/when you borrowed my robe
omoisometeki	I have been steeped with the hues of love[44]

This is the end of the little vignette about Izumi Shikibu. What are we to make of it? It is by placing it within the broader context of some of the other stories that appear within this section and in other versions of it in contemporary texts that we may come closer to understanding the thematic concerns that inform the different versions of this tale. The same section on "people moved by poetry" includes a story about the governor of Iwami who goes on a pleasure trip to Iwamigata. Hearing that the women divers there are skilled in reciting poetry, he has them summoned to give a performance. He notices a young woman of seventeen whose appearance and speech shows a refinement that one would hardly expect of someone of her class. When she recites a poem he is so profoundly moved by her performance that he presents her with a purple robe. At this she recites the following poem:

murasaki no	what use have I
kumo no uwagi mo	for this purple robe
nani ka semu	of the high-born
kazuki nomi suru	being a humble being
ama no mi nareba	who merely dives for fish?

This moves him to such depths that he decides to take her back to the capital. She laments having to leave her parents behind; the governor allows them to join his party. The girl's poems produce a miraculous result: she ends up becoming his wife and bearing him several sons.[45]

In another story, which follows the one about Izumi Shikibu, the Cloistered Emperor Saga, while on pilgrimage to Kumano, hears a peasant reciting a poem on seeing plum blossoms flowering at Otonashigawa in Hongū:

otonashi ni	the plum blossoms
saki hajimekemu	that have begun to bloom
ume no hana	soundlessly,
niowazariseba	how would we know of them
ikade shiramashi	if it were not for their fragrance?

The Cloistered Emperor seeks out the man and decides to reward him. The man speaks of the difficulty of supporting his mother, upon which the emperor presents him with a document exempting him forever from taxes on his land. The narrator marvels at the unimaginable dispensation accorded to him. He ends by observing that people who heard this tale commented that although the man was the son of a peasant, he had been reared as a page (*chigo*) and hence was deeply conversant with the Way of Poetry.[46]

Several aspects of these tales are noteworthy. They point to the extraordinary value placed on the ability to create a poem that is sensitive to both the protocols of poetic diction as well as to its appropriateness to a particular circumstance or context. The efficacy of such extemporization is demonstrated by the fact that those who display these extraordinary skills are much admired and duly acknowledged through material rewards. Another significant feature of these narratives is the fact that it is men and women of the lower orders who surprise their superiors by displaying an understanding of *waka* that is normally associated only with the highborn.

Indeed, it is invariably within a hierarchical relationship that these narratives come to be framed: aristocrats are always the ones who are in a position to recognize the worth of the poems of the lowborn, who prove that poetry can often well from the hearts of ordinary folk, thereby demonstrating the truth of Ki no Tsurayuki's claim in the preface of *Kokinshū* that "the seeds of Japanese poetry (*yamato no uta*) lie in the human heart and grow into leaves of ten thousand words."[47] This is the context in which Izumi Shikibu, an aristocratic lady-in-waiting and renowned poet, is brought into contact with a humble farm boy who, through a clever play on the word *ao kari* is able to express his amorous interest in her using the courtly idiom of a love poem. It is Izumi's association with love poetry that makes her a particularly apposite recipient of such versification.

This tale appears in different versions in texts such as *Fukurozōshi, Kokonchomonjū* (A Collection of Notable Tales Old and New, ca. 1254) and *Jikkinshō* (Stories that Illustrate the Ten Maxims, ca. 1252), attesting to the different uses to which the topos of Izumi and the young boy could be put. The earliest version of the tale in *Fukurozōshi* does not vary significantly from the *Shasekishū* narrative except at the end where the narrator observes that after the young cowherd (rather than reaper of crops) had composed the poem it was said that it aroused feelings within Izumi Shikibu that were not entirely appropriate. However, he dismisses this possibility by pointing out that these were merely the babblings of common folk. What the narrator appears to find hard to believe is that an aristocratic lady-in-waiting such as Izumi could possibly fall for the charms of a mere commoner. Regardless of why this rumor is included in the tale, what is clear is that two motifs, a propensity to respond to erotic encounters and a profound sensitivity to poetry, were beginning to coalesce around the figure of Izumi.

In *Kokonchomonjū* and *Jikkinshō*, the amorous connections between the boy and Izumi are more explicitly drawn. After the boy recites the "*shigure*" poem, Izumi, it is said, was so moved that she called the boy to enter her house.[48] Her words, "*oku e*," are clearly an invitation to further intimacy. Although she is not explicitly described as an *irogonomi,* it is precisely Izumi's ability to show a sensitive appreciation of a good love poem and to be suitably aroused by someone who is capable of composing it that makes her a suitable peg on which to hang this tale. What the story seeks to demonstrate is not Izumi's looseness of character but rather the extraordinary power of poetry to transcend the boundaries of social status and the cultural privileges attendant on it. The tale that precedes the Izumi story in *Kokonchomonjū* provides ample ground for such a reading.

A man from Kawachi, of a low rank (*shina iyashiki mono*), is taken with a lady-in-waiting who is of a higher social class, and sends her a refined poem, expressing his love. She is so moved by his composition that she accepts his overtures and enters into a relationship with him. The man, we are told, visits her every single evening from Kawachi. The tale concludes by observing that he was a veritable *sukimono,* who composed a *waka* even when he was on his deathbed.[49]

The theme of the power of poetry to effect miracles takes many forms in medieval narratives. In *Shasekishū,* the gods respond favorably to those who compose poetry, lifting them out of poverty, saving their loved ones, or helping them win back the affections of errant lovers. The gods of Kibune Shrine, for example, were vested with the power to bring together estranged lovers and to establish conjugal ties (*en musubi*) between men and women. Among the many stories about Izumi's love affairs that circulated in the medieval period was the belief that she had been abandoned by her husband, Fujiwara no Yasumasa, and that she visited Kibune Shrine to win back his favor. An early rendition of this legend appears in *Shasekishū*. Rather than illuminating the character of Izumi, this tale, I argue, provides a particularly propitious occasion for bringing together a number of topoi that revolve around the connections between gods and *miko* (female shamans), the power of poetry to bridge lover's quarrels, and the importance of performing rituals and practices with due regard to the context of their performance.

The Tale

When Izumi Shikibu lost the affections of Yasumasa, she consulted a *miko* and organized for her to perform the Ceremony of Harmonious Relations (*keiai no matsuri*) at Kibune Shrine. Yasumasa heard about this and hid himself in the shade of a tree by the shrine and watched: an elderly *miko* formed a circle with sacred staffs made of red paper strips. After performing certain rituals, she beat her drum, lifted up her skirt, and beat her genital area, after which she spun around three times. She then told Izumi Shikibu to follow her example. Izumi blushed and did not reply. The *miko* said, "Having decided to go through such an important event, how can you now not do it, when we have progressed this far? If that was the case, why did you follow this course of action in the first place?"

Yasumasa was amused, expecting to see something out of the ordinary. Izumi, appearing deep in thought for a while, recited the following poem:

chihayaburu	filled with shame
kami no miru me mo	before the watchful eyes
hazukashiya	of the mighty gods!
mi o omou to te	grieving my circumstances
mi o ya sutsubeki	must I sacrifice myself/my dignity?

Yasumasa found the form (*tei*) of her verse so full of refined grace (*yū*) that he called out, "I am here," and his feelings for her as he took her home with him were by no means shallow. This is an example of following the proprieties while transcending them. If Izumi had adhered strictly to the rules and lifted her skirt and circled around, beating her genital area, Yasumasa would have continued to spurn her and she would not have succeeded in her intentions.[50]

Why does Izumi refuse to expose her genital area and choose to recite a poem instead, and why is she filled with shame when asked to perform the dance by the *miko*? Why is Yasumasa amused at the prospect of seeing her performing the dance, and what might be the source of the compiler's confident assertion that Yasumasa would not have taken Izumi back had she exposed herself? What is the didactic intent of the story? Addressing these questions, I hope, will shift our attention away from Izumi as a real, historical person and from the fruitless attempt to establish the truth or otherwise of her story as a spurned woman who seeks to win back her husband and direct us instead to an exploration of how she functions as the ideal trope for the text's exploration of the connections between woman, bodily performance, sex, and poetry.

The Power of Female Genitalia

There is a long textual history within the Japanese tradition that celebrates the power of female sexual organs to captivate the gods and win their favors. The female shaman or *miko* often performed the role of mediating between humans and gods, and the source of her power to intercede on behalf of humans was attributed to the awe-inspiring nature of her sexual organs. In this tale, the *miko* who performs a dance for Izumi is reminiscent of the female god Ame no Uzume, as recounted in the *Kojiki* (A Record of Ancient Matters), who exposes her breasts and, pushing her skirt band down to her genitals, dances in an effort to lure the Sun Goddess Amaterasu Ōmikami out of her cave. The gods who watch her cavorting are so filled with merriment that they burst into laughter; Amaterasu is unable to contain her curiosity and comes out of the cave, thereby bringing light to a world plunged in darkness.[51] In another account in the *Nihon shoki* (Chronicles of Japan), Ninigi, the grandson of Amaterasu, who intends to descend to earth, enlists the help of Ame no Uzume to challenge the god of the crossroads, Sarutahiko; Ame no Uzume bares her breasts and, pushing down the band of her garment below her navel, confronts him with a mocking laugh. Sarutahiko succumbs and ends up welcoming Ninigi to earth and marrying Ame no Uzume.[52]

There are also many folk legends in Japan about demons (*oni*), who are subdued by women exposing their genitalia; these legends attest to the widespread belief in the stunning potency of female sexuality.[53] The *miko*'s performance in *Shasekishū* clearly has a long lineage. It is by lifting her skirt and striking her genital area that she seeks to placate the gods and to mediate on behalf of Izumi. It is presumably in order to reinforce the efficacy of this practice that she asks Izumi to follow suit. As Fukutō Sanae observes, the practice of visiting shrines such as Inari and Kibune and performing dances, which involved exposing the female sexual organs in order to ensure marital harmony, was a common practice among women of all classes.[54] The fact that Izumi goes to Kibune to win back Yasumasa suggests that it would not be unreasonable for her to participate in this well-established practice. Clearly, the narrator of the tale thinks otherwise.

The "Modest" Noblewoman?

When Izumi is called upon to perform the dance prescribed by the *miko,* she is unable to do so. She blushes with embarrassment and recites a poem instead. We may be tempted to interpret Izumi's reluctance at baring her genitalia purely as a mark of the modesty and restraint that accompany her respectable aristocratic status. As we know, however, Izumi Shikibu was not a chaste housewife. In the popular tradition she was associated with sexual passion and was credited with having had several scandalous affairs. Marriage itself, as Izumi's case demonstrates, was a fluid category that allowed couples to have varying degrees of commitment to each other. Furthermore, there is nothing in the literature to suggest that virginity was valorized, or that great importance was placed upon chastity for an unmarried woman.

Izumi's blushing, which may call to mind the response of many a heroine in a Victorian novel, has little to do with prudery or coyness, born of a sense of shame surrounding the body and sex. As I have argued earlier, the naked body was not seen as the site of desire, and therefore something to be kept hidden. *Setsuwa* tales describe sexual activities and sexual body parts with complete openness, and what is particularly striking is that the exposed body provokes laughter rather than erotic desire. Mujū may be a Buddhist priest but he is no prude: when he moralizes he draws attention to common human failings such as envy and passionate attachment. He seems little interested in promoting "modesty" in women, or in valorizing monogamy and chastising inconstancy. He has no hesitation in recounting outrageous, humorous tales of sexual escapades. In one story in *Shasekishū*, a wife attempts to catch her husband at his infidelities by coating his penis with flour. The husband tries to trick her by having an affair with another woman and recoating his penis with flour as his wife had done, little realizing that his wife had put salt in the flour and is therefore able to taste the difference![55]

In another tale of infidelity a husband draws a picture of a cow on his wife's private parts during his absence. While the husband is away the wife has an affair. She gets the lover to reproduce the picture that her husband had drawn. Unfortunately the lover draws a standing cow while the one the husband had drawn was lying down. The story ends on a cheerful note, with the wife quipping that the cow could not possibly spend a lifetime lying down and the husband accepting her infidelity with levity and good humor. In the first story Mujū is critical of the wife who tries to control her husband, and he seems to endorse the husband's decision to leave her. In the second tale, he praises the easygoing and tolerant attitude of the husband, who finds the situation humorous.[56] Izumi's modesty requires another explanation, which is far removed from modern discourses of sexuality in which sexual organs are kept hidden precisely in order to titillate, by holding out the promise of being ultimately revealed.

The Body and Identity

A closer look at the poem Izumi composes suggests that Izumi's embarrassment stems from the fact that if she were to perform the *miko*'s dance, the gods would witness her humiliation at having gone to such lengths to arrange for a ceremony to win back her husband. The enactment of the physical ritual, she fears, will expose even more starkly the desperation of her situation and of her willingness to sacrifice her own sense of self and dignity in order to regain the affections of her husband. It is through the clever play on the word *mi* in her poem that she indicates what is at stake in performing the ritual of lifting her skirt and striking her genitals. It is the shame attached to losing her dignity and compromising her standing in the world, rather than the exposure of the body itself, that would appear to be Izumi's paramount concern.

The implications of Izumi's stance in this story come into even clearer focus when juxtaposed against another account of a woman who is willing to go to absurd lengths to secure the affections of her husband. In *Shinsarugakuki* by Fujiwara no Akihira (989–1066), the sixty-year-old first wife of a court official, who is much older than her husband, runs around performing ceremonies at a number of shrines in order to reestablish a sexual relationship with him. She enlists the help of the god of love, Dōsōjin; she makes offerings to the elephant god, Shōden (also known as Kangiten, the elephant-headed god Ganesha), who was worshipped as the deity of conjugal harmony; and she dances at the Fushimi Inari Shrine, beating her sexual organs with an abalone shell, whose hollow was metonymically linked with the female sexual organs (*awabikubon*). She swings a bonito fish, associated with the penis, in a ceremony to win back her husband's love (*aizome no hō*).

The wife is the butt of cruel humor because of the dissonance between her physical state and the lengths to which she is willing to go in order to regain the attention of her younger husband. Her upper and lower teeth are missing, her hair is likened to the morning frost, and her breasts resemble cow's udders. The text recommends that she shave her snow-white hair and calmly become a nun. It is the ignominy of the situation that the first wife puts herself in, the unreal expectations she harbors, her continued interest in sex (she is described as an *irogonomi*) at an age when such desires are deemed unseemly, and the extraordinary tenacity with which she performs a host of rituals clearly exhibiting her unhappiness and frustration that occasion harsh criticism. In the end, all her efforts are to no avail, and she fails to reclaim her husband's attentions.[57]

Izumi's recitation of a poem, by contrast, is a mark of dignity, and both the quality of the poem as well as the sentiments it expresses cannot but yield results—Yasumasa is deeply moved and takes Izumi back. Izumi's success with Yasumasa, in keeping with the many stories about *waka* in *Shasekishū*, also serves a larger end: that poetry is able to supersede even the potency of the female sexual organs in pleasing and impressing the gods, and fulfilling human desires serves as the ultimate testament of its extraordinary power.

The Moral of the Tale

Restoring this story about Izumi to the context within which it appears in *Shasekishū* also reveals the limits of reading this narrative purely as one about Izumi or about women and their sexuality. Izumi's refusal to perform the *miko's* dance in this tale is intended to demonstrate the virtue of being flexible in following rules and proprieties, and making judgments about their appropriateness, based not on abstract principles but rather on the context in question. The Izumi story is one of three tales about the need to transcend the blind and rigid observation of rules and to make the necessary accommodations, as occasion demands, and follow them in spirit. In one example, a sacred banner in a temple, which has been purified in preparation for the copying of the *Lotus Sutra,* catches fire. A novice working there asks an old monk whether they should purify themselves again before entering the sacred hall in order to put out the fire.[58] Here, what is at issue is the stupidity of the novice who worries about rules at the risk of letting the temple burn down, rather than adapting the regulations to suit the situation.

In another instance, when Prince Hōjo is being ordained at the Tōdaiji he is initially asked to remove his sandals, following customary practice, with no regard for the fact that the platform is piled high with snow. In the end, the proprieties are not followed to the letter and the prince is allowed to keep his sandals on. The narrator approves of the monk who makes the wise decision of letting the prince keep his footwear on, not insisting that the prince walk barefoot in the snow.[59] The point being made in the Izumi story is that the performance of the sexual dance that the *miko* requires of Izumi is inappropriate for someone like her who belongs to the world of the aristocracy. For she has been endowed with the most powerful of magical powers, poetry, to secure what she desires. It is Izumi's deft use of poetry to express both her love of Yasumasa as well as her keen awareness of and sensitivity to her own situation that in the end proves most efficacious for a woman of her standing in winning back her husband.

The many stories that appear in *Shasekishū* may at first glance appear inconsistent, confused, and contradictory. Poetry is consonant with the Buddhist Way and is to be understood as a sacred practice. At the same time, it appears to reward those who are skilled poets not only with spiritual advancement but also with worldly benefits. Love is a deluded practice that creates attachment to worldly pleasures. However, love poems seem particularly efficacious in bringing together lovers who are estranged. Men and women, monks and *chigo*,[60] parents and children, indeed all those who are caught up in the web of love and affect, are often reunited in *setsuwa* tales through the power of poetry. These seemingly contradictory claims are a feature not only of the stories in *Shasekishū* but also of Japanese medieval narratives in general. If we are to make sense of these seeming contradictions, we need to question the sharp divisions we make between the religious and the secular and to rethink what we mean by Buddhism as a *religion* in the context of medieval Japan. This is a question I touch upon in the epilogue to the book.

Izumi, Dōmyō, and the Question of "Incest"

A striking feature of the stories we encounter in *setsuwa, otogizōshi,* and *karon* (treatises on Japanese poetry) is that a relatively limited repertoire of tales is endlessly recycled and given new twists, thereby opening up possibilities for addressing a diverse range of questions from a multiplicity of angles. These questions concern the place of poetry, sex, women, gods, and buddhas within the Buddhist epistemic framework, and it is within this context that a body of tales about Izumi came to be reworked and re-presented in medieval Japan.

The tale of Izumi's affair with the peasant boy who recites the *"shigure"* poem, for example, had several afterlives. In the medieval tale *Jippon ōgi* (Ten Fans) in the *otogizōshi* genre, the story comes to be reconfigured such that the boy turns out to be none other than Izumi's son, whom she abandoned as a baby.[61] As in *Shasekishū*, this tale speaks to the extraordinary power of poetry to transcend class boundaries; furthermore, the boy's ability to compose elegant verse becomes explicable in light of the fact that his mother is an outstanding poet. It is through the miracle of poetry that mother and son are reunited.

There are also several stories in the medieval repertoire in which Izumi has an affair with a younger man who turns out to be the son she cast away in her youth. These tales take many forms and provide a rich terrain for the playing out of a series of interrelated themes about the relationship between buddhas and gods, the power of the *Lotus Sutra,* the charms of the *irogonomi,* the magical efficacy of poetry, the nature and significance of unusual conjugal ties, and the inexplicable workings of karma. Rather than being distortions or misrepresentations of the real Izumi, what these tales demonstrate is Izumi's figural capaciousness that gives protean life to a wide range of themes and concerns that were central to medieval imaginings.

An early account of the relationship between Izumi and the monk Dōmyō appears in *Shasekishū.* Here Izumi, who is described as a beautiful woman given to amorous affairs (*kōshoku naru bijin*), visits Dōmyō and knocks on the door of his hermit dwelling at the outskirts of the Hōrinji temple where he piously performs his religious observances. Seeking to seduce him, she recites a poem in which she incorporates a phrase from the *Lotus Sutra* within her composition.[62] Dōmyō, recognizing what she has in mind, secludes himself in a mountain temple called Kaseyama. Izumi seeks him out and recites a poem in which, in the manner of a *michiyuki,* she evokes the place names Mikanohara, Izumigawa, and Kaseyama that make up her poetic journey to Dōmyō's retreat. These poetic place names provide Izumi, the *irogonomi,* with an opportunity to display both her amorous disposition as well as her poetic skills—the wind blowing off the river is cold (*kawakaze samushi*); cold in *waka* poetry is associated with the trope of a night spent alone, and hence an apposite associative link with *kaseyama* (literally "Mount Lend"), which expresses her desire that Dōmyō lend her his robes (*koromo kaseyama*), that is to say, share his bed with her. In the end, Dōmyō finds her poems so compelling that he gives in to her.[63]

As if through a loose thread of association, the narrative about Izumi and Dōmyō now shifts to a more comical register by adapting a story from *Konjaku monogatari* about a provincial governor who discovers that his lady is having an affair with the intendant of Gion Shrine. In *Shasekishū,* Hōshō (Yasumasa) and Dōmyō become rivals in love. Dōmyō, who is described as an earnest fellow (*mameotoko*), visits Izumi regularly. One day Hōshō, who is also much taken with her, arrives suddenly. Having nowhere to hide, Dōmyō climbs into a Chinese armor chest. Hōshō understands precisely what is going on, but rather than expose Dōmyō, he orders his men to carry the chest to the Gion Shrine and offer the armor to the deity there. When the officiating monks at the shrine open the chest they find not armor but the monk Dōmyō instead.[64]

The narrative moves on to Dōmyō's extraordinary skill in reciting the *Lotus Sutra.* Passing by the gates of Hōshō's house in his carriage, Dōmyō raises his voice and majestically recites a passage. A certain monk hearing his recitation intones the following poem:

mon no soto	hearing his voice
kuruma ni norite	outside the gate
koe kikeba	as he rides in his carriage
ware mo tawataku o	I realize I too must leave
idenubeki kana	the burning house

This monk, we are told, was the son of Izumi Shikibu, who composed the famous poem *kuraki yori kuraki michi,* and his father was none other than the priest Dōmyō.

The three vignettes from *Shasekishū* that I have outlined above serve as exemplars of a particular mode of reading/listening to medieval texts, which call for an orientation that is unfamiliar to us. For what is foregrounded in these narratives is not Izumi and Dōmyō as real people, presented as flesh and blood characters, but rather their metonymic links to particular themes and motifs that make them appropriate vehicles for the celebration of the power of poetry and of the *Lotus Sutra.* In other words, Izumi and Dōmyō are best seen not as historical characters who have been distorted by medieval writers but rather as textual figurations, whose endlessly malleable forms make them ideal vehicles through which to address the problems and concerns of the narratives within which they are embedded.

The first episode about the seduction of Dōmyō by Izumi, for example, tells us nothing about Izumi as a person, imbued with specific physical attributes or a particular psychological makeup. That she is an *irogonomi* already alerts us to the fact that she stands for the ability to be deeply interested in and committed to both love and poetry. She is the vehicle through which the text demonstrates how a deep knowledge of the *Lotus Sutra,* cleverly deployed to compose a *shakkyōka* (that also doubles up as a love poem), as well as the virtuoso manipulation of place names to convey amorous longing, can bring about miraculous transformations. In other words, Dōmyō as priest and Izumi as *irogonomi* are to be understood as figural sites for the unfolding of larger truths about the efficacy of poetry and the power of the *Lotus Sutra.* To read this literally or historically as an instance of how "Izumi Shikibu is cast in the role of a sexual predator, targeting a reluctant priest sworn to celibacy"[65] fashions the struggle described in this scene in purely personal terms, as something happening between two people, rather than as the playing out of a tension between the practice of poetry as "wild words and specious phrases" and its recuperation as an irresistible force, which derives its power from being inextricably tied to sacred texts. To argue that "her motive may be spite, or she may simply be inspired by the challenge that Dōmyō poses to her own powers of seduction,"[66] is to assume that Izumi in the text exists as a real person, whose intentions and motives, attributed to her (presumably by the author of the text), are open to psychological speculation.

The amorous coupling of Dōmyō and Izumi serves, I would argue, as a particularly apposite site for exploring the connections between the *Lotus Sutra* and poetry, which, more than the love affair between two individuals, is of central importance to Buddhist narratives.[67] This becomes abundantly clear in the third episode in the *Shasekishū* where Dōmyō's extraordinarily majestic chanting of the *Lotus Sutra,* and the context in which his recitation occurs, inspires a priest to compose his own poem in which he cleverly associates the scene of Dōmyō departing in his carriage outside the gates with his own desire to leave the burning house. Here he is of course alluding to one of the most famous parables within the *Lotus Sutra,* where a rich man saves his children from a burning house by promising them all kinds of carts that he knows they are attached to. After luring them out of the house, he gives each of them a splendid gold-decorated ox-drawn carriage instead. The splendid carriage he offers is the Greater Vehicle, or the Mahāyāna teachings. The Lesser Vehicles, rather than being rejected, serve as *hōben,* expedient means through which ordinary beings, who are still attached to worldly things, can be led to the ultimate truth of Mahāyāna.

The link that the priest establishes between Dōmyō's carriage and Dōmyō's recitation of the *Lotus Sutra,* on the one hand, and the parable of the burning house and the Greater Vehicle inscribed within this religious text, on the other, sets in motion another chain of associations. The text claims that the priest was the son of Izumi Shikibu and that his mother was known for her famous poem *kuraki yori kuraki michi,* which captured perfectly the teachings of the *Lotus Sutra.* It is the connection between Izumi's *kuraki yori kuraki michi* poem, inspired by the *Lotus Sutra,* and Dōmyō's majestic recitation of this sacred text that makes possible the link between Izumi and Dōmyō within the medieval imaginary, laying the ground for their amorous union. It would not be too far-fetched to suggest that it is the coupling of poetry and the sutra that gives birth to a priest who embodies within his own persona a profound sensitivity and understanding of the inextricable ties that bind the Way of Poetry with the Way of the Buddha.

The conjunction of Izumi, Dōmyō, and the *Lotus Sutra* in medieval narratives takes many forms. In *Uji shūi monogatari* (Tales of Uji), for example, their amorous relationship, coupled with Dōmyō's reputation as a formidable chanter of the *Lotus Sutra,* provides the narrative framework within which questions of ritual purity and pollution and the status of roadside deities vis-à-vis the more established gods that form part of the Buddhist pantheon come to be played out. In this tale, the power and status of the more established Buddhist gods Indra and Brahmā are asserted over the guardian of the fifth ward (Gojō no Dōsojin), a popular local deity of liminal spaces, who was worshipped as a protector against illness and as the god of fertility and love. Dōsojin is able to listen to Dōmyō's recitation of the *Lotus Sutra* only because Indra and Brahmā, who would normally come to hear his intoning, keep away due to the pollution brought about by Dōmyō's failure to wash himself after a night spent with Izumi, before beginning his recitation. The story ends with an admonishment from the venerable Tendai master Eshin (Genshin) that *nenbutsu* or sutra recitation must never be performed when one has broken the precepts or performed impure acts.[68]

The presence of Dōsojin in this tale is not fortuitous, especially when we take into account the fact that in many of the stories about Izumi and Dōmyō they turn out to be mother and son. For this kind of coupling goes back to the foundational myths of the land in which the sibling gods Izanami and Izanagi stir up the oceans to give birth to the Japanese islands. The coupling of siblings who were closely associated with fertility formed the basis for the tales of the origins of Dōsojin. Izanami and Izanagi came to be identified as the gods of union (*musubi no kami*) and the gods of couples (*fūfū no kami*), and it is with these gods that Dōsojin came to be aligned in popular worship as a god of fertility.[69]

Indeed, it is questionable to what degree even the use of the term "incest," as if it were a universal category, is appropriate in the context of the coupling of Izumi and Dōmyō. The terms *kinshin sōkan* (近親相姦) and incest (インセスト) are of recent provenance and do not appear in the texts under discussion. The sexual coupling of siblings, as we have observed, is central to the foundational myth of the birth of the Japanese islands. Incest, with all its connotations of taboo, sin, and personal guilt, is equally absent in Buddhist texts.

Dōmyō in the *Uji shūi* narrative is described as a monk who is deeply steeped in amorous love (*iro ni fuketaru sō*) and as an impressive intoner of the *Lotus Sutra*. It is the confluence of these two attributes that attracts the god of fertility, Dōsojin.[70] The tale is emblematic of the ambiguities embedded in such tales. Here, ritual impurity is condemned, and the superiority of Brahma and Indra is established over Dōsojin. However, the traces of *iro* as somehow connected to the sacred are never entirely erased. Indeed, as we shall see, they find their full-fledged articulation in other medieval texts where The Way of Sex (*irogonomi no michi*) is elevated to the Way of the Buddha. The amorous pairings of Ono no Komachi and Ariwara no Narihira, and Izumi Shikibu and Dōmyō, and their transformation into the female and male gods of love in other narratives, suggests the complex ways in which the accommodation between sex and enlightenment, and between the gods and the buddhas, came to be negotiated in medieval narratives.

In the late medieval text *Izumi Shikibu*, for example, the knowledge that she has inadvertently slept with her son becomes the seed of Izumi's enlightenment—she turns to the Buddhist Path and becomes the disciple of the holy man Shōku and writes her *kuraki yori kuraki michi* poem as an offering to the tutelary deity of Mount Shosha. There is nothing in the text to suggest that "the narrator expresses indignation at the nature of Izumi Shikibu and Dōmyō's affair."[71] What is at stake here is not human agency in this life but the accumulated effects of karma derived from past lives. The lesson Izumi learns from her unwitting act of coupling with her son is the truth of karma, the idea that the seeds sown by past deeds in former lives will affect the actions one takes in this life, and this awakens her to the realization that she must escape the cycle of births and deaths and attain salvation. Here what the text appears to foreground is the efficacy of *hōben* or expedient means, whereby the act of unknowingly establishing amorous ties with one's own son becomes an instantiation of the unaccountable workings of karma. Likewise, Dōmyō's infatuation with a woman who turns out to be his mother, the text suggests, is undoubtedly an unusual occurrence, which can only be explained through the mysterious operations of karma, which can bring about such improbable ties.[72]

Indeed, in some Buddhist tales, the topos of "incestuous" couplings becomes the site for exploring the deeper truths that underlie the unforeseen effects of karma accumulated from previous lives. In the story of the two monks Myōtatsu and Jungen in *Hōbutsushū*, for example, one of them unwittingly violates his mother; the other contemplates the endless cycle of births and deaths and recognizes the Buddhist truth that all beings are subject to transmigration over many lifetimes, and therefore are bound to be related to one another at some point. Asking himself the rhetorical question, "Is there anyone who is not my mother or my father?" (*Izure no hito ka waga bumo naranu wa aru*), he proceeds to take his daughter as his wife. Both monks attain salvation and are born in Amida's Pure Land.[73] The many versions of the sexual relationship between mother and son, enunciated under the proper names "Izumi" and "Dōmyō," attest to the power of such narratives to speak to the extraordinary diversity of themes and concerns that preoccupied medieval writers, proselytizers, and readers/listeners alike.

Izumi Shikibu as *Yūjo*

In many of the literary/religious narratives of the late medieval period in Japan, there is an extraordinary transformation whereby well-known noblewomen of an earlier age, such as Izumi Shikibu and Ono no Komachi, come to be reconfigured as *yūjo*.[74] The alignment of Heian court women with *yūjo* no doubt owed much to the fact that as Hitomi Tonomura suggests, "there was only a little distance between court ladies—expected to mother aristocratic offspring—and outside entertainers. Both were sexually available to male aristocrats and similarly highly accomplished in literature, the arts, and music."[75] Furthermore, in both their physical appearance and style of clothing—the eyebrows drawn as a smudge on the forehead, the long flowing hair, the short jacket (*kouchigi*), and the scarlet trousers (*hakama*)—*yūjo* were virtually indistinguishable from ladies-in-waiting and female officials at court.[76]

The fluid and porous nature of the boundaries that separated the two is already apparent in the poetic exchanges between Fujiwara no Michinaga and ladies-in-waiting such as Izumi Shikibu and Murasaki Shikibu. *Izumi Shikibu shū*, for example, includes a poem by Izumi written, the headnote tells us, in response to Michinaga's inscription of the word *ukareme* (a term synonymous with *asobi* and *yūjo*) on her fan. In her diary, Murasaki Shikibu recounts how she playfully rebuffs Michinaga's suggestion that she is a *sukimono*. While clearly not synonymous terms, both *ukareme* and *sukimono* in these contexts are meant to suggest that the ladies in question have a propensity to flirt and involve themselves in amorous affairs.

I would suggest that the conjoining of Izumi Shikibu and *yūjo* in medieval texts, made possible by a perceived overlap in their activities and status, became particularly important to medieval narratives because it opened up new discursive possibilities for bringing together a number of disparate topoi—woman, sex, poetry, and salvation—around which many of the problems and concerns that preoccupied Buddhist texts could be articulated. As I demonstrated earlier, many poet/priests were actively engaged in arguing that poetry in no way contravened Buddhist practice. Creatively using the interpretive modes available to Buddhist thought—*hōben* (expedient means), *honji suijaku* (original ground-manifest traces), *funi* (nonduality), and so on—writers sought to demonstrate that the Way of Poetry was consonant with the Way of the Buddha. The problem of *waka* as a worldly pursuit that constituted "wild words and specious phrases" was, of course, never entirely resolved and set aside, which may account for the almost obsessive reiteration, in medieval texts, of its power to confer both spiritual and material advancement to those who practiced it.

The arguments offered within Buddhist discourse for justifying sex and amorous activities were often analogous to the ones made for dealing with the problem of poetry as a worldly practice. Sex became an expedient means leading to enlightenment; often, following the logic of nondualism, the Way of Eroticism (*irogonomi no michi*) came to be conflated with the Way of the Buddha (*hotoke no michi*). Poetry was always the crucial mediator that allowed for sex to be aligned with enlightenment. This was not fortuitous because *irogonomi*, while clearly associated with sexual attachment and pleasure, was also integrally associated with a keen appreciation and mastery of *waka* poetry. It is my contention that it is precisely because the *yūjo* incorporated within her persona this dual face of both poetry and sex that she became the prime locus for exploring the relationship of these practices with both delusion and enlightenment.

In Japan many scholars have made invaluable contributions to what has now become a large body of literature on *yūjo*.[77] There are now three monographs, one in French and two in English, as well as a number of articles in English on the subject.[78] The question of the origins of *yūjo*, their early connections with the imperial court, their transformation into wandering figures, and the religious significance of their profession, are only some of the issues that have absorbed scholars working on *yūjo*. I do not intend to revisit this vast terrain in this brief concluding section of the chapter. What I hope to explore instead, through a reading of a selected number of tales, is how the terms "woman," "*yūjo*," "poetry," "sex," and "salvation" circulated in medieval texts in different configurations, and how the complex maneuvers and strategies that were available to the Buddhist exegetical tradition transformed the significations accorded to each term in different contexts. That Izumi could stand, at one and the same time, both for a woman steeped in sinful practices, as well as a bodhisattva, and a god of poetry and love points to her figural capaciousness, which, I argue, came to be fully exploited in medieval narratives to speak to issues that transcended any interest in her as a real historical person.

It is not fortuitous that in the many stories about *yūjo*, regardless of whether her activities were regarded as sinful or as signs of her enlightened state, it was poetry and song that served as the mediums through which questions of a soteriological nature come to be resolved. In *Hōbutsushū* (A Collection of Treasures, ca. 1183), attributed to Taira no Yasuyori, the *asobi* Tonekuro from Kanzaki is described as someone given to amorous and sexual pleasure (*iro o konomite*), and ignorant of the Buddha's teachings. When she is attacked and fatally injured by pirates as she plies her boat with a man in the western seas, she sings a song (*imayō*) in which she expresses her intent to intone or chant (*nenzu*) the praises of the Amida Buddha, who has vowed to save all sentient beings, and to welcome them to the Western Paradise. Her song bears results for, at her death, music emanates from the direction of the Western Paradise, and purple clouds rise above the ocean.[79] We can assume that she attains salvation and is born in Amida's Paradise.

The text attributes her birth in Amida's Paradise to the promise made by the Buddha Muryōju (Amida) in the *Daihōshaku Sutra* (Accumulated Great Treasures Sutra) to save even those who have not sown the roots of goodness or achieved merits in this life, as long as they turn to Amida for salvation. It is the desire to be saved, expressed through the form of an *imayō,* matched by the promise offered by the *Daihōshaku Sutra* to save all sentient beings that finds its perfect expression in the story of an *asobi,* who until now has paid little attention to the Buddhist teachings, and whose profession is tied to amorous and sexual pleasure. What the narrative seeks to establish above all is the power of a sutra that promises salvation to all, men and women alike.[80] The story ends with a Chinese verse by Gochūshō-ō (Prince Tomohira), which sings the praises of the Amida Buddha, "who saves even those who commit the ten evils; his power is even fiercer than the gales that sweep away the clouds and mists; one utterance of the *nenbutsu* resonates within his being, and brings forth a response, in the same way as the vast ocean gladly receives within itself a single drop of water."[81]

The imperative to read stories such as these as reflections of the status of *asobi,* and by extension of women in general, is born of contemporary questions and concerns. What if we were to set these aside and ask instead why stories about *asobi* were of such great interest to Buddhist exegetes? The life of an *asobi,* spent tossed about on the waters, worked as the perfect exemplification of the uncertain and unstable nature of the phenomenal world. Her profession, likewise, could stand in for human desire and deluded attachment to the world of *shiki.* It is my contention that *asobi* were important to Buddhist narratives because they functioned as particularly efficacious tropes for illustrating the larger truth of the compassion of Amida Buddha, who saved all sentient beings, regardless of their failings.

I am arguing that what these texts seek to highlight was not primarily the problem of the *sinfulness* of the *yūjo.* It was rather that narratives about *yūjo* could be pressed into the service of addressing the larger problem of both the allure and danger of being attached to sex and amorous pleasures, and more generally to the phenomenal world. No single ideological framework was available from within which to offer one unitary solution to this intractable problem, and this may account for the diverse forms the figure of the *yūjo* took in these narratives. The story of the famous holy man Shōkū in *Kojidan* (A Discussion of Past Matters), a collection of *setsuwa* compiled by Minamoto no Akikane around the years 1212–1215, takes another route, different from the one offered in *Hōbutsushū,* to stage and resolve the problem of sex. Here it is through the figure of the *yūjo* that Shōkū learns about the sacred nature of sex. Praying that he might behold a living bodhisattva, he is informed in a dream oracle that he should go to see the leader of the *yūjo* at Kanzaki if such is his wish. When he arrives at the house of the leader, he finds that a rowdy banquet is in progress. The leader of the *yūjo* group is engaged in singing an *imayō* lyric. When Shōkū joins his palms in obeisance and shuts his eyes, the *yūjo* before him appears in the form of the bodhisattva Fugen (Samantabhadra) and he can hear her reciting the sutras. Every time he opens his eyes she appears to be a *yūjo* singing an *imayō*. Deeply moved, with tears in his eyes, he gets up to leave. The *yūjo* follows him out and tells him not to tell anyone of his experience. She then passes away, and the air is filled with an amazing fragrance as she ascends to the Pure Land of the Amida Buddha.[82]

The power of this *setsuwa* narrative lies in the way in which it stages a series of oppositions and polarities that it then dismantles and reveals as fictions. The *yūjo*'s *imayō*, sung for the entertainment of her clients, is at first glance clearly associated with the sexual and with the world of attachment. However, when the holy man listens to it with his eyes closed he hears not secular songs but Buddhist sutras. By extension, the *yūjo*'s professional activities, of which reciting songs is one, turn out to be no different from Buddhist practices. Implicit in this tale is the claim that *imayō*—like *waka*—have the ability to express the profound truth of the Buddhist doctrine, demonstrated by the *yūjo*'s enlightened state.

It is a measure of the richness and ingenuity of the medieval Buddhist exegetical tradition that the debates and resolutions that were proffered around the question of the role of poetry and of sexual practices drew on different arguments from within a range of doctrinal positions, all of which claimed a place within Buddhist thought and practice. The position that all dharmas were interdependent and permeated one another, thus resulting in the ultimate unity of the whole universe (*jikkai gōgu*),[83] and the doctrine of the threefold truth undoubtedly contributed to advancing the claim that even the most unusual or unconventional of practices could be entirely consonant with the Buddhist Way. The assertion in the *Kojidan* story that *imayō* were no different from the sutras and that the *yūjo* was in fact a bodhisattva undoubtedly drew upon Tendai formulations of the idea that the true state of things could only be apprehended through mundane realities, which were always in a state of flux, and that the world of phenomena and the world of enlightenment were identical (*shōji soku nehan*).

The Tachikawa sect, which became increasingly popular in the twelfth and thirteenth centuries, and which developed from within Shingon, took the arguments about radical nondualism and wedded them with *Onmyōdō* Yin/Yang female/male symbolism to stake a bolder claim for the practice of sex as a path to enlightenment. The idea that one could acquire Buddhahood within this very body (*sokushin jōbutsu*) and that worldly passions constituted enlightenment (*bonnō soku bodai*) were literalized by Tachikawa exponents to mean that it was through the body and bodily practices that one could realize one's Buddha nature. From this they drew the conclusion that any distinction between sexual activity and sexual abstinence was a false one, and that it was precisely through sexual intercourse that enlightenment could be attained.[84]

Although the Tachikawa sect was declared heretical and suppressed by the fourteenth century, its ideas had a profound influence on medieval commentaries that offered novel interpretations of classical literary texts. What is particularly fascinating about these commentaries was the ingenuity with which analogy, allegory, and wordplay were used to render classical texts such as *Ise monogatari* and *Kokin wakashū* into complex, Shingon esoteric texts whose truths could be revealed only to the initiated.[85] This mode of seeking elaborate and hidden correspondences, which may appear irrational and far-fetched to modern readers, suggests another, to us unfamiliar, style of thought that harnessed a wide and eclectic range of Buddhist arguments bringing together poetry and sex to claim an integral connection between them and enlightenment.

In the *Gyokuden jinpi no maki* (Jewelled transmission of deep secrets), attributed to Fujiwara no Tameaki (ca. 1230s–after 1295), for example, it was by bringing together two elements within the myth about the primordial heavenly couple Izanagi and Izanami—the fact that they each recited a poem, after which they united sexually and gave birth to the Japanese islands—that the text is able to "conflate the cosmogonic procreative act with the origins of poetry and the origins of sexuality" and to lay the foundations for the argument that "the Path of Eroticism and the Path of Poetry were intertwined as one."[86] Drawing on *honji suijaku* thought, the text establishes a series of correspondences between Sumiyoshi Daimyojin and Izanagi, and between the latter and Dainichi Nyorai. This allowed for the incorporation of Ariwara no Narihira into the sacred pantheon by claiming that Narihira was an avatar of Izanagi, Sumiyoshi, and finally Dainichi Nyorai, the central Buddha of Shingon himself.[87]

The creation of Narihira as a deity who wrote *Ise monogatari* as an expedient means to guide people to the Buddhist Path also required, in this mode of exegesis, a transformation of the *Ise monogatari* from a tale of amorous exploits into an esoteric text, which held within it the profound truth of the Buddha's Way. The *Gyokuden jinpi no maki* does precisely this by claiming to reveal the secret sexual meanings hidden in the graphs *i* and *se* of *Ise monogatari:* "the graphs for i and se in the title *Ise monogatari* incorporate the Twin Realm mandalas (*ryōbu*). The womb and Diamond [Realm Mandalas] are created through the Way of Men and Women [i.e., through sex]. 'I' is 'womb' and 'woman.' 'Se' is 'diamond' and 'man.'"[88]

One version of the medieval commentary *Wakachikenshū* (Collection of Revealed Knowledge of *Waka;* ca. 1260s?), transmitted by Teika to Tameie and then to Tameaki, shows the influence of Shingon Tachikawa in Tameaki's supplement to the introduction of the text. Here he claims that "Narihira is identified as two Bodhisattvas: the Bodhisattva of Song and Dance in Paradise and the Horse

Headed Kannon. Seeing the plight of humanity . . . he was born as a human into this world . . . and eventually brought consolation to 3,733 suffering women. He recorded his activities in *Ise monogatari* in order to disseminate the [esoteric] meaning of eroticism (*irogonomi*) to later generations."[89] As Klein points out, this is one of the first examples of "etmyological allegoresis" at work.[90] For the identification of Narihira as Horse-Headed Kannon may have been inspired by the fact that Narihira was head of the Right Horse Guards. In Tameaki's commentaries, the poet Ariwara no Narihira, who is frequently identified as an avatar of various bodhisattvas and kami, including the Horse Headed Kannon and Dainichi Nyorai, is paired with Ono no Komachi, his female counterpart, who is presented as an avatar of Nyoirin Kannon. We see precisely this kind of pairing in the *otogizōshi Komachi sōshi* where, at the end of the tale, we are told that Komachi was a manifestation (*keshin*) of the bodhisattva Nyoirin Kannon and that Narihira was a manifestation of the Eleven-Headed Kannon.[91]

I have summarized above the nature of medieval forms of argumentation because they offer important insights into how the narratives of that age were intended to be read, that is, not as personalized accounts of particular individuals but rather as instantiations of the Buddhist Truths that they enabled. It was by arguing for the innate interconnectedness between poetry, eroticism, and the Buddhist Path—the Way of Poetry=the Way of Eroticism, the Way of Poetry=the Way of the Buddha, the Way of Eroticism=the Way of the Buddha—that medieval commentaries sought to resolve the problematics of poetry, sex, and enlightenment.

The ideas articulated in these texts had a considerable impact on the popular culture of the Muromachi period, particularly Noh and *otogizōshi*.[92] The tantric practices of the Tachikawa sect, which were an application of the idea of radical nonduality and enlightenment within one's own body, provided popular medieval tales with the conceptual language for envisioning the radical possibility of enlightenment through the practice of sex. It is within this context that we need to situate some of the stories about Izumi Shikibu as *yūjo* that came to be circulated in the centuries after her death.

Jōruri monogatari, composed in the late medieval period, for example, recounts a story about Minamoto no Yoshitsune, who, as a young lad, tries to seduce Princess Jōruri by telling her a story about Izumi. In this tale Izumi Shikibu is described as a noblewoman of great beauty and a highly accomplished poet. However, when she performs memorial services for her late mother and father, they communicate to her through a dream, telling her that they have fallen into hell because Izumi has spurned the love of countless men who have lost their hearts to her. In the dream, the parents implore her to "make a vow to love all men, without distinction, from the highest to the lowest" (*takaki iyashiki oshinabete aijōgan o tatsu*), thereby ensuring their becoming buddhas in their own bodies (*sokushin jōbutsu*).

Izumi decides to become a nun. Just as she is about to cut her hair the Amida Buddha appears before her and reminds her of her parents' words. Izumi leaves home, sets up a hut on Fifth Avenue in the capital, and puts up a sign, announcing that she will tie a knot of intimacy with one thousand men. In three years and three months she entertains nine hundred and ninety nine lovers. The final encounter is with a mute who oozes terrifying sickness from every pore. The sight of this hideous apparition shakes Izumi's resolve to sleep with every man, without discrimination. The mute (who can speak after all), however, reminds her of her vow, and mobilizes the arsenal available within Buddhist discourses to convince Izumi of the essential difficulty of women attaining enlightenment. Women, he claims, are deceptive beings who, while appearing as bodhisattvas on the outside, are in fact demons within. They are encumbered by the five obstructions, and their bodies exude blood, which is polluting. His speech has the desired effect. Izumi experiences a change of heart and sleeps with him. In the end, the mute reveals himself to be none other than the Kannon of Kiyomizu Temple. He praises the strength of her filial resolve and assures her that both she and her parents will attain enlightenment within their own bodies. Izumi follows him up to Kiyomizu, and filled with deep gratitude and joy she composes a poem in which she likens her own state to one who, after a brief sleep, has discovered the joy of entering the True Path.[93]

It is worth considering the diversity of the themes and motifs central to Buddhism that is brought together in this narrative. Izumi Shikibu here is not explicitly described as a *yūjo,* but her setting up a hut on Fifth Avenue in Kyoto clearly suggests that she has located herself in an area where women offer their sexual services to men. Conflating the popular legends of Ono no Komachi, who was said to have spurned her male suitors, with the love life of Izumi, the narrative turns on its head her withholding of sex from her male pursuers by demanding of her that she sleep *without discrimination* with a thousand men in order to ensure their salvation. Indeed, the rhetorical force of the narrative, as I argue, derives from a series of such inversions and transformations that overturn conventional understandings of the nature of reality, and by extension of the distinctions between the phenomenal world and the world of enlightenment. Woman as *yūjo*/Izumi Shikibu, standing as she does for certain failings and shortcomings, becomes the ideal medium both for articulating a series of dualities and then deconstructing them to reveal their provisionality, thereby reaffirming the truth of the nondual Dharma.

The *yūjo* as *irogonomi,* given her association with sex and with amorous affairs, is an obvious site for exploring the nature of deluded attachment. She is at the center of many conversion narratives, where she recognizes the sinfulness of her ways and becomes a nun, devoting herself to the Buddhist Path. There is, however, another equally compelling argument within Buddhist discourse that suggests that sex, when associated with the courtesan, is a potent metaphor not of delusion but of nondiscrimination, which manifests itself through actions that are undertaken with complete detachment and compassion. The courtesan, who falls outside of the conventional social order, turning her back on family, home, and procreation, is often positioned as the antithesis of the householder, who remains trapped within the world of *samsāra.* In this she is not unlike the nun who also rejects family life in order to follow the Buddhist Way.

In *Jōruri monogatari* the Way of Sex far surpasses the path of renunciation, for in the end it ensures that Izumi and her parents attain Buddhahood within their own bodies. The figure one thousand to account for the number of men Izumi is called upon to sleep with draws attention to itself for its hyperbolism. The textual strategy here is to take the mundane and worldly practice of sex out of its ordinariness and render it sacred through excess. It is in tales such as these that we see the traces of tantric Buddhist ideas and practices, which celebrated the performance of sex as the highest path to enlightenment. It is not insignificant in this context that the *yūjo*'s/Izumi's bravura performance is an affirmation not of amorous pleasure but rather of the proper execution of her professed vow to sleep with all men, without discrimination.

The diseased and evil-smelling man who insists that Izumi sleep with him performs a number of functions in this tale. It is through him that the *yūjo*'s capacity for undiscriminating compassion is put to the ultimate test. There are many precedents for this in Indian Buddhist narratives in which a bodhisattva gives away his body as an act of extreme self-sacrifice to save others. Often the demand, by a deity, that he sacrifice parts of his body turns out to be a ruse to test the seriousness of his intent, and, in the end, he is rendered whole by an Act of Truth.[94] Kokan Shiren's *Genkō shakusho* (1332), a thirty-volume history of Buddhism in Japan, which includes so-called biographies of holy men and women, offers an account of Empress Kōmyō's vow to cleanse the dirt from the bodies of one thousand men. Like the story in *Jōruri monogatari,* her final challenge comes in the form of a leprous man who requests that she bathe him and suck the pus from his boils. Unable to refuse she acquiesces. The man turns out to be the Buddha Ashuku, who radiates beauty and fragrance. Filled with joy she has a temple, Ashukuji, built in his honor.[95] Here too the invocation of the figure one thousand is a rhetorical move to demonstrate that acts of self-sacrifice must perforce be grounded in excess.

The repulsive figure who oozes sickness in *Jōruri monogatari* also serves as the standard-bearer for all the conventional arguments launched against women—they are polluted through the blood they exude during menstruation and childbirth; they cannot be saved in their female forms because of the "Five Obstructions"; they must be reborn as men before they can attain enlightenment; and so on. However, in the end, he himself becomes the dominant metaphor for the truth of nonduality. The vituperative nature of his diatribe against women is intended to bring into even sharper focus the fact that all the objections he raises are in the end chimerical. For the Path of Sex assures women, and by extension, the *yūjo*/Izumi, Buddhahood in *their own* bodies. His outward manifestation as a disfigured mute notwithstanding, he is none other than Kiyomizu Kannon, thereby embodying in his own form the nondual Dharma. Rather than seeing him as playing "a leading role in effecting Izumi Shikibu's sexual and psychological degradation," and interpreting his speech as "particularly demeaning," and one that "deprives Izumi Shikibu of her remaining dignity,"[96] I would argue that both Kannon and Izumi Shikibu serve as rhetorical devices, making possible a series of inversions that allow for the affirmation of the ultimate truth of nonduality over conventional realities.

The arguments I have made in this chapter are often at odds with what has now become a dominant strain in contemporary scholarship on women in medieval Japan, in which what I call the textual figure of Izumi is treated as if she were a representation of a real woman. I have sought to argue otherwise by suggesting that Izumi Shikibu was of interest to medieval writers not because they wanted to construct a life-and-blood, authentic portrait of her as a historical person with particular psychological and sexual dispositions, or because they were engaged in an ideological agenda to distort the truth of her lived reality. Rather, her own historical circumstances and the empirical truth of her corporeality provided the basis for transforming her into a particularly potent figure of speech that brought together, under the sign "woman," questions that were of the utmost importance to the medieval world, namely, how sex and poetry as worldly pursuits could be reconciled with the Way of the Buddha.

Izumi's poetry did not belong to her as an individual but was available to be used creatively to fit a wide range of scenarios that illuminated precisely this question of the relationship between worldly attachment and the goal of enlightenment. Kamo no Chōmei, as we have observed, was well aware of the fact that the *kuraki yori kuraki* poem was commonly attributed to the "real" Izumi Shikibu. That the *asobi* at Muro, in his *Hosshinshū*, recites the same poem when she approaches a holy man's boat to seek his help in attaining enlightenment, without acknowledging the historical Izumi, is a testament to the myriad ways in which both Izumi and her poems were seen not as repositories of individual identity and authorship but rather as part of a shared repertoire that could be performed in different ways, each iteration producing different notes and diverse resonances.

Another analytical approach that I have sought to challenge here is the claim that Buddhism was misogynistic, in the sense that it sought to oppress women and to position them consistently as inferior to men. In a hierarchically ordered universe, it was hardly surprising that women were not the equals of men. Establishing women's inferiority to men was not the central issue for texts that used the figure of Izumi. Buddhism did not engage in a "*wilful* [italics added] domestication of *yūjo* to turn them into 'ritual scapegoats' by presenting them as at once defiled beings and sacred bodhisattvas."[97] The narratives about Shinto gods and buddhas were not attempts by "Buddhist mythmakers" to subjugate and "rationalize a disruptive Dionysian cult of fertility that they simultaneously condemn as a sinful practice and uphold as an accomplishment leading to spiritual enlightenment."[98] For Buddhism was hardly a monolithic, anthropomorphized, purposeful entity, possessed of agency and consciousness, which sought to impose its will on those it wished to oppress and marginalize. Rather, the diversity of the debates and arguments, the insistence with which they were endlessly rehearsed, and the seemingly contradictory positions that were adopted in medieval texts attest to the workings not of a hegemonic discourse but of an unresolved and often highly stylized staging and rehearsing of themes and concerns about sex, poetry, and enlightenment that continued to be of enduring interest to Buddhist exegetes.

If woman in medieval texts was an endlessly malleable category, and if the workings of Buddhism in medieval texts are accessible to us only through the play of genres, tropes, and other rhetorical devices that these texts used in order both to pose and to grapple with questions that it deemed to be of utmost importance, then Buddhism cannot be reduced to a singular discourse that finds in woman the stable object that is there to be either suppressed, co-opted, or ignored. Treating poetic tales as historical sources, woman as a trans-historical category, and Buddhism as a monolithic and hegemonic discourse have made it all too easy for us to ascribe to both women and Buddhism motives and desires that are born of our own modern concerns and political imperatives. In trying to capture some of the preoccupations and concerns of medieval writers and exegetes, I have attempted to come closer to the organizing categories through which they made sense of their world, which is far removed from our own.

CHAPTER FIVE

"Meditating on the Impure Body"

The Generic Transformations of a Medieval Topos

The body as a foul thing, filled with feces, pus, blood, worms, and so on, appears as a recurring motif in Buddhist doctrinal texts. These texts seek to impart the lesson that the body/self, like all worldly phenomena, is fundamentally insubstantial and short-lived, and that its capacity to arouse intense desire makes it the ideal vehicle for demonstrating the deluded nature of all attachment. Grasping the true nature of the body, in the Buddhist view, is an essential step along the path to enlightenment.

However, this does not mean that the body in the Buddhist tradition is consistently the object of revilement, for it is also the privileged site upon which enlightenment comes to be inscribed. The hagiographies of holy men and women all emphasize the fact that the bodies of enlightened beings, in death, defy the process of decomposition, and rather than disintegrating and becoming malodorous, remain whole and exude heavenly fragrances. The cult of relics attests to the magical powers of the enlightened body, which even in its fragmented form holds out the possibility of extending the experience of enlightenment to those who, through acts of devotion, partake of its sacred nature. The body in Buddhist canonical texts is the site of multiple pedagogies—as a signifier of impurity it serves to highlight the futility of desire and attachment to the world; at the same time, it is also the prized vehicle for the performance of rituals and practices that lead to the realization of Buddhahood that is inherent in all beings.[1]

This chapter takes as its central theme one aspect of the body's pedagogical potential, namely, the lessons to be learned from meditating on the impurity of the body (*fujōkan*). However, rather than the doctrinal expositions on the impurity of the body and on the practice of meditating on corpses, both of which form part of the Buddhist teachings in scriptural writings, the focus of this chapter is on the ways in which the concept of bodily impurity and the need to meditate on it comes to be thematized in Japanese visual and literary narratives of the medieval period.

I am particularly interested in charting how conceptions of the body, woman, and desire, which circulate in these texts, are part of a shifting constellation of meanings, and how the significations with which they are endowed are shaped by the conventions and tropes that characterize the different genres within which they are embedded. It is by examining the widely divergent discourses on the Buddhist theme of the impurity of the body, and of the dangers of worldly attachment in medieval narratives, that I seek to demonstrate the contingent and changing nature of these categories.

I begin with a brief account of how the concept of the foul and impure nature of the human body is articulated in the Buddhist scriptures and commentaries, before turning to the ways in which this theme is taken up, particularly in works in the *monogatari* and *setsuwa* genres. I focus, at some length, on the tropes of death and dying in the *Tale of Genji* to demonstrate how a text, whose central theme is the workings of amorous and erotic entanglements, creatively rearticulates Buddhist discourses on the impurity of the body and on its capacity to resist decomposition to produce not revulsion and detachment but rather an increased longing for the lover who is no more.

I turn next to two *setsuwa* collections, *Hosshinshū* (A Collection of Tales of Religious Awakening), attributed to the famous poet/priest Kamo no Chōmei (1156–1216),[2] and *Kankyo no tomo* (A Companion in Solitude), believed to have been written by Priest Keisei in 1222.[3] I focus on these texts for two reasons: first, because unusually for prose narratives in medieval Japan, they engage directly, and in a sustained fashion, with the theme of *fujōkan;* second, the fact that they stand at the interstices of two contending discourses make them ideal sites for considering how the dynamics of intertextuality operates: for the notion of *fujōkan* as it comes to be represented in these tales is shaped both by Buddhist scriptural writings as well as by literary texts written in the courtly tradition. Styles of writing are, of course, intrinsically tied to modes of thinking and, as I seek to argue, when *Hosshinshū* and *Kankyo no tomo* borrow from the narrative strategies and conventions of courtly *waka* and *monogatari* genres, their reading of *fujō* deviates from the critique of the body, of attachment to women, and of the seductions of amorous love, articulated in the sutras and commentaries.

Fujō in Canonical Texts

The *Anguttara Nikāya* (The Book of the Gradual Sayings),[4] one of the central texts in the Pali canon, refers to the body as an infected wound that never heals, as a boil with nine openings out of which foul and evil-smelling matter constantly oozes.[5] In the *Mahāprajnāparamitopadesa* (Commentary on the Great Wisdom Sutra; Ch. *Ta-chih-tu-lun;* Jp. *Daichidoron*),[6] we have a vivid description of the foulness of our bodies from the very moment of conception: during copulation, the male worm, a white essence, issues forth like tears and the female worm, a red essence, gushes forth like vomit and it is out of the fusion of these two worms, which are like tears and vomit, that our flesh is born. The commentary then describes the intrinsically foul nature of the body after it is born, filled as it is with feces, urine, pus, blood, fat, entrails, worms, and so on. Finally, it portrays the foulness of the corpse in various stages of decay in order to establish that the body is impure at all times, even before birth and after death.

The fifth-century Pali text *Visuddhimagga* (Path of Purity), in which Buddhaghosa systematized the Theravāda formulation of sensory withdrawal and sensory observation, devotes a whole section of his work to the technique of meditating on the impurity of the body. Buddhaghosa proposes a schema for identifying the multiple stages of bodily decay after death—the swollen corpse; the bluish corpse; the festering corpse that exudes pus; the fissured corpse; the corpse gnawed and mangled by dogs, jackals, and so on; the corpse that has its various parts scattered about; the corpse that is both hacked and scattered; the corpse that is smeared with the blood that drips from it; the corpse infested with worms; and the bones either as a whole skeleton or as separate bones.[7] The topos of the nine stages of the process of death and corruption (Sk. *nava asubhbhāvanā;* Jp. *kusō*) is one that, as we shall see, occurs frequently in Japanese visual texts.

Part of the training of a Buddhist monk involved spending time in the charnel fields in order to observe, in minute detail, various stages of the putrefaction of the human body, thereby understanding its true nature. For example, as the *Visuddhimagga* tells us, meditating on the festering corpse, which emits a bad stench, is beneficial for those who lust after the sweet-smelling body of a person who uses flowers and perfumes. Meditating on the worm-eaten body, which now belongs to a manifold variety of worms, is a cure for anyone who is attached to his/her own body thinking, "It is mine."[8]

Meditations on the foulness of the body were part of a thoroughgoing critique of all sense perceptions, which were said to lead to acts that produced bad karma. In *Visuddhimagga*, Buddhaghosa emphasized not only the body's impurity but also the essential foulness of food, explaining how it was to be meditated upon through ten stages. For example, when we meditate on food, which is crushed by the teeth and smeared with saliva, we apprehend that it has lost all its visual beauty and "it reaches a state of extreme repulsiveness, like dog's vomit in a dog's trough."[9] Contemplating food once it has turned into excrement and urine is similarly a way of losing one's passion and greed for food. In Buddhaghosa's text every single impurity associated with the body receives elaborate treatment. There is a detailed description, for instance, on how to meditate on hair and apprehend its essential foulness.[10]

Buddhaghosa's discourse on the impurity of the body is bound neither by class nor by gender. He makes no distinction between young and old, high- and lowborn, or men and women, for he takes it as axiomatic that all bodies are essentially impure and subject to death and decay. As he points out in *Visuddhimagga,* "even a king, if he were to wander from village to village in a state of nature, with his hair all rough and dishevelled, would be undistinguishable from any rubbish-remover or outcast, because the body would be equally repulsive in either case."[11]

In the vast majority of texts that deal with the theme of *fujō,* however, women came to be singled out as exemplars of the truth of bodily impurity. It is not hard to see why this was so for it was the female form that was accorded pride of place as the locus of allure and beauty, and it was precisely for this reason that it had to be subjected to an elaborate deconstruction, which would lay bare its essentially foul character. It was the capacity of the female form to arouse desire and attachment that made it a synecdoche for the duplicitous and dissembling nature of the body tout court. The particular context within which the female body came to be seen as a particularly threatening presence was within the male monastic orders where the celibacy of monks was of the utmost importance.

In the *Anguttara Nikāya,* for example, the Buddha warns monks that woman's nature is such that under any circumstances she will ensnare the heart of a man. Women, he says, are the snare of Mara.[12] Warning against the defilement that will result from contact with women, the Buddha chastises a monk who has had sexual contact with women thus: "It were better for you, foolish man, that your male organ should enter the mouth of a terrible and poisonous snake, than that it should enter a woman. . . . It were better for you, foolish man, that your male organ should enter a charcoal pit, burning, ablaze, afire, than that it should enter a woman."[13]

Reflecting the same perspective, the earliest tales about the Gautama Buddha and his decision to renounce worldly life point to the moment when, on observing the saliva dribbling from the half-open mouths of the women in his harem, who are in deep sleep, he is awakened into the realization that women whom he had seen as epitomes of beauty were in fact no different from the corpses strewn about in the charnel fields.

Theragāthā, an anthology of poems in Pali composed by monks sometime between the lifetime of the Buddha and the third century B.C.E., expresses the same point. In one poem, the Buddha's disciple Mahāmoggāllana mounts a vehement diatribe against the courtesan Vimala, who allegedly has attempted to seduce him. Her body, he declares, is evil smelling, a bag of dung tied up with skin, her breasts, no more than lumps on her chest. The hyperbolic language through which the vilification of the female body occurs suggests the degree to which it was feared as an irresistible force that could not but arouse uncontrollable desire and affective attachment. It was through the strategy of highlighting the disjuncture between outward form and inner essence, and between the composite body and its fragmentation through dismemberment or disintegration, that the injunctions against attachment to the female form came to be elaborated in Indian scriptural texts.

Conceptions of *Fujō* in Japanese Doctrinal Texts

The concept of *fujō*, apprehended par excellence through meditation on the nine aspects of death (*kusō*), was familiar to Japanese monks through the sutras and commentaries, which were introduced from India to Japan via China. The religious commentaries composed in Japan, which refer to the theme of *fujō*, closely follow the Chinese scriptural texts. *Ōjōyōshū* (Essentials of Salvation), by the Tendai monk Genshin (942–1017), devotes several pages to the concept of *fujō*.

Genshin presents a graphic description of the sufferings experienced in the six realms of existence (*rokudō*). Describing the evils of the human world, he singles out impurity (*fujō*), suffering (*ku*), and evanescence (*mujō*) as objects for meditation. In the section on impurity, which is the lengthiest, he draws upon and sometimes directly quotes from the Chinese commentaries such as *Daichidoron* (Discourse on the Great Wisdom), *Maka shikan* (Cessation and Insight), and the Zen sutras to demonstrate how the body is composed of bones, sinews, joints, organs, and flesh; how it is essentially foul and comparable to a rotting and decaying house; and how it is inhabited from head to toe by worms even when we are alive. Finally, he turns to the body after death and depicts in graphic detail the decay and dissolution of the body. Here he follows the nine stages of decomposition (*kusō*) that became the standard objects of Buddhist meditation.[14]

Genshin writes:

One must certainly take note that this body is impure from start to finish. Men and women we love are all like this [fundamentally impure]. How can the body possibly arouse desire in a person of wisdom? For this reason it says in *Maka shikan*, "Until one has grasped this aspect [impurity], one's feelings of lust and attachment are extremely strong, but when one apprehends [this truth], then all desire ceases. It is like a person who, not having seen faeces, an unbearable sight, eats food, but then having inhaled their foul stench, ends up vomiting and can no longer eat." *Maka shikan* further says, "If one grasps this aspect, then arched eyebrows, dark eyes, white teeth, and red lips are all like decorating excrement with white powder; it is like dressing up a festering corpse in silk and damask. It is a sight unbearable to behold. It goes without saying, who would be able to draw close to it? There was the person who employed the Brahmin Mrga-landika to kill him.[15] How then can we possibly take pleasure in kissing and embracing? Meditating in this way is the medicinal soup that cures the illness of lustful desire."[16]

The horrific images of death and bodily decomposition that are evoked in scriptural texts find their most direct expression in the paintings of the nine stages of decay (*kusōzu*) that were executed in different forms, from handscrolls and hanging scrolls to printed books, between the thirteenth and nineteenth centuries in Japan. The *Kusōshi emaki* (Illustrated Handscroll of the Poem of the Nine Stages of a Decomposing Corpse) and *Jindō fujō sōzu* (Painting of the Impure Aspect of the Human Realm), which form part of the *Rokudōe* (Pictures of the Six Paths of Transmigration) that are to be found in the Tendai temple at Shōju Raigōji, are representative works within this genre.[17]

Both works begin with a depiction of an aristocratic woman whose beauty and refinement are portrayed through her long hair and many-layered robes. The scrolls chart her gradual decomposition after death, depicting the nine stages of her bodily decay, thereby highlighting the contrast between ordinary perception, which sees the body as a thing of beauty, and the ultimate reality of its impure and impermanent nature. These visual texts are heavily influenced by Buddhist commentarial writing: the *Kusōshi emaki*, for example, draws on *Maka shikan* and attempts to reproduce, through precise anatomical detail, the descriptions of the nine stages of decomposition elaborated in the commentary.

Jindō fujō sōzu is inspired by Genshin's *Ōjōyōshū*, but its pictorial style deviates from the scriptural tradition by incorporating landscape and the theme of seasonal change into its narrative on human decay. In this, the scroll draws on the poems on the nine stages of decay (*kusōshi*) attributed to the T'ang Chinese poet Su Tung-po.[18] The visual imagery often takes the form of an implicit dialogue with the poem text: when the poem speaks of the corpse in its early stage of discoloration, likening it to flowers fading in the third month, for example, it resonates within the painting in the form of an image of a newly deceased body being showered with cherry blossoms.[19] The fact that the Raigōji scroll engages in this way with poetry has implications for the way in which the theme of *fujō* comes to be represented.

The *waka* poems that accompany the Chinese verses are striking for their evocation of a mood of nostalgia and sadness, rather than horror and revulsion, when they speak about the body and *fujō*. Take, for instance, the following poems on the theme of "scattered bones," the ninth stage of decay of the human body, accompanying the pictorial depictions of decay in *Kusōshi emaki:*

> Behold,
> our lives like drops of dew,
> vanished with the morning.
> Only our bodies remain,
> scattered into the tall grasses.

> Bodies,
> they thought their own
> lie broken now.
> Among the slender reeds
> turning to dust.[20]

There is a slide here from a critique of the body's impurity (*fujō*) to a lament about its evanescence (*mujō*),[21] a shift that is characteristic of the conventions of *waka,* which register the passage of time through the melancholy trope of *mujō.* Love and the changing seasons exemplify the mutability of all things: their beauty captured briefly before it inevitably fades away forms the dominant aesthetic of both *waka* and *monogatari,* and it is this sensibility that informs the treatment of *fujō* in *Hosshinshū* and *Kankyo no tomo.* A close examination of the ways in which the topoi of death and dying work in the *Tale of Genji* may best illustrate the nature of the textual debts that *setsuwa* narratives such as *Hosshinshū* and *Kankyo no tomo* owe to the conventions of *monogatari,* and in the process elucidate how it is that they produce a pedagogy of the impure body, which is not always consonant with the one envisioned in canonical texts.

The Erotics of Death and Dying in the *Tale of Genji*

The many scenes in the *Tale of Genji* that describe in loving detail the sufferings of those who are dying and the physical state of the bodies of those who have died suggest the seriousness with which the text engages with the theme of human mortality. For the most part, however, it is not bodily decomposition but the Buddhist body of enlightenment, immune to bodily decay, that gets creatively reconfigured in the text as an aesthetic and erotic presence.

The courtly ideal of beauty in the Heian period, we are told, was plumpness. And yet, in the *Genji,* it is often the emaciated, thin, and indeed in some ways almost noncorporeal body that evokes the strongest feelings of desire and emotional commitment. As we have observed in Chapter 2, beauty when associated with frailty and helplessness is expressed through the term *rōtashi,* which is used to describe a particular kind of beauty that is seen to inhere in women. It is female beauty that serves par excellence as a metaphor for the fleeting and ephemeral nature of the world, and it is this resonance with the Buddhist teachings that makes the dying woman a topos of considerable significance within the text.[22]

If in Buddhist scriptural texts the knowledge that all things are impermanent and transient leads to the abandonment of desire and attachment, in romance narratives such as the *Genji,* this insight is put to use for entirely different ends to produce even greater attachment and longing for the female figure who comes to signify evanescence and change. Suetsumuhana is an unattractive flower because its red color never fades, and its blossoms are long lasting: the lady who is known by this unfortunate sobriquet shares the failings of that flower for she fails to fall ill and die; Yūgao's appeal, on the other hand, lies in the fact that like the flower *yūgao,* which fades before dawn, she too dies young while still at the height of her beauty.[23]

In the "Spring Shoots" chapter, when Murasaki is seriously ill, her color is described as having "deteriorated to a bluish pallor." Rather than evoking unpleasant suggestions of decay, this blue-white complexion is described as being extremely beautiful, and her skin, now turned translucent, gives her appearance an incomparably frail and beautiful look (*yo ni naku rōtage nari*). Murasaki's virtual release from her own corporeality, the fact that she is "as weak as a cicada shell" (a motif that appears repeatedly in the work), is what renders her unusually beautiful.[24]

Likewise, in the scenes of Ōigimi's slow death by self-imposed starvation, the aestheticization of frailty and insubstantiality is carried to fetishistic heights. "Her arms had become extremely thin, and appeared phantom like in their weakness. And yet, for all that, her colour remained unchanged, for she retained her whiteness, and her beauty and grace. She gave the impression of being a lifeless doll that was lying down . . ." (*kaina nado mo ito hosou narite, kage no yō ni yowashige naru mono kara, iroai mo kawarazu, shirō utsushige ni nayo nayo to shite . . . mi mo naki hina o fusetaramu kokochi shite . . .*).[25]

The most eloquent homage to beauty in the *Genji* occurs in the many death scenes that take center stage in this text. These scenes draw upon Buddhist hagiographical accounts of the holy deaths of men and women whose bodies resist decomposition, and instead of emitting foul odors, they exude heavenly fragrances. As Jacqueline Stone has argued, one of the sources of Buddhism's powerful appeal was that it held out the promise of "mastery of death."[26] The final moments before one's departure from this world were deemed to be of critical importance, for if faced with right mindfulness, they could ensure one's salvation. Equally, however, even a lifetime of religious practice could be rendered useless, and could result in rebirth in one of the inauspicious realms, if at the approach of death, the mind was distracted by fear, desire, or pain. As Stone suggests, "The manner of the individual's death, including both his posture and the corporeal signs manifested by his dying, are considered indices to his spiritual condition. . . ."[27]

In death, the extreme whiteness of Murasaki's skin, the radiance of her face, and the lustrous quality of her hair all speak of her exquisite beauty. Murasaki's body shows no signs of decay: she is presented to us not as a corpse, which inevitably disintegrates, but rather as someone who is even more beautiful in death than she was in life. When she is cremated only a thin wisp of smoke rises from her funeral pyre, providing "little satisfaction for the bereaved one who had hoped to trace the smoke to the dreary evening sky and imagine his lover among the clouds."[28] Even if the smoke leaves behind hardly a trace, it provides another kind of solace, for it speaks to the insubstantiality of her form, attesting to the truth of evanescence. Murasaki, as she draws close to death, is likened to a dewdrop that is about to vanish.

As we shall see, her death scene mimics within the altered context of a romance narrative the strategies employed in Buddhist literature to depict the passing away of holy men and women who attain birth in the Pure Land.[29] Rather than serving as an object lesson for apprehending the transitory nature of human life and the futility of romantic attachment, Murasaki's death does not lead Genji to take the tonsure, despite his devout disposition and his avowed intent to abandon worldly life. It leads instead to even greater longing and attachment to his lost love.

The motifs and images that characterize Murasaki's death scene are replayed and amplified in the descriptions of Ōigimi as she dies in the remote setting of Uji. Here the narrative links Kaoru's despair at seeing Ōigimi die more directly with Buddhist insights into the nature of death and suffering. He prays to the Buddha, urging that if Ōigimi's death is indeed meant to lead him to abandon worldly life, then he should be shown something of her that will fill him with horror and cause him to awaken from his sorrow. However, Ōigimi's body does not provide Kaoru with the signs that might make possible his religious redemption. Gazing upon her as she is close to death, he observes that her hair gives off the same fragrance that it carried when she was alive. Ōigimi remains frail to the last and, like Murasaki during her cremation, very little smoke rises from her.[30]

Ōigimi's death has the opposite effect of that intended by the religious narratives of death leading to renunciation (*hiren tonsei tan*), in which the sight of the inevitable decay of the body of the female lover becomes the occasion for the man to abandon worldly life and take the tonsure. Despite his fervent prayers, Ōigimi's death makes Kaoru cling even more firmly to the world of amorous attachment, driving him to find substitutes for her in the figures of her sister Nakanokimi and her half sister Ukifune.

Male deaths in the *Genji* receive considerably less attention; Kashiwagi is the notable exception. Kashiwagi's body, rendered weak and feeble, is described as a cicada shell in order to evoke the beauty of his insubstantiality. Like Murasaki and Ōigimi, his body too resists all signs of unseemliness even when he is dying. Those who are seriously ill, we are told, normally have an unkempt appearance, with dishevelled hair and beard. Kashiwagi, however, still has his *eboshi* firmly in place and, in his wasted condition, looks paler and more distinguished than before. His beauty is further enhanced by the pitiful faintness of his breath. Of particular interest is the term *yase saraboitaru* to refer to his extremely thin and wasted body.[31] *Sarabou* signifies the whitening of the bones of a corpse from exposure to the elements.[32] It is surely significant that a term that in the Buddhist context signifies the state of decay that the body inevitably undergoes is applied to the living body and reinvented here as an aesthetic category. The term *sarabou* draws attention to the frailty of Kashiwagi's form and the pure whiteness of his complexion, and these in turn become emblematic of his aristocratic refinement and grace.

The emotional and erotic charge of death and dying as aesthetic tropes in the *Genji* cannot be understood outside of the Buddhist world view within which the text is located and with which it creatively engages. The deaths of Fujitsubo, Murasaki, Ōigimi, and Kashiwagi are beautiful not only because they are "enshrouded in the language of poetry"[33] but also, equally significantly, because they are imbued with religious significance. Steeped in Buddhist imagery, their deaths are holy events that call to mind the accounts of enlightened beings who pass away and are born in the Pure Land (*ōjōden*).[34]

When Fujitsubo dies she does so calmly and quickly, "like a flame that is extinguished" (*tomoshibi nado no kieru yō nite hate tamainureba*).[35] By echoing the words from the *Lotus Sutra* describing the moment of the Buddha's passing away, Fujitsubo's death is elevated to the highest spiritual level. Despite her transgressive relationship with Genji, and the guilty secret that she must carry all her life, in death she is saved, for her religious devotions through her grave illness and her munificence assure her an immaculate death. The depth of her piety and generosity, we are told, is so widely acknowledged that even mountain ascetics (*yamabushi*) cannot but mourn her loss.[36]

Murasaki, of all the characters in the *Genji,* comes closest to being the ideal *bosatsu* figure of romance. She is often described as someone who appears as she is, without any calculation (*nani gokoro nashi*). However, she is far from being untouched by Genji's infidelities: the text offers many instances where she is betrayed and hurt by her own guileless and trusting nature.[37] That she is able to cultivate compassion and forbearance in the face of Genji's inconstancy, and that she displays an intensely pious disposition, marks her as one destined for a particularly holy death.

The seriousness of her intent to take religious vows and her initiative in organizing the ceremonies for the recitation of the *Lotus Sutra* (*Hoke Hakkō*) demonstrates her commitment to the Buddhist Way, which offers the possibility of disengaging from worldly attachments and preparing for death. Despite the horror of being possessed by the spirit of the Rokujō Lady and the suffering caused by a protracted illness that it brings in its wake, in the end she performs an exemplary death. In the final hours that she spends in the company of the Akashi empress and Genji, she is a picture of dignity and grace, composing poems with her visitors. The final moment comes when she lies down and draws (literally) the curtain on her life, "fading away like the dew." Spring, cherry blossoms, and, in the end, dew, with which she is associated, mark her as the ideal heroine who dies beautifully while still relatively young, exemplifying the Buddhist truth of the transitory nature of all things.

The text's engagement with Buddhism, however, does not rest solely in transforming the trope of evanescence into a thing of beauty. For there are intimations in the text of death's seamier side: the inevitable process of decomposition that marks the bodies of ordinary beings is a muted but unsettling presence, casting its shadow over Yūgao and Aoi. Perhaps it is in the nature of spirit possession that it cannot but leave its ugly mark on the one who has aroused such intense jealousy (Murasaki is of course the notable exception). Aoi's death, brought on by the angry spirit of the Rōkujo Lady, is touched by suggestions of violence. Just before her death she is overcome by a tightening of her chest, and she has a convulsion.[38] No one is around when she dies, and as she has given the appearance of being dead many times during the frequent attacks that she has suffered, it is only when her body gradually changes (*yō yō kawari tamau koto domo no areba*)[39] that her parents reluctantly accept that she is indeed gone. Persisting in the hope that she might yet be brought back to life, her father commissions esoteric rites for her revival even though it is clear that her body is "in a bad state" (*sokonaware tamau*).[40] In the end they take her to the Toribe fields to be cremated. The descriptions of Aoi's final moment and of her bodily decomposition are hinted at with the utmost decorum. Understated as the words for the change her corpse undergoes might be, there is no doubt that her body shows signs of decay.

Like Aoi, Yūgao too is possessed by the spirit of the Rokujō Lady and is taken gravely ill. Consumed with despair and longing, Genji lies down next to her, only to discover that her body is growing ever colder and that she has stopped breathing. Later when he embraces her and urges her to come back to life he finds that she has gone quite cold, and that, as a result, she feels increasingly unpleasant to touch (*hieirinitareba kehai mono utoku nari yuku*).[41] Soon after, however, when Genji's attendant Koremitsu carries her into the carriage, the narrator comments on the slightness of her form, and on the fact that far from appearing in any way repulsive, she in fact exudes a frail beauty (*ito sasayaka nite, utomashigenaku rōtage nari*).[42]

Later when Genji goes to the place where her dead body has been taken, he seems to disavow ever having found her body in death unpleasant. The text explicitly states that he experiences no fear and that her beauty remains, as before, unchanged (*osoroshikige mo oboezu, ito rōtage naru sama shite, mada isasaka kawaru tokoro nashi*).[43] There is a certain tension here between the text's acknowledgement of the change that Yūgao's body undergoes and the claim that in fact her beauty remains unblemished. A romance narrative must maintain the fiction that there is no cooling of Genji's youthful passion and affective intensity even in the face of the death of the loved one, and this is achieved by recuperating the beauty of Yūgao's body and holding its inevitable decay in a state of suspension.

Death and dying in the *Genji* are profoundly imbricated in Buddhist thought, and it is with this connection that I am concerned, for it allows us to see how the *Genji* reworks, within the altered context of the *monogatari*, Buddhist conceptions of the body and death: for both the view that the body is necessarily subject to the laws of mutability that govern all phenomena and the belief that a holy death can ensure that the body remain pure and resistant to change and decomposition are creatively woven into the very texture of the amorous entanglements that lie at the heart of the *Genji*.

In the section that follows, I consider how the *setsuwa* tales of Chōmei and Keisei, which draw upon both scriptural texts and the courtly genres of *waka* and *monogatari*, shift back and forth between two different discursive modes, reconciling the view articulated in Buddhist canonical writings that the body is essentially impure and foul, and that it should properly arouse feelings of disgust and revulsion, with the very different sensibility that informs courtly genres where love, desire, and attachment, and the women who are central to their generation, become the sites of nostalgia and longing for that which is lost.

The Scriptural Context of *Hosshinshū* and *Kankyo no tomo*

The stories in *Hosshinshū* and *Kankyo no tomo* demonstrate considerable familiarity with the sutras, religious commentaries, and hagiographic tales that deal with the theme of *fujōkan*. They often reproduce the standard arguments regarding the impurity of the body found in religious texts: Chōmei frequently cites passages from *Ōjōyōshū* while Keisei draws directly upon *Maka shikan*.[44] It is striking that it is when the tales seek to demonstrate the impurity of the body as a universal condition, unmarked by gender difference, that they reproduce the horrific images of decomposition found in the religious commentaries. The story in *Kankyo no tomo* (1:19) about a lowly temple attendant, who devotes himself secretly in his spare time to meditating on "undescribably horrible corpses," for example, focuses on the ungendered body as a metaphor for the deceptive nature of the phenomenal world.[45] Asked by his master to demonstrate the fruits of his labor, the servant monk covers a bowl of gruel with a tray and meditates on it for a while. When he uncovers it, all the food has turned into white worms. Seeing this, the master entreats the servant monk to guide him to enlightenment. Quoting from several religious commentaries, Keisei writes:

> In the section entitled *Shidai zenmon,* the great Tendai master says, "If an ordinary, foolish person goes to the edge of a graveyard and looks at the rotting dead bodies scattered about, it will be easy for him to attain some insight."[46] This was indeed the case with the servant monk. Then again, in the *Maka shikan,* in explaining the word *kan* (insight), Chih-i said, "Even the mountains and rivers are all impure. Likewise food and clothes, too, are impure. Food is like white worms. Clothing is nothing but the skin of evil-smelling animals." The insight gained by the temple servant was thus truly great, and it is precisely because of this that it corresponded exactly with the words in the holy text. So it was that a Buddhist priest in India explained, "Utensils are like skulls. Food is like worms, and clothing is like snake skin." Indeed the Chinese Vinaya master Tao-hsuan taught, "Trees are nothing but the bones of man. The earth is nothing but the flesh of man."[47]

The proof of the servant monk's enlightenment lies in the fact that he apprehends the true nature of the foulness of the body, food, clothing, and other material pleasures exactly as outlined in scriptural texts.

Chōmei's story in *Hosshinshū* on *fujōkan* entitled "About the Priest Shinkai Who Did Not Leave Any Traces Behind" is a long account of the problems associated with attachment to the body. Chōmei, like Keisei, argues that the body is fundamentally impure and unreliable. Little other than a temporary shelter sought by a traveller for the night, the body is unworthy of any attachment. After death it becomes food for birds and beasts, and in the end is reduced to becoming dirt by the wayside.[48] In the section on meditating on *fujō,* which forms part of a larger narrative about the monk Genpin, who develops an attachment to the wife of a grand councillor, he draws heavily on *Ōjōyōshū* to claim that:

> In general, the human body is like a rotting house fabricated from flesh and bones. The various internal organs are like poisonous snakes coiled up.[49] Simply because it is covered by one thin layer of skin, it hides its myriad impurities. Although one may paint the face with white powder and perfume the body and clothes with incense, is there anyone who does not know that this is deceptive ornamentation? The foods we seek from the mountains and the seas are all transformed into filthy rotting things when a night has passed. [Decorating the body] is like putting excrement inside a painted vase and wrapping a decaying corpse in brocade. Even if, for example, one were to wash such a body with the water of the great oceans, it would not become clean. Even if one perfumed it by burning incense, it would soon smell rotten.[50]

A significant transformation takes place, however, when *Hosshinshū* and *Kankyo no tomo* deal with the themes of amorous love and attachment between men and women. Both texts acknowledge the deluded and pointless nature of amorous relationships and point out that they are at variance with the Buddha's teachings. However, as we shall see, by adopting the mode of storytelling of *monogatari,* and the poetic vocabulary of *waka,* they considerably undermine the critique of love and desire and of the female body, all of which are at the heart of the discourse of *fujō* in scriptural texts.

Narratives of Love in *Hosshinshū* and *Kankyo no tomo*

In *Hosshinshū,* Chōmei uses the literary conventions of Heian romances to chart the trajectory of a love affair. A man, who was once intimate with a lady of great refinement, eventually abandons her, leaving her to pass her time forlornly, lamenting his fickleness. One day he happens to go past her house and is told that the mistress wishes to see him. Surprised and curious, he enters the gate. Chōmei's narrative proceeds in a style common to *monogatari:* the weeds have grown thick, and the garden has a rough and neglected air. The sight of this heightens his inexplicable feeling of sadness (*nan to naku aware fukaku namu masarikeru*). When he enters the house, he encounters his lady kneeling as she recites from the *Lotus Sutra.* The descriptions of her beauty that follow could easily belong to a work such as the *Genji.* "She had become somewhat thinner and frailer. As a result, the pure and fragile beauty of her form, and the manner in which her hair cascaded down, made her quite unlike the woman he had been intimate with earlier. Her beauty was without parallel" (*sukoshi omoyasetaru mono kara, ito kiyoge ni rōtage naru katachi sugata, kami no koborekakaru sama nado, moto mishi hito to mo oboezu, tagui naku miyuru ni*).[51] This leads the man to wonder what madness had induced him to leave her, and he begins to tell her of his love. The lady ignores him, continues to recite the *Lotus Sutra,* and then breathes her last. The tale concludes with the following moral:

> One often hears of instances of a lady turning into a stone because of her love for a man or becoming a malevolent spirit. Although, without a doubt, love is a deeply sinful practice, the fact that this lady was able to make it the means for entering the Pure Land, and the fact that she ended her life in the way she wanted, suggests that she was possessed of truly wondrous intent. If only people who have suffered because of love emulated her, and prayed for birth in the Pure Land, what noble spirit they would display.[52]

Like many a heroine in the *Genji* the noblewoman turns to the religious life because of the suffering brought by a failed love affair. Unlike her counterparts in *monogatari,* however, she is much more successful in her unequivocal rejection of her lover. Moreover, the tale asserts that she achieves a holy death, as a result of her "wondrous intent," which allows her to focus single-mindedly on birth in the Pure Land through the recitation of the *Lotus Sutra.* The aristocratic virtues of grace, refinement, and depth of feeling, which are central to courtly depictions of amorous affairs, are not incidental to the affective intensity that her piety evokes in her lover and in the narrator of the tale. It accounts in no small measure for the fact that, far from offering an unequivocal condemnation of love, the narrative ends up salvaging it by claiming that love can serve as the karmic link (*en*) that makes possible birth in the Pure Land. The arguments mounted in favor of love here are analogous to the ones found elsewhere in *Hosshinshū,* where the practices of music and poetry are valorized as privileged modes through which religious awakening occurs.[53]

Keisei's story in *Kankyo no tomo* "about the religious awakening of the nun who lived in the mountains of Tsu province" begins as a standard narrative of religious conversion caused by the death of a loved one. In this instance, a woman, who loses her husband at the height of her youth, comes to the realization that the love between man and wife is by its very nature ephemeral. She casts aside her children and her possessions and lives in the depths of the mountains in a rough straw hut she builds for herself.

After praising her for the depth of her resolve, and her ability to detach herself from worldly attachments, in sharp contrast to women who are, as a rule, caught up in hopes and expectations that cannot be fulfilled, the text embarks on a lengthy excursus into the admirable depths of conjugal love displayed by famous lovers, immortalized in the poetic tradition. It is worth quoting this passage at length here, for it is a striking illustration of the ways in which Keisei's narrative undoes the moral it purports to preach:

In truth, we hear of many instances of couples who want to grow old together, pledging that they be buried in the same grave and praying that they may be together again in the next world. Their acts are full of expectations for the future, but in fact they constitute a deep crime.

The Emperor HsuanTsung pledged that if he were born in the skies, he would like to be a bird, which would fly in unison with its female partner. In the land of Yamato we have the case of the lady who lamented, "If it be a wild field, then I shall be a quail calling plaintively";[54] the lady who left behind the following words: "I am eager to see the color of the tears of love";[55] and the lament of the person who wrote, "It is indeed sad to think of you sleeping alone in the bed that you once shared with me."[56] If we do not perform memorial services with total sincerity for a dead person, then it is indeed hard for that person to cease being attached to the world and to become a Buddha.

Throughout their lives people constantly think about love. Comparing their love to the flames of Mt Fuji,[57] they display a heart that is tortured by love. Or they liken themselves to the Kiyomi Barrier[58] and wear their tears on their sleeves. Despite this, they turn into smoke that rises forlornly from the Toribe fields[59] and disappear like the dew in the fields of Asajigahara.[60] How they must suffer during their lives! The sorrow of those who are endowed with great sensitivity (*nasake fukakaran hito*) must become much greater and deeper, depending on the time and situation they are in.

Not long after Prince Atsunori began a relationship with the Fifth Imperial Princess, who lived in her secluded pavilion, he passed away.[61] Before his death, he wrote in his own hand the following poem on the sash of the curtain in the place where she lived: "If your repeated promise that you will never forget me is true, then mourn for me when you see the mountain mist."[62] Having been told this story, even a man as lowly as myself cannot help but recall it every time I see the dawn in spring or the mists spreading over the edge of the mountains.[63] I am also unable to forget the love that these two people bore each other in the past. It is deeply moving to consider how much more so the princess's heart must have been tortured when she saw the mists in spring . . . these relationships are at once pitiable and shamefully neglectful of the Buddha's Dharma.[64]

At one level, it is possible to read the narrative quoted above as a straightforward Buddhist morality tale, which warns against the sinfulness of amorous love, desire, and attachment. The fact that Keisei resorts to literary themes and motifs taken from the courtly repertoire to make his point about the deluded nature of amorous love can be explained on pragmatic grounds: Keisei is, after all, writing these stories for the edification of a highborn noblewoman, who is likely to be steeped in romances and in *waka* poetry, popular among women of her class, and what better way to help her to appreciate the message embedded in the exemplary tale of a nun renouncing the secular world than by couching his tales in a language familiar to her? Implicit in such a reading, of course, is the assumption that the Buddhist message constitutes the substance of the story and that its literariness is merely a matter of form.

However, the sheer excess of the virtuoso performance draws attention to itself: the innumerable literary references and poetic allusions, far from being merely formal devices, actually shape the way in which Buddhist conceptions of love come to be reformulated in the tale. Keisei begins with a reference to the famous love story of Hsuan Tsung and Yang Kuei-fei, immortalized by Po Chü-i in his poem *The Song of Unending Sorrow*. Immensely popular at the Heian court, this story became emblematic of tragic love and the impossible dream of being totally at one with one's lover, captured in Hsuan Tsung's poem where he prays that he be reunited with Yang Kuei-fei in heaven like a pair of legendary birds, each with one eye and one wing, always flying together. Turning to Japanese precedent, Keisei alludes to an episode from *Ise monogatari* in which a lady, after receiving a poem from a man who has lost interest in her, responds with a poignant poem of her own in which she expresses her longing for him.

The text is particularly attentive to the extraordinary sensitivity and the depth of feeling that members of the imperial family show to their loved ones and the degree to which *waka* poetry is central to their expression of love and longing. By claiming that whenever he sees the mists rising over the edge of the mountain he unfailingly remembers the poem composed by Prince Atsunori for the princess, the narrator is able to demonstrate his sensitive appreciation both of courtly poetry and of the grief of the princess who mourns her dead husband. His humble insistence that someone as "lowly" as himself cannot possibly match the degree of sensitivity and refinement displayed by emperors and princesses in fact merely serves to reinforce his own claims to a shared courtly sensibility, which spontaneously generates a heightened understanding of the truth of evanescence through the experience of love, and equally importantly, through its expression in the language of poetry.

There is a certain tension between the moral of the tale, which strains to declare that relationships between lovers are at once "pitiable and unmindful of the Buddha's Dharma," and the bulk of the narrative, which is a moving evocation of a world from the past in which lovers express the pain of the loss of loved ones through poetry. Keisei presents love and its passing in an elegiac mode, and in doing so he adopts the literary persona of a refined aristocrat who, even after having renounced worldly life, still finds himself deeply moved by the beauty and ephemerality of love. Indeed, the adoption of a courtly literary stance has implications for the way in which the theme of the impurity of the female body and the need to meditate on it in order to apprehend the true nature of the phenomenal world comes to be interpreted in texts such as *Hosshinshū* and *Kankyo no tomo*. This, as we shall see below, is in striking contrast to the tales of female beauty and impurity in the Indian tradition.

Fujōkan in Indian Buddhist Texts

The apprehension of both the beauty and impurity of the female body is often achieved in Indian Buddhist texts through vivid descriptions of the erotic body and its subsequent dissolution through decomposition and dismemberment. A technique often used in the Indian texts is to render repulsive and grotesque the very physical attributes that once generated desire in men, presenting them as discrete elements, severed from the body, and now subject to the greedy attention of vultures and kites. In the sixth-century Tamil Buddhist text *Manimēkalai*, for example, a young lad who wanders into the cremation grounds encounters a young woman whose body parts are scattered about. He hears "the drawn-out shriek of a vulture piercing and consuming a naked mound of venus, the unrestrained howl of an evil dog who had snatched and torn apart a severed arm stacked with bangles, and the crunch of the hungry kite seizing and eating beautiful, erect, young breasts adorned with sandalpaste."[65]

The courtesan *Manimēkalai,* who renounces her profession in order to become a Buddhist nun, attempts to cure a young man of his deluded attachment to her beauty. She does so by showing him an old hag who was at one time regarded as exceptionally enchanting. She points to the inevitable decay of the physical attributes that once made the old woman renowned for her physical attractiveness. For example, she draws the young man's attention to the eyebrows that were once like victorious bows, but which are now like dried-up prawns; to the teeth that were once like pearls, but which now look like uneven yellowed seeds on a gourd; to eyes that were once like water lilies, but which now are runny and swollen; to the breasts, which droop like empty bags; and so on.[66]

Both the eroticization of the body and its undoing through horrifying images of its dismemberment in the Indian Buddhist narrative tradition are related to the particular conventions that are used to evoke the beauty of the female body. Sanskrit love poetry, to which these narratives are indebted, evoke erotic *rasa,* the aesthetic mood, flavor, or sentiment that marks the experience of love through stylized images of the physical attributes of the female body. Courtly Sanskrit texts eroticize the female body by using an elaborate set of similes to celebrate its beauty: breasts are likened to golden jars, to the protuberances over the frontal sinuses of an elephant, or to the buds of celestial coral trees; necks are as shapely as conch shells; waists are like sacrificial altars, narrow in the middle and broad at the top; and thighs are like the stems of the plantain or banana tree, round, smooth, and tapering.[67] While images from nature are important to Sanskrit love poetry, these images are inextricably tied not only to human emotions but also to the body.

In courtly Sanskrit poetry both the pain and the pleasure of love are imagined in highly corporeal terms. In the Sanskrit poetry of Amaru (sixth to seventh century), for example, a woman's sense of being abandoned by her lover is expressed with an abundance of images that highlight the physical nature of her bond with him:

> my breasts
> just budding
> became full
> against your chest
> in embraces . . .
> my arms
> let go
> of my mother's neck
> that they might
> cling to you.
> my deceiver—
> what can I do?
> you do not even walk
> down my street any more.[68]

Buddhist texts, drawing on the stylized images of the female body found in Sanskrit literature, locate the eroticism of the body in its physical characteristics.

When they seek to warn against the dangers of attachment to sex and the body, it is through a skillful distortion of these erotic images that the body is transformed into the site of the grotesque.

As we observed in Chapter 2, the body in courtly texts, such as the *Tale of Genji,* is apprehended not primarily through its physical attributes but rather through its performative modes, and through clothes, to which it is metonymically linked. *Waka* is central to the expression of erotic and affective longing and attachment in the *Genji,* and one of the conventions of this poetic form is that the human realm and the natural and cosmological order are always interlinked. In the following poem by Ukifune, for example, both the pain and pleasures of times past are captured through the complex interplay of robes, signifying sexual intimacy, and plum blossoms, redolent of the scent of spring:

sode fureshi	the one whose sleeves brushed against mine
hito koso miene	I do not see, it is true
hana no kaori no	and yet I sense his presence
sore ka to niou	in the scent of his sleeves/
haru no akebono	and of the dawn in spring[69]

The intimacy Ukifune shared with her lover is conveyed not through vivid images of their sexual passion, as in the poem by Amaru quoted earlier, but elliptically, through the image of lovers' sleeves brushing. Images from the natural world—the sight and smell of the red plum blossoms—bridge the temporal distance between the past and present and bring, unbeckoned, Ukifune's absent lover to her side. Nature here is not imagined in opposition to culture for both wo/man and nature are bound together by the same principles that order the cosmos. The connection between the scent of the plum blossoms and the lover's perfumed sleeves is not one of similitude or likeness. The word *niou,* which stands for the fragrance of both, refuses any distinction between the world outside and the emotional state within.

Poems are not lyrical expressions of a unique and singular self, whose emotions are found reflected in nature. As Thomas LaMarre suggests when he speaks of the logic that governs Ki no Tsurayuki's poetics in *Kokinshū,* "humans do not use images or descriptions to convey prior emotions; sensible forms come first, and emotions must follow their patterns and rhythms, for sensation provides the link to extrahuman forms."[70] The feelings expressed in *waka* are diffuse and decentered, often echoing the rhythms and patterns observable in nature, and it is for this reason that both seasonal and love poems partake of a shared affective universe shaped by the inevitable passage of time.

In following the conventions of *waka,* love and attachment between men and women in *Kankyo no tomo,* as we observed in the story about the lady of Tsu, always echo the patterns observable in the natural world. The tears that drench the sleeves of lovers are associated with the waves at Kiyomi barrier, and the flames of love are none other than those emitted by Mount Fuji. Given the inextricable connections between love and poetry in the medieval Japanese literary tradition, and the extraordinary value attached to poetry within it, any unequivocal rejection of love and passion would be tantamount to turning one's back upon the revered practice of *waka* itself. The use of the language and imagery of *waka* in Chōmei and Keisei's *setsuwa* on *fujō* to talk about amorous desire transforms the topos of love from a deluded practice that produces attachment to one where it becomes an aesthetic trope of nostalgia and longing.

Likewise, by adopting the narrative structure of *monogatari,* the figure of woman in *Hosshinshū* and *Kankyo no tomo* becomes the exemplar of refinement, grace, and poetic skill, all qualities that are central to the proper performance of courtly love in *monogatari.* In keeping with the conventions of this courtly genre, her erotic and affective powers do not rest in her body's physical attributes; the beauty of the female body is not understood as a material entity and hence cannot be deployed to produce its obverse—disgust and revulsion. Women in the *setsuwa* of Chōmei and Keisei generate love and desire in men. However, they fail to become the sites of bodily impurity and come to be metonymically associated instead with the inevitable passing of love, and by extension with the ephemeral nature of all things in the phenomenal world. Rather than revulsion, women generate sorrow and melancholic appreciation in equal measure for all that is no more. It is with this profound transformation of the trope of *fujō* that I am concerned in the section that follows.

Fujōkan in *Hosshinshū* and *Kankyo no tomo*

In a story in *Hosshinshū* in which Chōmei engages directly with the theme of meditating on the impurity of the female form, a high-ranking and much-revered priest Genpin confesses to a grand councillor that he has become obsessed with thoughts about the councillor's wife, whose "wondrous form" he has had occasion to glimpse (*katachi ito medetakute mietamaerishi*). The councillor, who has always looked to Genpin for religious guidance, immediately promises to make the necessary arrangements to satisfy Genpin's wishes. The wife of the councillor, who agrees to her husband's scheme, leads Genpin to a place that is appropriate for such a rendezvous. The text tells us that "she was beautifully made up and attired with great care," and that Genpin does nothing but gaze at her intently for about two hours, expressing his repentance from time to time by clicking his nails (*tanji*).[71] He then leaves without doing anything, vindicating the councillor's belief that he is a deeply enlightened priest. The narrative about Genpin and the councillor's wife ends with the following conclusion: "Genpin must have meditated on the impurity of things (*fujōkan*) and thereby overcome his lustful attachment."[72]

In this tale there is a conspicuous absence of any description of the physical features of the councillor's wife or the nature of her beauty. All we are told is that Genpin is enraptured by her "wondrous form," and that she appears before him beautifully dressed and made-up. This is entirely consonant with the way in which the beauty of the body is communicated in romance narratives such as the *Tale of Genji.* Nor is there any description of how Genpin mentally transforms a beautiful woman into a foul and impure body and what that visual transformation involves; the compiler merely surmises that Genpin must have meditated on the impurity of the body (*fujō o kanjite*) and thereby overcome his lust and attachment.

The fact that Genpin does not need to meditate on an actual corpse to apprehend the truth of *fujō* is offered as proof of his highly enlightened state. At the same time, by withholding from the reader how Genpin envisages her decaying form, Chōmei's narrative is in tune with the courtly aesthetic of *waka* and *monogatari,* in which the beauty of the female form is communicated without reference to the body's physical aspects, and where any suggestion of the body's decomposition after death is, at best, hinted at elliptically through euphemisms.

It is only when Chōmei moves from the particular to the general that he turns to scriptural texts and offers a trenchant critique of amorous attachment by dwelling in graphic detail on the impurity of the body. The tale ends with the following admonition:

It goes without saying that when the spirit leaves the body and life has passed away, the body is thrown into the graveyard, there to lie forlornly. Becoming swollen and rotten, the corpse disintegrates; in the end it becomes a white skeleton. It is because human beings understand its true nature that they always shun corpses. It is said, "Foolish and ignorant folk who are drawn to sensual pleasures that are transient and who allow their hearts to be deluded are like flies in a toilet who are enamoured of feces."[73]

In another tale in *Hosshinshū,* a young nobleman, Ōe no Sadamoto,[74] falls in love with a woman whom he considers as being "without compare" (*tagui naku oboekeru onna*). After her death, unable to get over the loss of his beloved, he refuses to dispose of her body and keeps it with him, looking at it "as it changed with each passing day" (*higoro heru mama ni nariyuku sama o miru ni*). This leads him to an intuitive understanding of "the unattractive nature of this ephemeral world" (*ukiyo no itowashisa omoi shirarete*); he experiences religious awakening and takes the tonsure.

Again, the narrative proceeds in a manner that follows the protocols of the *monogatari* genre—a man loses interest in one woman and transfers his attentions to another, and it is through the understated phrase "without compare" (*tagui naki*) that we are told of her extraordinary physical and emotional allure. The echoes of another woman, Aoi, whose body gradually changes (*yō yō kawari tamau koto*) after death are audible in the way in which the decay of the wife's body is hinted at with the cryptic statement that Sadamoto watched as it "underwent changes with each passing day" (*higoro heru mama ni nariyuku sama o miru ni*). The effect of this on Sadamoto is not described and can only be imagined from the fact that he decides to abandon worldly life to become a monk.[75] Chōmei's tale offers a striking contrast to another version of this story found in the *setsuwa* collection *Konjaku monogatari*:[76]

> Not long ago, during the reign of Emperor Enyū, there was a person called Ōe no Sadamoto who was governor of Mikawa. . . . During this time, over and above his own wife with whom he lived, he fell in love with a beautiful woman who was in the prime of her youth, and whom he found most hard to leave. Extremely jealous, his wife suddenly broke their conjugal bond, and they separated. As a consequence, Sadamoto took the young woman as his wife and lived with her. When he was appointed to the post in Mikawa, he took her with him. While the woman was in the provinces she fell seriously ill, and for a long time she suffered greatly. Filled with grief, Sadamoto performed all manner of prayers on her behalf, but her illness was not cured, and with each passing day her beauty began to fade. Seeing her in this way, Sadamoto was deeply saddened. Eventually her condition became grave, and she passed away. After that, Sadamoto was so unbearably grief-stricken that for a while he did not have her buried, but lay by her side with her in his arms. As the days passed, when he kissed her mouth, a horribly foul stench emanated from it. At that point a feeling of revulsion arose within him, and he buried her, crying all the while. From that moment, he understood that the world was a sad place, and he suddenly experienced religious awakening.

It is worth noting that *Konjaku monogatari*, a collection of tales that was, in all likelihood, not the work of a single author, displays a remarkable heterogeneity in terms of both literary styles and thematic concerns. The stories on *fujōkan* in this work appear to revel in the grotesque details of the body's decomposition,[77] offering a marked contrast to the tales in *Hosshinshū* and *Kankyo no tomo,* which maintain a consistently decorous and understated tone even when they speak of the body's dissolution and dismemberment within the context of a love story. Without exception, in all the stories in *Hosshinshū* and *Kankyo no tomo* that are directly related to the theme of men taking the tonsure when they apprehend the fundamentally impure nature of their loved ones, the decay of the female body does not figure as the dominant topos, and what the tales evoke instead is a melancholic reflection on the passing of time and the beauty and sadness of worldly love. The following examples all demonstrate the degree to which these *setsuwa* narratives fail to produce an unequivocal denial of love and a revulsion toward the female body, which is at the heart of the practice of *fujōkan.*

Kankyo no tomo (1:20) recounts a tale about an insignificant, illiterate man who, despite his lowly status, has the requisite sensitivity and feelings to intuit the true meaning of the impurity of the body and to use this moment of religious awakening to leave his wife and follow the religious path. He writes:

Not too long ago, I think, there was a man in the province of Yamashiro who was very close to a woman. One day something happened, and he began to treat her coldly. "If this continues, I feel that our relationship will no longer be a tranquil one," the woman lamented. "Before either of us become too old and there is nothing to be done for it, perhaps it would be best if we separated and married someone else."

"As in former times, I find it extremely hard to leave you," the man replied, in surprise. "It is just that a particular incident has occurred that makes me feel distant towards you. Some time ago, I set off on a trip and on the way, rested awhile in the fields. Seeing the skull of a dead body that was lying there, I looked at it for some time. From that moment onwards, I lost interest in the world and thought about how fleeting our life is and how after death we will all be in that state. Looking at the skull, I thought about the kind of person it would have been while alive, and how that person would have been treated with respect and consideration. But now the person was no more than a frightening and disgusting skull. After that I thought I would check to see if your face was the same as the skull. I touched your face, and sure enough, there was no reason at all why the two would be any different! From that moment, somehow, my heart felt empty and indeed things have got to this stage for which you reproach me."

Thus a month went by. One day he said to his wife, "If on the basis of the merit gained from taking the tonsure, I am able to be born in Buddha's land, then at the time when I return to earth to take you along with me as my companion, I will be able to show you the depth of my feelings for you. So saying, he suddenly left as if vanishing into thin air. What an extraordinary heart this man possessed![78]

There is no denying that the man's method of apprehending the foulness of his wife's body, namely by *touching* her face and recognizing that it is no different from the skull he has encountered in the fields, is, within the framework of Japanese love narratives, deeply unsettling in its effect. Amorous love in this tale does not receive unqualified affirmation. Nonetheless, the text does salvage conjugal love, albeit on a different plane: when the man decides to leave his home and take the tonsure, he promises his wife that when he attains enlightenment, he will choose her as his eternal companion to live in Buddha's Paradise, and thereby demonstrate to her the depth of his attachment. In other words, he does not reject his wife completely: he holds out the promise of eternal togetherness in Amida's Paradise.[79] Furthermore, the text is at pains to extend the qualities of sensitivity and feeling, associated in medieval literary texts with exemplary lovers and poets of the aristocratic class, to a man of the lower orders.

After this understated account of the man's intuitive understanding of the impurity of his wife's body, the narrative continues in a poetic mode, eschewing the theme of *fujō,* focusing instead on the inexorability of the passage of time and the sadness that it evokes:

All human beings see sights such as these. After all, as we are not rocks or trees, when we see such sights, it is bound to make our hearts heavy. It goes without saying that the affection of a beloved one, that person's endearing form, the actions that one remembers vividly—all of it comes to an end with the death of the beloved, like a dream dreamed while dozing. This indeed should awaken the mind. Yet while this is so, sadly, after some time passes and earlier events become things of the past, we forget and begin to laugh again, albeit in soft tones. The fact that this young man contemplated [on the skull] deeply, without forgetting [its lesson], makes me feel that, like the bhikku in India from the past, he was tied by an unimaginable karmic link to someone who, in another life, had meditated on the impurity of things, and this link had now become the seed that caused him to leave this world. . . . It is indeed deeply moving to remember how Kumarajiva's mother,[80] while standing at some burial mounds, saw human bones turned white, and that this aroused her faith and led her to leave this fleeting world. In truth, anyone with sensitivity and feeling would experience religious awakening at the sight of a skull.

This elegiac mode changes only when he shifts registers and draws more directly from canonical texts to speak of the dissolution of the body, now unmarked by gender. Here too the dominant emotion that the body in death and decay arouses is not revulsion or disgust but rather feelings of sadness and shame:

> Thus Kōbo Daishi wrote, "When we try to visit old lovers from the past, that's what we find: white worms crawling about in a hole and blue flies flying inside the mouth—seeing this we feel both sadness and shame" (*hito tabi wa kanashimi hito tabi wa hazu beshi*).[81] The *Maka shikan* teaches us about the dead body from the time of its death when it starts decomposing, to the time when the bones have been gathered up and burnt. In truth anyone viewing a dead body would become sad. It is all the more impressive that the heart of an illiterate person [such as the one I have described] was awakened on its own [without any religious guidance].

Even when *Kankyo no tomo* and *Hosshinshū* challenge the tropes of love and female beauty by presenting the female body in its mutilated form, the body figures as a muted presence and is used in order to reflect not on its impurity but rather on the ephemerality of the phenomenal world and the sadness of its passing. Relating a story of love, jealousy, and revenge (2:21), Keisei recounts how a young woman was killed and mutilated by her mistress who was jealous of the fact that the girl was involved in an affair with her husband. The woman, we are told, is no longer in the shape of a human being:

> She was like a big tree, which had been cut up. Her arms and legs were missing. It was a filthy and unseemly sight that cannot be likened to anything. Even if water from the great ocean were poured on it and the body washed, it could not be purified. Even if looked at from afar, it was an unbearable sight. At that time, who could possibly think of sharing their coverlets and pillow with such a person?[82]

This shocking representation of *fujō* is, however, considerably undermined by the mode whereby the narrator expresses compassion for the mutilated young woman cast into the dry riverbed and his efforts to pray for her salvation. Keisei writes:

> The owner of the body cast aside on the riverbed was extremely pitiable. She must have experienced feelings of great sadness and resentment. She most certainly will not be reborn into one of the good realms. Moved by this recognition, without distinguishing the low from the highborn, I have

written down and gathered the names of those whom I have met before they died. I have secretly placed these names by my side, and although it is scarcely enough, I intone the mantras on behalf of the dead in the hope that they will be born into a higher realm. While doing this, even though I have never met her, I include the young girl whose dead body was cast aside on the riverbed in Karahashi, and I pray for her future. Each time I note down her name, my sleeves are drenched in tears; her face appears clearly before me as if I had just met her, and I am so moved that I weep profusely.[83]

Unlike the women who appear in Indian Buddhist tales, the young girl here is not a demonic temptress who meets retribution for her secret relationship with her mistress's husband. Instead, by portraying her as a victim of the thoughtlessness and cruelty of the world, Keisei is able to rework the trope of the sensitive lover in an altered context. The narrator's tears when he thinks about the dead woman call to mind the image of the inconsolable lover who weeps at the death of his beloved. By casting the narrator in the role of the sensitive and compassionate lover/monk who prays for the young woman's salvation and by using the imagery of love narratives, Keisei significantly softens the harsh lesson that the notion of the foulness of the female body is intended to impart.[84]

The tale in *Hosshinshū* about the religious awakening of the monk Tōnobō (5:1) employs a similar strategy when it evokes the horror of the sundering and mutilation of the female form. A minor official, Kunisuke, who moves to the provinces, loses contact with a lady he is involved with. One day he returns to the capital and by chance discovers her whereabouts. He goes into her cottage to talk to her, but the lady refuses to turn around and face him. Attributing this to her resentment at having been abandoned, he embraces her from behind and tries to comfort her in various ways. Eventually he pulls her toward him, only to discover that "both her eyes were missing. The sight was unbearable to behold: it was as if the branches of a tree had been torn down from their trunk."[85] The understated "the birds, as they are wont to do, had already done the deed," tells us why the lady's eyes are missing. There is no question that in the context of the *monogatari*-like narrative style adopted by Chōmei, this is a shocking revelation.

The overwhelming mood of the story is, nonetheless, one of sadness over the plight of the lady abandoned by her lover and her family and finally cast out in the fields, left for dead. Rather than being filled with revulsion and disgust at her state, Kunisuke is overcome with "sorrow and pain." He does not revile her, nor does he attempt to give her a moral lesson on the essentially impure nature of the female form. Instead, attributing their fate to evil deeds committed in a former life, he proceeds to take the tonsure.

The stories in *Hosshinshū* and *Kankyo no tomo,* as I have sought to demonstrate, draw heavily upon the tropes of love and desire as articulated in *monogatari* and *waka,* while at the same time attempting to offer a Buddhist critique of attachment. A striking feature of these texts is that, even when they purport to demonstrate the truth of bodily impurity, the body is curiously sidelined, for in following the literary protocols of courtly texts the body's physical attributes are not imbued with eroticism, and hence cannot be deployed for creating the horrific body.[86] In this, the stories in these *setsuwa* collections are a far cry from the tales on *fujō* that appear in Indian Buddhist narratives in which the beauty of the female body rests on elaborate descriptions of the hips, breasts, eyes, and so on, which can then be inverted in order to reveal the body's repulsive aspects through graphic and exaggerated images of its decay and dismemberment.

If desire and attachment, the central problems for Buddhism, are not located in the materiality of the body in *waka* and *monogatari,* and if it is upon these genres that *Hosshinshū* and *Kankyo no tomo* draw, what are the discursive modes available to these texts to render intelligible the practice of meditating on the body's ugliness and impurity? I have argued that the critique of desire in these *setsuwa* comes to be articulated by focusing not primarily on the impurity of the body but rather on the ephemerality of all phenomena (*mujō*). It is through the realization of the impermanent nature of worldly love that the protagonists of these tales experience religious awakening and take the tonsure. This is precisely the insight that meditation on the impure body is supposed to yield. However, in Chōmei's and Keisei's tales, the idea of evanescence performs a paradoxical function. It is at once a critique of desire and the very ground upon which desire is generated. The narrative techniques employed in these tales induce nostalgia and a sense of elegiac longing for all that inevitably changes and fades away. This longing is rendered in a highly aestheticized mode that displays a curious attachment to, even fetishization of, evanescence itself. In adopting the discursive strategies of *waka* and *monogatari,* texts that purport to illustrate the truth of *fujō* in fact never fully efface the erotic and affective charge that amorous longing and attachment produce in courtly texts. In so doing, these texts fail to offer the critique of woman, body, and desire that is at the heart of the scriptural teachings on the impurity of the body.

Epilogue

A man fucks a turnip. A young woman eats the turnip, falls pregnant, and gives birth to a boy. A snake is aroused and has sex with a woman. A priest makes love to a youth who falls pregnant, and gives birth to a baby who is in fact a nugget of gold. A beautiful woman turns out to be a deceitful fox; a youth a bodhisattva. Not unlike the world of classical and medieval Europe, peopled with "gods who can change form, centaurs that threaten to rape mortal women, old hags who can transform into beautiful virgins, wandering wombs, lactating monks, miraculous sex changes, monstrous births, saints being tortured oblivious to pain . . . ,"[1] popular tales from medieval Japan conjure up an altogether unfamiliar universe, filled with strange people and happenings.

What is most striking about medieval Japanese tales is their "otherness," which sometimes seems to defy even the most basic rules of logic and rational thought. How we read works that belong to a world so different from our own has been the central question that has animated this book. The intellectual questions that I asked of medieval texts were perforce driven by debates and concerns that belong to our own time. I chose what at first glance appeared to be some of the most fundamental categories through which all societies organize the world—body, sex, man, woman—to consider the connections between the body and eroticism, and between Buddhism and gender in these texts. However, it became clear that these categories, far from being universal, in fact carried multiple significations, many of which failed to correspond to our own understandings of them. Historicizing the terms "body," "woman," "sex," and "gender," and showing how their critical purchase derived from debates that were specifically part of the Western religious and philosophical traditions, was the necessary starting point of my project, because it was only then that I could begin to think through what these categories signified, and how they worked, in the context of medieval Japan. I argued that it was by taking the Buddhist view of the world seriously, and by locating medieval narratives within the broader debates and arguments that were generated within the Buddhist epistemic framework, that we could make sense of medieval Japanese texts and recognize the distinct set of rules, conventions, and organizing principles that gave them coherence and meaning.

It became apparent that the body, for example, was never the troubled site of debates in China or Japan in the way that it was in the European tradition. Nor did it come to be defined in opposition to the spirit, soul, or mind. While modes of representing the body were by no means uniform—in Buddhist sculpture it took a form that was readily recognizable, as something made of flesh, blood, and bones, while in the *Tale of Genji* it registered as a presence principally through robes and hair, to which it was metonymically linked—what always remained constant was the assumption that the mental and psychic attributes of the body were integral to its materiality.

The implications of reading the body in this way were far-reaching. It called for a reappraisal of what it meant to use categories such as sex, gender, man, and woman, which in part derived their meanings from the significations that the body acquired in the post-Renaissance West. As I argued in Chapter 1, it was from the eighteenth century that, in the West, the distinction between man and woman came to be grounded in the body, and sexual difference came to be a biological truth that could not be challenged or refuted. The body was now understood as an inert, material entity, aligned with nature, standing in opposition to and separate from the social or cultural realm. With new biological understandings of the body, women came to be irrevocably marked as the inferior sex. This was the context within which feminists in the 1970s launched arguments claiming that women's social roles, their gender, had to be differentiated from the truth of their sex. The binaries of body/mind, nature/culture, and man/woman were the necessary starting point for debates about the body, women, and sexuality that were generated within feminist discourse. These debates had a clear historical provenance and belonged to the past and present of the West. They would not serve to understand how these categories came to be configured in the context of medieval Japan.

If in the medieval Japanese tradition, man and woman were not constituted primarily through the difference of their sexual organs, if nature was not severed from culture, and if the body was not in any meaningful sense separate from the mind, categories such as "body" and "woman" could not be understood from within a Western philosophical framework and needed to be inserted within the Buddhist episteme to which they properly belonged. This allowed for a conception of the body as a malleable, fluid, and permeable entity, far removed from the immutable, passive, and stable object it was to become from the eighteenth century in Europe. The act of sex, as we shall see, could not be seen as an exclusive privilege accorded only to humans. In a world where humans and nonhumans intermingled and often morphed one into the other, the distinctions that are at the heart of our humanism, which grants agency and consciousness only to human beings, simply did not hold.

In what follows I would like to return to some of the stories with which I began this epilogue, as well as to others like it, to conduct a kind of experiment, one in which I offer two alternate readings of the same *setsuwa* tales. In one I use the categories woman, body, and sex, keeping intact the significances that they carry for us today, while in the other I seek to defamiliarize these terms, using the emendations and problematizations that I have offered in the book, on occasion going further to suggest that these categories even when historicized may not be entirely adequate in explaining how those who inhabited the medieval world made sense of it. This exercise, which engages with narratives that I have hitherto not considered in the book, may help to bring into sharper focus some of the questions and arguments that have been at the heart of this intellectual project.

Let me begin with a pair of stories from *Konjaku monogatari,* which involve sexual intercourse between a snake and a human. In the first tale, a woman is overcome by a sudden urge to urinate. She squats behind a wall and is suddenly unable to move from that position for several hours. Her young servant is distraught and does not know what to do. A warrior appears on horseback. He tries to get the woman to stand up, but her face is ashen white, and she looks as if she is about to die. He notices a snake's head poking out of the hole in the wall. He understands what has transpired: "When the woman was taking a leak, the snake saw her vagina (*mae*) and desire (*aiyoku*) welled up inside it, and so she lost her senses. That's why she can't stand up." The man kills the snake and the woman recovers.[2]

In the second narrative, a young priest falls asleep in a large room away from people in Miidera temple. He dreams that he is having sex with a beautiful woman. He fucks her (*totsugite*) well and finally ejaculates. Upon waking up he finds a snake lying beside him, dead, with its mouth open. Utterly startled and terrified, he notices that his front is wet, and that the snake has spewed out semen from its open mouth. He understands what has transpired and decides not to tell anyone about this. In the end, he confides in one of his close friends, another monk, who is equally terrified when he hears the tale.[3]

A standard interpretive move in reading these tales would be to group together vagina, woman, man, and penis and treat them as the key words that are likely to unlock for us the central meaning embedded in these narratives. These words are readily translatable into our contemporary categories of sexuality and gender. Once we have taken for granted that snakes and other nonhumans are simply metaphors for commenting on the relationship between men and women, these tales lend themselves quite seamlessly to being read as ideologically driven representations of medieval attitudes toward women and sexuality.

This approach is reflected in the following analysis of the second story: "In the tale of the sleeping monk at Miidera, the reaction of the man to the open mouth of the dead snake suggests feelings about women and sex embraced by many Nara and Heian period Buddhists. Women represent evil, relentless desire, and the loss of control. The vagina is repelling in its association with the snake's mouth. The bestial attack on the penis of an unsuspecting man alludes to the view of women as physical creatures who pursue men sexually to prevent them from attaining enlightenment."[4]

The presumption here is that the mouth of the snake, in this instance, represents the vagina, and that the monk's reaction is little more than a reflection of Buddhism's misogyny. In the tale of sexual intercourse between the snake and the woman, on the other hand, the snake is seen as being clearly phallic. In either case what these stories, and others like it attempt to do, in this view, is to absolve Buddhists from fully taking responsibility for their own sexual desires by blaming women instead.[5] In Chapter 1 as well as in the substantive chapters of the book, I have already indicated why I think the treatment of "woman" as a fixed and stable identity that works in the same way in all texts is unsustainable and why the concept of female agency or oppression cannot be taken for granted. Buddhism, too, I have argued, cannot be treated as a purposeful, homogenous entity that aims consciously or otherwise to vilify women. Here, I would like to pursue another line of reasoning, asking what interpretative possibilities open up if we suspend a purely anthropocentric reading of these tales and consider how, and in what terms, intercourse between humans and animals is imagined in these narratives.

To label sex between a human and an animal as an act of bestiality is to smuggle in unwarranted, modern assumptions about sexuality, in which the intermingling of man and animal is tantamount to sexual perversion, a form of deviant behavior that contravenes the norm. The stories from *Konjaku monogatari* do not speak of such sexual activity as aberrant human behavior, for desire and sexual intercourse are not seen as the sole preserve of human beings alone. It is striking that the text attributes feelings of sexual and affective desire (*aiyoku*) to a snake. *Aiyoku* is a Buddhist term often used for feelings of intense love/desire between parents and children, men and women, and monks and *chigo*. *Aiyoku* constitutes a form of deluded attachment that leads humans and nonhumans alike to be caught in the endless wheel of transmigration. The use of the term *aiyoku* in speaking about the snake suggests that the animal is not a metaphor for male desire, for like humans animals too are endowed with feelings and desires.

Moreover, the term *totsugu*[6] is used not only to describe sex between two humans but also when a snake enters a woman's vagina,[7] or when a man fornicates with a turnip.[8] This is entirely in accord with Buddhist cosmology, which took for granted that gods and humans coexisted, and that plants, animals, deities, and humans were shape-shifting forms that could sometimes morph one into the other. There are many examples in *Konjaku monogatari* and other collections of *setsuwa* of humans who are reborn as animals and who are widely recognized by others as having undergone this transformation as a result of karma from their past lives.

Ashis Nandy's observation that "deities in everyday Hinduism . . . are not entities outside everyday life, nor do they preside over life from the outside; they constitute a significant part of it . . ."[9] is equally true for Buddhism in medieval Japan. When women turn into foxes, and humans reveal themselves to be manifestations of the gods and buddhas in medieval texts, these are not mere flights of fancy or manifestations of irrational superstition. They point to a different way of ordering, knowing, and inhabiting a world in which living beings and buddhas are seen as occupying the same physical space and conceptual terrain.

The doctrinal basis for such ideas came from different sources, among them Chih-i's formulation of the ten worlds concommitant (*jikkai gogu*), in which each of the ten realms was seen as mutually interpenetrating and encompassing such that no ontological distinction was possible between, say, the world of hungry ghosts, the world of demons, and the world of humans, gods, and buddhas. In this schema what was presupposed was that "the nine realms of unenlightened beings possess the Buddha nature inherently, while the Buddha possesses the nine realms of unenlightened beings."[10]

Regardless of whether the concept of *jikkai gogu* was widely known or accepted, there is no doubt that a constitutive feature of the medieval imaginary was the intermingling of the realms of humans, ghosts, gods, and buddhas. In the twelfth-century picture scrolls of hungry ghosts (*gaki zōshi*),[11] *gaki* are depicted as grotesque, skeletal figures with enormous bellies and needle-thin throats. They are driven to eating excrement and carrion, and are tortured by demons and vultures. But the realm they inhabit is imagined as being an integral part of the human world. Quietly consuming excrement while people defecate, begging food from monks, mingling with the crowds in a busy marketplace, licking water that is offered to the statue of the Buddha, they are inextricably woven into the fabric of medieval society and are not dissimilar to the starving beggars who once populated medieval towns and cities—at once pariahs, and at the same time integral parts of the community as a whole (Figure 7).[12]

Figure 7. *Gaki zōshi* (Picture Scroll of the Hungry Ghosts), 12th century, Tokyo National Museum.

The fascination with stories about snakes and humans lay precisely in the fact that they challenged the mundane truths of everyday reality. These tales brought home the possibility that in a world where humans, animals, spirits, and ghosts coexisted, they might be brought into the closest proximity. What better way to literalize the comingling of humans and animals, and the dangers attendant on it, than through sexual intercourse? Fear, awe, and amusement were what *setsuwa* tales elicited in equal measure when they narrated extraordinary and miraculous events, which were at once unexpected, but at the same time entirely within the realm of the possible.

Could this explain why the narrator of the tales discussed above has nothing to say about men or women, but offers instead rather mundane and practical advice on how to avoid such encounters? The woman who is penetrated by the snake suffers, and hence the suggestion that one should not pee facing a wall. The priest is terrified when he discovers that he has ejaculated inside the mouth of a snake. It does the snake no good either, for the story tells us beasts cannot tolerate human semen and die when it enters their bodies. The moral of the tale is to avoid sleeping in places that are far away from human habitation.

Setsuwa recount both the pleasures and dangers of living in a world in which humans and other beings shared a common space, and in which the inexorable forces of karma could work in unexpected ways, bringing human beings in contact with bodhisattvas and demons alike. The central drama enacted in the tales

I have briefly considered is not one in which men's desires are rationalized by targeting women who are held solely responsible for their arousal. Rather it is the potential danger attendant on the collision of the human and nonhuman realms that these texts seek to illustrate through their accounts of the curious trafficking between human and animal worlds.

In what follows I would like to consider another set of stories from *Konjaku monogatari,* in which a story about a man who displays his penis appears alongside one about a man who loses his headgear. In the first tale the courtier Minamoto Akisada pulls out his penis during an official ceremony. Fujiwara Norikuni, another courtier who witnesses this event, cannot help but laugh out loud. When he is asked why he finds it fit to laugh in the midst of an official ceremony, he cannot simply say that Akisada took out his penis. The narrator explains that what people said about this event was that one should not engage in such frivolous play (*tawamure*), with no regard to the appropriateness of the context in which it is performed.[13]

This tale appears to accord with our own sensibilities on a number of counts. It seems to map on to our own clear distinctions between the public and the private spheres, in which sex and the body's "private parts" are best kept hidden, confined to the privacy of the bedroom. The shock of recognition the story elicits in us has a great deal to do with our own understanding of sex as a public secret, which when exposed through a public display of sexual organs constitutes a transgression.

Our reading is overdetermined by the fact that for us sexuality serves as the master code that explains the source of all human desires and impulses. From this starting point it seems natural to group together all stories in which sex and sexual organs appear in a particular text and to find in them the workings of sexuality, which is identified as the driving force that gives meaning and coherence to the tales. In what follows I would like to question the obviousness of this methodological approach by considering instead the story of the exposure of the penis together with that about the loss of a hat. Counterintuitive as this may seem, this is the order in which these tales appear in *Konjaku monogatari.* Reading them in conjunction with one another destabilizes our assumptions about sex and sexual organs as the sites of individual identity; it also makes possible imagining other more unfamiliar forms that selfhood can take in medieval texts.

The tale in question is one in which Tokimune, a court official, accidentally knocks off the headgear of another member, Kiyotada, during a formal ceremony. This, we are told, elicits raucous laughter and causes commotion among those in attendance. Kiyotada picks up his headgear and, without completing his formal duties, runs away. The two live on to a ripe old age, and this event continues to be recounted for a long time.[14] This is only one among a number of stories in *Konjaku monogatari,* whose central themes are the ludicrousness of losing one's own hat and becoming the butt of laughter, or of the ignominy of having one's headgear removed and thrown away by others.[15]

That the display of a penis has the power to reduce those who witness the spectacle to uncontrollable laughter seems to us perfectly understandable given that sexual organs are so-called private parts, whose public exposure contravenes codes of acceptable behavior, and in that sense can be transgressive of the normative order. Less fathomable is the idea that those who lose their headgear experience humiliation and loss of face, and that those who see or hear of such occurrences find these incidents outrageous and deeply amusing. Courtly headgear, *kamuri*[16] or *eboshi,*[17] however, are not merely things that cover men's heads or simply culturally prescribed forms of adornment. They are akin to robes in that they are metonymically linked to the male body and to a meaningful sense of self (Figure 8). The body (*mi*), as I have argued, signifies personhood, understood as something constituted through an awareness of its standing in the world. If *eboshi* and *kamuri* are metonymic of the male body and central to a sense of self, then it is not surprising that their removal or loss signals exposure and humiliation.

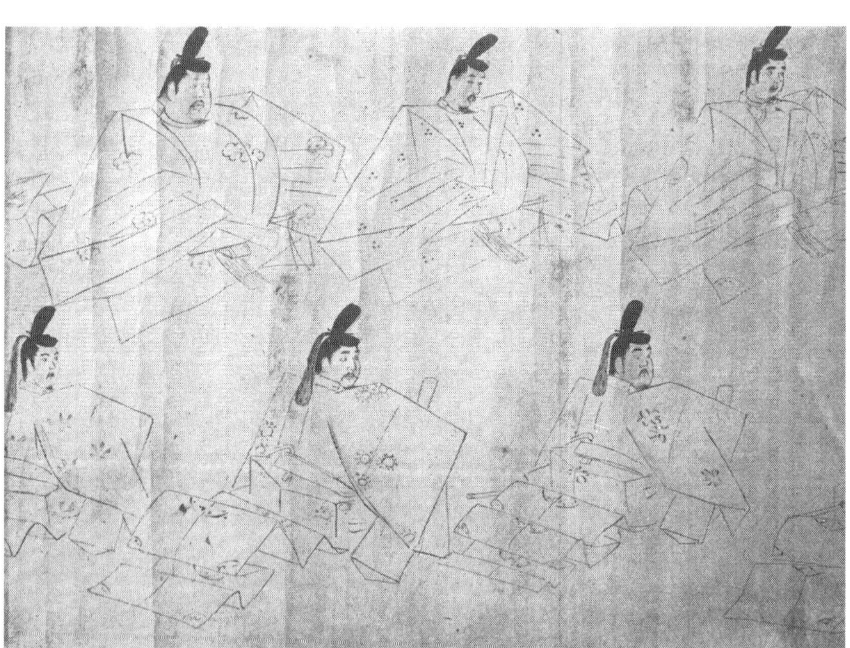

Figure 8. *Kuge Retsuei zu* (Portraits of Court Noblemen), 13th century, Kyoto National Museum.

The flaunting of the penis, it turns out, is of less consequence than the loss of a hat. Sex and the genital organs are not the sites of shame or transgression: it is only unacceptable to expose oneself in the context of a courtly ceremony (not to be conflated with the public sphere). In other contexts there is little censure or opprobrium attached to sexual activity or sexual body parts. Headgear, on the other hand, is ideally never to be removed, even when a man is alone. It is the hat rather than the penis that appears to signify male identity, calling into question any natural connection between masculinity and the penis; both the body's materiality and the meanings it carries turn out not to be universal, forcing us to read seemingly familiar objects differently. The *Tale of Genji,* we realize, is telling us something significant when it points out that, unlike others who might display a dishevelled appearance in sickness, Kashiwagi keeps his *eboshi* firmly in place even on his deathbed. It is through a seemingly unimportant item of clothing that we recognize the full import of *eboshi* in the social world of aristocrats, as a central site of male dignity, decorum, and self-worth.

As I suggested in Chapter 2, men who forcibly have sex with women in *Konjaku monogatari* are criticized not for violating women's bodies but rather for stealing their clothes, and praised when they leave behind the robes of the women they have forced themselves upon. That Lady Nijō in *Towazugatari* describes her experience of being sexually violated by the retired Emperor Go-Fukakusa through the idiom of clothes, despairing at the fact that her thin robe is badly torn, and that she will be left with nothing in the world, not even her name, demonstrates the degree to which notions of the body, self, and robes are inalienably linked. It also points to the vast gap that separates their world from our own, for to us rape is first and foremost a violation of the physical body, which is the locus of individual identity.

In the texts of medieval Japan there are bodies that are best apprehended through robes and hats, animals and humans who engage in sexual intercourse with one another, and youths who give birth to gold after having sex with monks. One of the opportunities and pleasures of reading literatures of a very different time and place is that they make possible a defamiliarization of categories that have become naturalized and obvious, and unsettle reading and interpretive practices to which we have grown habituated. Seizing this opportunity makes it possible and necessary to seek new and different ways of making sense of, and deriving pleasure from, the faraway, long-ago texts that we encounter. I have been arguing that when we encounter modes of being that are very different from our own, we cannot presume that our analytic categories—body, woman, gender, and sexuality—will be adequate to our understandings of the literary/religious narratives we seek to explicate. We need, I have been suggesting, to remain attentive to the moments when these categories are stretched, sometimes to the point where they cannot render us any intellectual service, for they fail to illuminate the past we seek to represent and understand. This does not mean that the romantic hermeneutic aspiration to "step into their shoes" is an option available to us either, for we cannot encounter different worlds other than through our time and in terms of our own categories of thought. It is in the space between these two problematic alternatives that we must shuttle, not disavowing our intellectual traditions but allowing the strangeness of other worlds to discomfit and unsettle our categories and provoke critical examination of them. The result may be a better understanding of worlds other than our own, as well as a better understanding of the capacities and the limits—including, perhaps, unsurpassable limits—of our modes of comprehension, and a recognition that we too, as much as them, are inescapably in and of our times.

Notes

Introduction

1. James Schultz makes the same point in his critique of the anachronistic ascription in European medieval studies of modern conceptions of desire to twelfth-century German tales of courtly love. See Schultz, *Courtly Love, the Love of Courtliness, and the History of Sexuality* (Chicago: University of Chicago Press, 2006), 63–79.

2. François Jullien's emphasis on the disposition of things, which produces particular effects in the world, is useful for thinking about desire and affect in ways that do not privilege human initiative and agency. Jullien, *The Propensity of Things: Towards a History of Efficacy in China,* trans. Janet Lloyd (New York: Zone Books, 1995), 260.

3. Konishi Jin'ichi, *A History of Japanese Literature, The Archaic and Ancient Ages,* vol. 1, trans. Aileen Gatten and Nicolas Teele (Princeton, N.J.: Princeton University Press, 1984), 58–62.

4. The two worlds of *ga* and *zoku* were, of course, by no means mutually exclusive, and as Konishi argues, often a *ga-zoku* aesthetic prevailed, making possible the incorporation of both forms into a single text.

5. Classical works, which combined prose and poetry, often came to be categorized loosely, sometimes gaining the appellation *niki* or *nikki* (journals or diaries), and at other times *uta monogatari* (poem tales) or simply *shū* (collections of poems). *Ise shū,* for example, has a significant prose narrative section but, as the name suggests, was thought of as a collection of poems until the late Edo period when it came to be referred to as *Ise nikki* (The Diary of Lady Ise). *Setsuwa* did not exist as a genre until the Meiji period.

6. In using the word "episteme" in this context I do not mean to suggest that knowledge in the Buddhist world belonged solely to the realm of ideas, separate from material, embodied practices.

7. William LaFleur, *The Karma of Words: Buddhism and the Literary Arts in Medieval Japan* (Berkeley: University of California Press, 1983), 9.

8. For a discussion of how these two mutually exclusive fields of study emerged in Japan and how they shaped scholarship on Kamo no Chōmei, see Rajyashree Pandey, *Writing and Renunciation in Medieval Japan: The Works of the Poet-Priest Kamo no Chōmei* (Ann Arbor: Center for Japanese Studies, University of Michigan, 1998), 3–5. There is a much greater attempt in recent scholarship to bridge the divide between literary and Buddhist studies, but well-entrenched academic divides often militate against interdisciplinary conversations.

9. See, for example, the articles in Mitamura Masako, Kawazoe Fusae, and Matsui Kenji, eds., *Genji kenkyū,* 10 vols. (Tokyo: Kanrin shobō, 1996–2005).

Chapter 1. Rethinking Body, Woman, Sex, and Agency in Medieval Japanese Narratives

1. It is not my intention here to provide a survey of the extensive literature that has burgeoned around the body, nor do I seek to offer a sustained analysis of the body's enmeshment in webs of discourse and power, and the medical, religious, and material practices within which bodies were produced in the context of medieval Japan, for that would require writing an altogether different book.

2. Friedrich Nietzsche, *The Will to Power*, trans. W. Kaufmann (New York: Random House, 1968), 131.

3. Some of the standard works of reference on the body in the Anglo-American academy are Bryan Turner, *The Body and Society* (Blackwell: Oxford University Press, 1984); Michael Featherstone, Mike Hepworth, and Bryan Turner, eds., *The Body: Social Process and Cultural Theory* (London: Sage, 1991); and Chris Shilling, *The Body in Culture, Technology and Society* (London: Sage, 2004). The growing importance of the study of the body as a separate field of inquiry is reflected in the continued popularity of the academic journal *Body and Society*, which was launched in 1995.

4. Caroline Bynum's work on Christianity in the medieval period, for example, offers a counternarrative to the characterization of all medieval Christian discourse as dualistic. She argues that far from despising the body and wishing to escape from it, Christian theologians in fact "assumed the flesh to be the instrument of salvation . . ." Medieval uses of gender categories, likewise, she suggests, were complex and took a number of different forms, and there is little evidence to suggest that medieval thinkers conceived of the body as matter or as female. Furthermore, medieval theorists who debated questions of eschatology did not privilege the soul and abandon the body but argued instead that at the end of time, the body we possess in this world would be resurrected along with the soul with which it would be united. Bynum, "Why all the Fuss about the Body? A Medievalist's Perspective," in Victoria Bonnell and Lynn Hunt, eds., *Beyond the Cultural Turn: New Directions in the Study of Society and Culture* (Berkeley: University of California Press, 1999), 251–255.

5. See Susan Bordo, *The Flight to Objectivity: Essays on Cartesianism and Culture* (New York: SUNY Press, 1987), 45–73, for a discussion of how Cartesian dualism marked a significant break from medieval understandings of self and the world.

6. For a bold argument about how the culture of dissection and the science of anatomy helped produce new conceptions of interiority and self, and how these pervaded every aspect of intellectual thought and artistic practices, uniting disparate figures such as Rembrandt, John Donne, and Descartes, see Jonathan Sawday, *The Body Emblazoned: Dissection and the Human Body in Renaissance Culture* (London and New York: Routledge, 1995).

7. Chris Shilling, *The Body and Social Theory*, 2nd ed. (London: Sage, 2003), 11.

8. Foucault's challenge to the commonly held assumption that the body "obeys the exclusive laws of physiology and that it escapes the influence of history" comes from his examination of the multiplicity of regimes to which the body is subjected, such that "nothing in man—not even his body—is sufficiently stable to serve as the basis for self-recognition or for understanding other men." See Michel Foucault, "Nietzsche, Genealogy, History," in Sherry Simon and Donald F. Bouchard, eds., Donald F. Bouchard, trans., *Language, Counter-Memory, Practice: Selected Essays and Interviews by Michel Foucault* (Ithaca, N.Y.: Cornell University Press, 1977), 153.

9. Indeed much of the new work being done on the body today brings together the disciplines of neuroscience and the humanities/social sciences, to overcome precisely the artificial separation between nature and culture that has shaped these disciplinary formations. Of particular interest in this regard is the work being done on affect and emotions, which explores the interplay of the biological basis of emotion with its cultural formation, treating the two as integrally linked, rather than casting them within the binary of nature versus culture. See, for example, Brian Massumi, *Parables for the Virtual: Movement, Affect, Sensation* (Durham, N.C.: Duke University Press, 2002). For an overview of some of the major debates emerging in this new line of inquiry, as well as a comprehensive bibliography of work in this field, see Nicole Eustace, Eugine Lean, Julian Livingstone, Jan Plamper, William Reddy, and Barbara Rosenwein, "AHR Conversation: The Historical Study of Emotions," *American Historical Review* 117:5 (December 2012): 1487–1531.

10. When I speak of the "East Asian" tradition, I am referring here to the complex nexus of Daoist, Buddhist, and Confucian ideas that circulated in China, Korea, and Japan in the premodern period. In arguing that the "East Asian" tradition was different from the Western one, I wish to avoid any suggestion that the non-West occupies a position of radical alterity that renders it incommensurably different from and, by implication, wiser and superior to the West. Such idealizations would only serve to reproduce, through inversion, the oppositions familiar to us in Orientalist discourse.

11. Roger Ames, "The Meaning of the Body in Classical Chinese Philosophy," in Thomas P. Kasulis, Roger Ames, and Wimal Dissanayake, eds., *Self as Body in Asian Theory and Practice* (New York: SUNY Press, 1993), 168. As Ames argues, "Since body and mind were not regarded as different 'kinds' of existence in any essential way, they did not generate different sets of terminologies necessary to describe them. For this reason, the qualitative modifiers that we usually associate with matter do double duty in Chinese to characterize both the physical and the psychical." Ames, 163.

12. Thomas P. Kasulis, "The Body—Japanese Style," in *Self as Body in Asian Theory and Practice*, 303.

13. Shigehisa Kuriyama, "The imagination of the body and the history of embodied experience: the case of Chinese views of the viscera," in *The Imagination of the Body and the History of Bodily Experience* (Kyoto: International Research Center for Japanese Studies, 2001), 18–19.

14. Mark Seldon, "Tales of Shen and Xin: Body-Person and Heart-Mind in China during the last 150 Years," in Michael Feher, with Ramona Naddaff and Nadia Tazi, eds., *Fragments for a History of the Human Body*, pt. 4 (New York: Zone Books, 1989), 267.

15. John Hay, "Is the Body Invisible in Chinese Art?" in Angela Zito and Tani Barlow, eds., *Body, Subject, and Power in China* (Chicago: University of Chicago Press, 1994), 51.

16. Ibid., 67.

17. John Rosenfeld, *Portraits of Chōgen: The Transformation of Buddhist Art in Early Medieval Japan* (Leiden: Brill, 2011), 147.

18. Willa Jane Tanabe, "The Persistence of Self as Body and Personality in Japanese Buddhist Art," in Roger Ames, Wimal Dissanayake, and Thomas Kasulis, eds., *Self as Image in Asian Theory and Practice* (New York: SUNY Press, 1994), 406–420.

19. Sarah Horton, *Living Buddhist Statues in Early Medieval and Modern Japan* (New York: Macmillan, 2007), 1–2.

20. For a more detailed consideration of how the mind and body work together, see Thomas P. Kasulis, "The Body—Japanese Style," 299–319.

21. In Japanese Tendai and Shingon formulations, the body, always understood as a mind-body complex, became a particularly prized vehicle for the performance of rituals and practices that were seen as enactments and expressions of an already enlightened state. As William LaFleur puts it, "This ensconsing of truth in physical form was for Kūkai [the founder of the Shingon sect of Buddhism in Japan] never a move downward or an incarnation from some loftier, more spiritual, plane but a natural and in no way condescending articulation of the truth in the physical world. It was also a way of maintaining the radical nondualism of the Mahāyāna tradition; body and mind were not permitted to become separate or opposable realities." LaFleur, *The Karma of Words,* 21–22.

22. Elizabeth Grosz, *Volatile Bodies: Toward a Corporeal Feminism* (Bloomington: Indiana University Press, 1994), 3–7.

23. In the medieval scientific tradition, "all human exudings—menstruation, sweating, lactation, emission of semen, etc.—were seen as bleedings; and all bleedings—lactation, menstruation, nosebleeds, hemorrhoidal bleeding, etc.—were taken to be analogous. Thus, it was not far-fetched for a medical writer to refer to a man menstruating or lactating, or to a woman emitting seed." Caroline Bynum, "The Female Body and Religious Practice in the Later Middle Ages," in Michel Feher, with Ramona Naddaff and Nadia Tazi, eds., *Fragments for a History of the Human Body,* pt. 1 (New York: Zone Press, 1989), 185–187.

24. For a discussion of the one-sex model, see Thomas Laqueur, *Making Sex: Body and Gender from the Greeks to Freud* (Cambridge, Mass.: Harvard University Press, 1990), 19–20, 25–62, 63–113, 114–142, and 150–154.

25. As Laqueur puts it, "Nature [here] is not therefore to culture what sex is to gender, as in modern discussions." See *Making Sex,* 29.

26. Kenan Malik argues that race discourse became particularly vocal in the nineteenth century, when science and evolutionary theory, in particular, were harnessed to support the idea of a natural order underlying social and economic inequalities. See his *The Meaning of Race: Race, History and Culture in Western Society* (New York: New York University Press, 1996).

27. See Laqueur, *Making Sex,* 149–150.

28. Joan Wallach Scott, "'Gender' A Useful Category of Historical Analysis," in Joan Wallach Scott, ed., *Feminism and History, Oxford Readings in Feminism* (Oxford: Oxford University Press, 1996), 156.

29. In her influential book on a feminist reading of Buddhism, Rita Gross defines her own project as a "feminist valorization of Buddhism." The task of valorization, as she sees it, is to recognize that a religious tradition, however sexist or misogynistic, may not be "irreparably so" and hence can be returned to its "original state" before it became tainted by patriarchy. The search is thus on for a "usable past" in which stories from within Buddhism that have hitherto been sidelined or ignored in male-centered accounts are returned to the center and re-presented as viable models for the empowerment of women. Rita Gross, *Buddhism after Patriarchy: A Feminist History, Analysis and Reconstruction of Buddhism* (New York: SUNY Press, 1993), 3–4.

30. See, for example, the following works: Michele Marra, "The Buddhist Mythmaking of Defilement: Sacred Courtesans of Medieval Japan," *Journal of Asian Studies* 52:1 (1993): 49–65; Rajyashree Pandey, "Women, Sexuality and Enlightenment: *Kankyo no tomo,*" *Monumenta Nipponica* 50:3 (Autumn 1995): 325–356; Terry Kawashima, *Writing Margins: The Textual Construction of Gender in Heian and Kamakura Japan* (Cambridge, Mass., and London: Harvard University Press, 2001); Barbara Ruch, ed., *Engendering Faith: Women and Buddhism in Premodern Japan* (Ann Arbor: Center for Japanese Studies, University of Michigan, 2002); Ber-

nard Faure, *The Power of Denial: Buddhism, Purity, and Gender* (Princeton, N.J.: Princeton University Press, 2003); Rajyashree Pandey, "Poetry, Sex and Salvation: The 'Courtesan' and the Noblewoman in Medieval Japanese Narratives," *Japanese Studies* 24:1 (May 2004): 61–79; Janet Goodwin, *Selling Songs and Smiles: The Sex Trade in Heian and Kamakura Japan* (Honolulu: University of Hawai'i Press, 2007); and Keller R. Kimbrough, *Preachers, Poets, Women and the Way: Izumi Shikibu and the Buddhist Literature of Medieval Japan* (Ann Arbor: Center for Japanese Studies, University of Michigan, 2008).

31. For a useful survey of trends in the study of women's history in Japan from the prewar to the present day, see Haruko Wakita, Ryūichi Narita, Anne Walthall, and Hitomi Tonomura, "Appendix: Past Developments and Future Issues in the Study of Women's History in Japan: A Bibliographical Essay," in Hitomi Tonomura, Anne Walthall, and Wakita Haruko, eds., *Women and Class in Japanese History* (Ann Arbor: Center for Japanese Studies, University of Michigan, 1999), 299–313.

32. Denise Riley, for example, argues that "'women' is a volatile collectivity in which female persons can be very differently positioned, so that the apparent continuity of the subject of 'women' is not to be relied on; 'women' is both synchronically and diachronically erratic as a collectivity, while for the individual, 'being a woman' is also inconstant, and can't provide an ontological foundation." And lest we despair that the feminist cause is irrevocably lost if we jeopardize the stability of the category "women," Riley insists upon its indeterminacy, arguing that "this instability has a historical foundation, and that feminism is the site of the systematic fighting-out of that instability . . ." Denise Riley, *"Am I that Name?": Feminism and the Category of "Women" in History* (Minneapolis: University of Minnesota Press, 1988), 2–5. In a similar vein, when Joan Scott considers the status of "experience" in the practice of history writing, she argues that those who privilege experience as incontrovertible evidence "take as self-evident the identities of those whose experience is being documented and thus naturalize their difference. . . . The evidence of experience then becomes evidence for the fact of difference, rather than a way of exploring how difference is established, how it operates, how and in what ways it constitutes subjects who see and act in the world." See Joan Wallach Scott, "The Evidence of Experience," in Gabrielle Spiegel, ed., *Practicing History: New Directions in Historical Writing after the Linguistic Turn* (New York: Routledge, 2005), 202.

33. Charlotte Furth, *A Flourishing Yin: Gender in China's Medical History, 960–1665* (Berkeley and Los Angeles: University of California Press, 1999), 52.

34. Ibid., 7.

35. *Onna* often refers to a young woman. *Otoko*, like *onna* also often signifies a young man, or at any rate one who has yet to retire from the secular world. *Otoko* can also mean a manservant or attendant.

36. All references to *Genji monogatari* (hereafter referred to as *GM*), are based on the following text: Yanai Shigeshi, Murofushi Shinsuke, Ōaki Yūji, Suzuki Hideo, Fujii Sadakazu and Imanishi Yūichirō eds., *Genji monogatari*, Shin koten bungaku taikei, vols. 1–5, 4th ed. (Tokyo: Iwanami shoten, 2001). All translations, unless otherwise stated, are my own. See *GM*, vol. 1, 329.

37. *GM*, vol. 4, 148.

38. For a comprehensive and authoritative account of the complex ways in which nature works as a metaphor in *waka*, and particularly in the ways in which animals and plants are associated with both particular seasons and genders, see Haruo Shirane, *Japan and the Culture of the Four Seasons: Nature, Literature and the Arts* (New York: Columbia University Press,

2012), 45–55. For a study of the many ways in which the trope of *ominaeshi* was used in *waka* poetry, and in particular its connections with the topos of "the five obstructions," see Edward Kamens, "Dragon-Girl, Maidenflower, Buddha: The Transformation of a Waka Topos, 'The Five Obstructions,'" *Harvard Journal of Asiatic Studies,* 53:2 (1993): 389–442.

39. Tani Barlow makes the same point when she talks about the ways in which new conceptions of the modern Chinese woman entailed a reconfiguration of the category woman whereby, in line with the sexual discourses that emerged in the West, her identity came to be grounded in her sexuality. See her "Theorizing Women: Funü, Guoja, Jiating," in Angela Zito and Tani Barlow, eds., *Body, Subject and Power in China* (Chicago: University of Chicago Press, 1994), 266.

40. Through a close textual reading of *waka* poetry, Michel Vieillard-Baron argues that it is the stance that the poet adopts in the composition, rather than his/her biological sex, that renders the work masculine or feminine. See his "Male? Female? Gender confusion in classical poetry (*waka*)," *Cipango—French Journal of Japanese Studies* 2, English selection (2013): 1–23.

41. The "five obstructions" (*itsutsu no sawari*) refer to the impossibility for women to attain rebirth as a Brahmā, Indra, Māra, Cakravartin or Wheel-turning King, and, most significantly, Buddha.

42. That this association of woman with sex has become commonplace in interpretations of medieval poetry and literature in general is reflected in the translation by Helen McCullough of Ki no Tsurayuki's description of Ono no Komachi's poetry in the Japanese preface of *Kokinshū.* The original text says *tsuyokaranu wa onna no uta nareba narubeshi* (the fact that her poems are lacking in strength must be due to the fact that they are women's poems). In Helen McCullough's translation the weakness of her poem is attributed to her "sex." There is little reason to assume that Tsurayuki attributes the weakness of Ono no Komachi's poems to something inherent in the female condition that derives from her biologically determined sexual makeup. That poems written in the male as opposed to the female voice are different is not in question. My argument is that these differences are based on certain stylized poetic performances rather than on immutable sexual characteristics. Kojima Noriyuki, ed., *Kokin wakashū,* Shin nihon koten bungaku taikei, 5 (Tokyo: Iwanami shoten, 1989), 4. Helen Craig McCullough, trans., *Kokin Wakashū: The First Imperial Anthology of Japanese Poetry* (Stanford, Calif.: Stanford University Press, 1985), 7.

43. See Leon Hurvitz, trans., *Scripture of the Lotus Blossom of the Fine Dharma (The Lotus Sutra)* (New York: Columbia University Press, 1976), 201–202.

44. Robert A. F. Thurman, trans., *The Holy Teaching of Vimalakīrti: A Mahāyāna Scripture* (University Park and London: Pennsylvania State University Press, 1976), 56–63.

45. See Vanita Seth, "Difference with a Difference: Wild Men, Gods and Other Protagonists," *Parallax,* 9:4 (2003): 75–87, for an analysis of the development of racialized understandings of the body in the eighteenth and nineteenth centuries in which "Nature, be it the physical body or the physical environment, was no longer an agent with volition and intent, but a mute and passive object for study and classification" (85).

46. This is Thomas Laqueur's description of the sexed body in the nineteenth century. Laqueur, *Making Sex,* 51.

47. Yoshida Kazuhiko argues that the principle of *modori* or "return" (used in Kabuki and Bunraku theater) in which, through a dramatic performance, a character's true character is revealed after several twists and turns, is not dissimilar to the strategy used in the Devadatta

story to achieve its rhetorical effects. See his "The Enlightenment of the Dragon King's Daughter in the Lotus Sutra," in Ruch, *Engendering Faith,* 303.

48. Bernard Faure, for example, recognizes the problems of treating "woman" as a unified category and of treating gender as the only prism through which to read medieval texts, and yet the question of women's victimhood or agency looms large in his work. He claims that "women were full-fledged historical actors, and we should not be too quick in concluding that they were passive victims" and that "some resisted with more or less success . . . while others seem to have been 'active' victims, wilful agents of their own victimization (or of that of their 'sisters')." See Faure, *The Power of Denial,* 331–332. Citing the case of Kumano *bikuni,* for example, Faure argues that while purporting to work "on behalf of women," they "contributed, albeit unwittingly to their debasement . . ." (53). A little later, returning to the subject of Kumano *bikuni,* he writes, "They tried to conceal the sexist nature of the dogma by presenting their message as one of feminine emancipation . . . these nuns contributed to the subjection of women to Buddhist male ideology" (78). Keller Kimbrough follows Faure's approach, arguing that "while Kumano *bikuni* and other female proselytizers were obviously and perhaps unavoidably complicit in propagating aspects of traditional Buddhist misogyny, they were simultaneously engaged in its subversion. . . . Kumano *bikuni* were pro-woman within an overwhelmingly misogynistic context." Kimbrough, *Preachers, Poets, Women and the Way,* 215.

49. Dipesh Chakrabarty and Sanjay Seth seek to inquire into the meanings and consequences of the fact that historiography cannot take seriously a world in which gods and spirits are treated as active agents, even where the human agents concerned attribute their actions to them. Chakrabarty, *Provincializing Europe: Postcolonial Thought and Historical Difference* (Princeton, N.J.: Princeton University Press, 2000), 72–96. Seth, "Reason or Reasoning? Clio or Siva?" *Social Text* 78 (2004): 85–101.

50. I am drawing here on Saba Mahmood's work on a women's piety movement in contemporary Cairo, which offers particularly valuable theoretical insights into how we might think critically about women's agency, oppression, and resistance. See her "Feminist Theory, Embodiment, and the Docile Agent: Some Reflections on the Egyptian Islamic Revival," *Cultural Anthropology* 16:2 (May 2001): 202–236.

51. Ibid., 206.

52. This is what Judith Butler seeks to do when she argues that power has to be understood not as something that dominates the subject but rather as something that brings the subject into being. Subjectivation for Butler is produced through performativity, that is to say, through the iteration of particular modes of conduct and bodily comportment that reinforce gender and other social norms. See Judith Butler, *Bodies that Matter: On the Discursive Limits of "Sex"* (New York: Routledge, 1993), 220.

53. Both Tomiko Yoda and Thomas LaMarre make the same point about the limits of understanding agency through the liberal model of subjectivity. In talking about poetics in the Heian period, Thomas LaMarre argues that "it is not uncommon for scholars to treat poetics as the site of political contestation and to analyze poetic exchanges in which poets air their grievances in a competitive arena. Such competition is often construed by contemporary scholars as a form of resistance—usually to the ruling elite—and is interpreted in terms of the individual versus the group; in effect, they presume a modern apparatus of resistance." He chooses to read poetic exchanges not "as a form of resistance but rather as a mode of participation in a poetic order of things." See his *Uncovering Heian Japan: An Archaeology of Sensation and*

Inscription (Durham, N.C.: Duke University Press, 2000), 7. Yoda argues that "the *Genji* offers a highly intricate and multilayered portrayal of interpersonal conflicts—especially in what is expected to be among the most powerful forms of affective bonding—without constituting the agents who think and speak as autonomous, heroic, and psychological subjects" and that "the tensions and negotiations between lovers that the poetic dialogues articulate, in other words, cannot be understood through the modern binary between individualism and collectivism or resistance and conformism." See her *Gender and National Literature: Heian Texts in the Construction of Japanese Modernity* (Durham, N.C.: Duke University Press, 2004), 145.

54. See Barbara Ruch, "The Other Side of Culture," in Kozo Yamamura, ed., *The Cambridge History of Japan: Medieval Japan*, vol. 3 (Cambridge: Cambridge University Press, 1990), 510.

55. See, for example, Ishida Mizumaro, "Bikuni kaidan: ama no tokui na seikaku," in *Musashino joshi daigaku kiyō* 18 (1978): 1–15; Hosokawa Ryōichi, "Sairinji sōji to ama," in Ōsumi Kazuo and Nishiguchi Junko, eds., *Shirīzu josei to Bukkyō, Sukui to oshie*, vol. 4 (Tokyo: Heibonsha, 1989), 143–151. Lori Meeks suggests that the multivalent significations attached to the act of becoming a nun defy a simple explanation of nunhood as synonymous with victimhood. See her "Buddhist Renunciation and the Female Life Cycle: Understanding Nunhood in Heian and Kamakura Japan," *Harvard Journal of Asiatic Studies* 70:1 (June 2010): 1–59.

56. See Faure, *The Power of Denial*, 53.

57. As Christina Laffin argues in her study of the nun Abutsu, "Abutsu's transitions between some form of tonsure to a return to sexual life show the fluidity of the categories of 'lover,' 'nun,' and 'wife' . . ." See her *Rewriting Medieval Japanese Women: Politics, Personality, and Literary Production in the Life of Nun Abutsu* (Honolulu: University of Hawai'i Press, 2013), 83.

58. As Walter Johnson suggests, "the term 'agency' smuggles a notion of the universality of a liberal notion of selfhood, with its emphasis on independence and choice . . ." See Johnson, "On Agency," *Journal of Social History* 37:1 (2003): 115.

59. For a brief discussion of the many texts that proliferated around the question of the sinfulness of Murasaki Shikibu's *Tale of Genji*, see Haruo Shirane, ed., *Envisioning the Tale of Genji: Media, Gender, and Cultural Production* (New York: Columbia University Press, 2008), 17–19.

60. In an interview with Nicholas D. Kristof, Setouchi Harumi says that Genji's liaisons were rape, not seductions. See Nicholas D. Kristof, "Kyoto Journal; The Nun's Best Seller: 1,000-Year-Old Love Story," *New York Times*, May 28, 1999. See also Komashaku Kimi, *Murasaki no messēji, Asahi Sensho* 422 (Tokyo: Asahi Shuppan, 1991).

61. More nuanced readings have attempted to restore something of the historical and cultural contexts within which women writers positioned themselves as narrating subjects in sexual encounters. See Royall Tyler, "Marriage, Rank and Rape in *The Tale of Genji*," *Intersections: Gender, History and Culture in the Asian Context* 7 (March 2000): 1–10, who argues that coercion was an acceptable strategy for men in a culture where to accede to men's sexual advances too readily was frowned upon, and furthermore, that it was the initial coercive overture that ensured the long-term commitment and support of men within a polygamous world. Margaret H. Childs argues that vulnerability and passivity were regarded as highly valuable traits in women in the *Genji* because they served to enhance women's appeal, arousing in men feelings of protectiveness and love. See Childs, "The Value of Vulnerability: Sexual Coercion and the Nature of Love in Japanese Court Literature," *Journal of Asian Studies*, 58:4 (November 1999): 1059–1079. Hitomi Tonomura considers how Lady Nijō recasts her coercive sexual encounter with Go-Toba as something emblematic of her sexual allure that allows her to con-

struct a positive narrative of self. See her "Coercive Sex in the Medieval Japanese Court: Lady Nijō's Memoir," *Monumenta Nipponica* 61:3 (Autumn 2006): 283–338.

62. Kimura Saeko reviews feminist readings of the *Tale of Genji* to argue that reading Genji as a rapist muddles the distinction between literary narratives and reality and goes against the basic principles of literary analysis, and that such readings are an application of modern discourses of sexuality onto Heian texts. She suggests that greater reflection is required on the relationship between literary analysis and feminism. See her "Genji monogatari to feminizumu," *Kokubungaku kaishaku to kanshō* 73:5 (2008): 72–81.

Chapter 2. The Erotics of the Body in the *Tale of Genji*

Epigraph. GM, vol. 3, 338.

1. As Robert Brower observes, Japanese court poetry is not interested in "either the identification of the people in love or a description of them." It is unimaginable, he says, for a medieval European romance with "its interminable descriptions of the woman from top to toe." See Robert Brower and Earl Miner, *Japanese Court Poetry* (Stanford, Calif.: Stanford University Press, 1961), 452.

2. Daud Ali points out that embracing, kissing, scratching, biting, coitus, slapping, moaning, oral sex, and so on constituted the well-defined and elaborate rituals necessary for the production of desire, and the proper consummation of sex in *Kāmasutra* and classical Sanskrit poetry. See Daud Ali, *Courtly Culture and Political Life in Early Medieval India* (Cambridge: Cambridge University Press, 2004), 213–214.

3. Michel Foucault, *The Will to Knowledge: The History of Sexuality,* vol. 1, Robert Hurley, trans. (London: Penguin Books, 1998), 35.

4. Speaking of French libertine literature of that period, for example, Peter Cryle writes, "The moral (or social) requirement that sexual scenes not be described in full, coexists, and often happily cohabits, with the pleasure of suggestive understatement." See Peter Cryle, *The Telling of the Act: Sexuality as Narrative in 18ᵗʰ and 19ᵗʰ Century France* (Newark: University of Delaware Press, 2001), 184.

5. Paolo Santangelo makes much the same point about the Chinese attitude to love and desire. See "The language of body as repulsive/seductive language: the case of the literati in late Imperial China," in Kuriyama Shigehisa, ed., *The Imagination of the Body and the History of Bodily Experience* (Kyoto: International Research Center of Japanese Studies, 2001), 60.

6. For a discussion of nudity as a form of clothing in Greek art, see Larissa Bonfante, "Nudity as Costume in Classical Art," *American Journal of Archaeology* 93:4 (October 1989): 543–570.

7. John Berger sees the story of Adam and Eve as central to the creation of the concept of nakedness. Nakedness comes into being when the body becomes the object of the gaze of the other, and in European art, he argues, it is the figure of the nude woman that is singled out as the object of the male gaze. What is more, the nude woman so internalizes this gaze that she only recognizes herself as someone being viewed. See John Berger, *Ways of Seeing* (London: Penguin Books, 1972), 45–64.

8. See Margaret Miles, *Carnal Knowing: Female Nakedness and Religious Meaning in the Christian West* (Boston: Beacon Press, 1989), xi.

9. See Kenneth Clark's *The Nude: A Study in Ideal Form* (New York: Pantheon Books, 1956), 3–4.

10. There is by now a large body of feminist and poststructuralist critique that challenges some of the foundational assumptions that underlie Western art and its valorization of the nude. See Ruth Barcan, *Nudity: A Cultural Anatomy* (Oxford: Berg, 2004), 36–42; Lynda Nead, *The Female Nude: Art, Obscenity, and Sexuality* (London and New York: Routledge, 1992); and John Berger, *Ways of Seeing*, 45–64.

11. Ruth Barcan, *Nudity: A Cultural Anatomy*, 31–32.

12. See François Jullien, *The Impossible Nude: Chinese Art and Western Aesthetics*, Maev de la Guardia, trans., (Chicago: University of Chicago Press, 2007), 14.

13. Ann Hollander, *Seeing Through Clothes* (Berkeley: University of California Press, 1993), 336–337.

14. Mario Perniola, "Between Clothing and Nudity," in Michel Feher, with Ramona Naddaff and Nadia Tazi, eds., *Fragments for a History of the Human Body*, pt. 4 (New York: Zone Books, 1989), 243.

15. See *Murasaki Shikibu nikki* in Hasegawa Masaharu and Imanishi Yūichi, eds., *Tosa nikki, Kagero nikki, Izumi shikibu nikki, Sarashina nikki*, Shin nihon koten bungaku taikei 24 (Tokyo: Iwanami Shoten, 1989) 297–298. See also Richard Bowring, *Murasaki Shikibu: Her Diary and Poetic Memoirs* (Princeton, N.J.: Princeton University Press, 1982), 114–115.

16. Caroline Bynum argues that there is "reason to think that medieval people saw Christ's penis not primarily as a sexual organ but as the object of circumcision and therefore as the wounded, bleeding flesh with which it was associated in painting and in text." See her "The Body of Christ in the Later Middle Ages: A Reply to Leo Steinberg," *Renaissance Quarterly* 39:3 (1986): 407.

17. See Ikeda Shinobu, "The Image of Women in Battle Scenes: 'Sexually' Imprinted Bodies," in Joshua Mostow, Norman Bryson, and Maribeth Graybill, eds., *Gender and Power in the Japanese Visual Field* (Honolulu: University of Hawai'i Press, 2003), 43.

18. *GM*, vol. 1, 117.

19. Ibid., 157.

20. Ibid., 93.

21. Edwin Cranston, trans. *A Waka Anthology: Grasses of Remembrance*, vol. 2, pt. B (Stanford, Calif.: Stanford University Press, 2006), 699.

22. *GM*, vol. 1, 93.

23. Cranston, *Waka Anthology*, 699.

24. Poem 507 *Kokinshū*, anonymous poem.

25. Poem 554 *Kokinshū* by Ono no Komachi.

26. *GM*, vol. 1, 144.

27. *Goshūishū* (Later Collection of Gleanings, 1086), 20: 1164.

28. *GM*, vol. 1, 307. As Royall Tyler points out, this poem functioned as a magic spell to be repeated by the person who had seen a spirit, and whose help was enlisted "to knot the overlapping hems at the front of his or her robe." See Royall Tyler, trans., *The Tale of Genji* (New York: Viking, 2001), 174.

29. *Kokinshū*, 992.

30. *GM*, vol. 1, 318.

31. For an analysis of the significance of the production of clothes by women in Heian texts and their implications for the narrative construction of female subjectivity, see Carol Cavanaugh's stimulating article, "Text and Textile: Unweaving the Female Subject in Heian Writing," *Positions* 3:6 (1996): 595–636.

32. *GM,* vol. 2, 85. The poems are translated in Cranston, *Waka Anthology,* 775–776.

33. *GM,* vol. 2, 86.

34. See Yamada Yoshio, Yamada Tadao, Yamada Hideo, and Yamada Toshio, eds., *Konjaku monogatari shū,* Nihon koten bungaku taikei, vol. 5 (Tokyo: Iwanami shoten, 1979–1980), 174–176.

35. Ibid., 177–178.

36. For an analysis of the politics of class and gender in this picture scroll, see Chino Kaori, "Chōshō suru kaiga: Obusumasaburō emaki ni miru jendaa to kurasu," in Ito Seiko and Kōno Nobuko, eds., *Onna to otoko no jikū: Nihon josei shi saikō,* vol. 2 (Tokyo: Fujiwara shoten, 1996), 121–187.

37. Both European and Japanese medieval texts present beauty and ugliness through a set of conventionalized images. The courtly ideal of feminine beauty in medieval England, for example, was the maiden, a virgin, with the purest of white skins, long golden hair, gray eyes, red lips, and a long and slender body with small breasts and a protruding belly. Ugly women were old, with loose, wrinkled skin and breasts like deflated bladders. See Kim Phillips, *Medieval Maidens: Young Women and Gender in England 1270–1540* (Manchester: Manchester University Press, 2003). The portrayal of ugly women in medieval Japanese texts draws on Chinese conventions. The *kanbun* text *Shinsarugakuki,* for example, describes the elderly first wife of a court official in unflattering terms—her teeth are missing, her hair is white, and her breasts hang down like a cow's udders.

38. Joshua Mostow makes a similar point when he argues that eroticism in the *Genji* is produced through association, poetic images, and postures of longing, such as the chin resting in hand, suggesting brooding thoughts. It is not the body that is important here. It is the general ambience in which figures are placed, their clothes, and the erotic context that allows us to imagine where their love and longing will lead them. Unpublished paper, "National Erotics, Gender and Representations of Sexuality in Heian Japan."

39. *GM,* vol. 2, 72.

40. *GM,* vol. 1, 255.

41. See Yuhara Miyoko, *Ōchō monogatari bungaku in okeru yoshibi no kenkyū* (Tokyo: Yūseido, 1988), 51–103.

42. *GM,* vol. 4, 391.

43. Tyler, *Tale of Genji,* 875.

44. For a discussion of *rōtashi,* see Inukai Wataru, "Genji monogatari no utsukushi to rōtashi," *Heian bungaku kenkyū* 11:1 (1953): 29–38. Also, Matsumura Seichi, "Genji monogatari no rōtashi," *Kokugo to kokubun* 42:6 (1965): 1–12. For a discussion of *rōtashi* and the role of vulnerability in the *Tale of Genji,* see Margaret H. Childs, "The Value of Vulnerability," 1059–1079.

45. *GM,* vol. 1, 172.

46. Ibid., 306.

47. Ibid., 310.

48. *Miko,* who performed shamanistic rituals and communicated with *kami,* were allowed to wear their hair loose and flowing freely, for it is there that the *kami* were thought to temporarily reside. Letting the hair down in order to invite a lover or his spirit to dwell in it is a favorite trope in many poems in *Manyōshū.* For an analysis of hair symbolism in ancient Japan and its importance in the poetry of *Manyōshū,* see Gary Ebersole, "Long black hair like a seat cushion: Hair symbolism in Japanese popular religion," in Alf Hiltebeitel and Barbara Miller, eds., *Hair: Its Power and Meaning in Asian Cultures* (Albany, N.Y.: Suny Press, 1998), 75–103.

49. This claim, of course, requires a caveat, for while clothes were the measure for gauging the beauty of men *and* women, hair constituted a highly gendered ideal of beauty associated exclusively with women. Men's hair in Heian times was never visible, for it was always covered by headgear, *eboshi,* which was worn at all times, including while asleep. Even when Kashiwagi is on his deathbed, for example, he makes sure that his *eboshi* is in place, for its loss would suggest a serious compromise of his honor and dignity.

50. See Kawazoe Fusae, *Sei to bunka no Genji monogatari: kaku onna no tanjō,* 2nd ed. (Tokyo: Tsukuma shobō, 1999), 129–143.

51. *GM,* vol. 1, 157.

52. The terms *shukke* (renunciant) and *ama* (nun) had multivalent significations in the Heian and Kamakura periods. The phrase "taking the tonsure" does not adequately capture the many stages that could signal women's gradual retreat from worldly life. The first step was to cut the hair up to the shoulders (*amasogi*); this could be followed by a second ceremony in which the head would be shaved completely. The onset of a serious illness, old age, or intimations of death could occasion this final step. See Katsuura Noriko, "Tonsure Forms for Nuns: Classification of Nuns according to Hairstyles," in Barbara Ruch, ed., *Engendering Faith: Women and Buddhism in Premodern Japan* (Ann Arbor: Center for Japanese Studies, University of Michigan, 2002), 122–125. For an illustration of differences between full tonsure and *amasogi,* see page 120.

53. *GM,* vol. 1, 157.

54. See Katsuura, "Tonsure Forms for Nuns," 114.

55. *GM,* vol. 2, 119.

56. Ibid., 120.

57. *GM,* vol. 5, 375.

58. *GM,* vol. 3, 377.

59. *GM,* vol. 1, 128.

60. For a discussion of the different interpretations to which this poem lends itself, see Toda Akiyoshi, "Izumi Shikibu zō no henyō: setsuwa kara no manazashi," *Hikakubunka* 11 (2003): 119–140.

61. *GM,* vol. 4, 137.

62. Ibid., 149. This is a gesture also performed by the young Murasaki after the night when Genji first sleeps with her.

63. Ibid., 150.

64. Ibid., 149.

65. Ibid., 150.

66. For another reading of this episode, see Mitamura Masako, "Yūgiri monogatari no jendaa kisei: osanasa, wakawakashisa to iu hihan kara," *Kokubungaku kaishaku to kanshō* 69:8 (2004): 6–13. Mitamura argues that Ochiba no Miya's "obstinacy" is a sign of her strong individualism and willpower. I prefer to read this scene not as an instance of "individual" resistance but rather as the text's way of pushing the possibilities of romance and revealing love's darker side through the figures of women such as Ochiba no Miya and Ōigimi.

67. It is noteworthy that it is when Genji affects a parental relationship with the young Murasaki that he strokes her hair and undertakes to trim it himself. *GM,* vol. 1, 297.

68. *GM,* vol. 4, 138.

69. *GM,* vol. 5, 362–363.

70. Ibid., 363.

71. I draw here on the work of Mitamura Masako and Kawazoe Fusae, who both discuss the significance of the topos of hair in the *Hatsune* chapter. See Mitamura Masako, "Kurokami no *Genji monogatari*: manazashi to tezawari kara," *Genji kenkyū* 1 (April 1996); Kawazoe Fusae, *Sei to bunka no Genji Monogatari*.

72. Translated in Tyler, *Tale of Genji*, 433; *GM*, vol. 2, 381.

73. *GM*, vol. 2, 382.

74. Ibid.

75. Ibid., 384.

76. Ibid.

77. Genji treats the many women who are in his care with kindness and consideration and visits them all, assuring them of the sincerity of his feelings. It is worth noting that his response to them is tied not only to their physical appearance but, equally importantly, to their status: "He felt for all of them, each according to her station (*izure o mo, hodo hodo ni tsukete aware to oboshitari*). *GM*, vol. 2, 389. The connections between eroticism, gender, power, and status in the *Genji* are themes that I explore at length in the chapter that follows.

78. Ibid., 386.

Chapter 3. The Erotics of Power in the *Tale of Genji*

Epigraph. GM, vol. 2, 389.

1. There would be little dispute in academic work on the *Genji* today with Haruo Shirane's claim that "in highly allusive, poetic, aesthetic, and less than apparent ways, the *Genji* dilates on the question of political power." See Haruo Shirane, *The Bridge of Dreams: A Poetics of 'The Tale of Genji'* (Stanford, Calif.: Stanford University Press, 1987), 23.

2. This reading of the *Genji* is exemplified in Ivan Morris's *The World of the Shining Prince: Court Life in Ancient Japan* (Oxford: Oxford University Press, 1964).

3. This is the approach taken by Michele Marra in his *Aesthetics of Discontent*, where he argues that political disaffection and dissent are voiced in aesthetic terms, or at the level of culture, only because they cannot do so through overt political discourse. For him, the way to grasp the politics at work in the text is by looking at those elements extraneous to it, such as its production and transmission, and its sociopolitical context, rather than at the formal features and generic conventions of the text itself. See Michele Marra, *The Aesthetics of Discontent: Politics and Reclusion in Medieval Japanese Literature* (Honolulu: University of Hawai'i Press, 1991), 7–8.

4. Michel Foucault, *Power/Knowledge: Selected Interviews and Other Writings 1972–1977*, Colin Gordon, ed. (New York: Pantheon Books, 1972), 98.

5. Ibid.

6. Today we are, at least in theory, committed to the idea that equality is a precondition for "true" romance; the play of power so central to the generation and enactment of eroticism therefore is not an acceptable part of social relations and has to be thematized as a separate domain of sexual play that involves practices such as sadomasochism and so on.

7. Lynne Miyake makes a similar point when she argues that the composition of *Tosa nikki* by a man who takes on the persona of a woman demonstrates how gender is not connected to sexual identity but is something that is textually produced. See her "The Tosa Diary: In the Interstices of Gender and Criticism," in Paul Schalow and Janet Hunter, eds., *The Woman's Hand: Gender and Theory in Japanese Women's Writing* (Stanford, Calif.: Stanford University Press, 1996), 41–73. Likewise, in the anonymous twelfth-century fictional tale *Torikaebaya*

Monogatari (The Tale of "If Only I Could Change Them Back"), the daughter of the Minister of the Right, Himegimi, is raised as a boy and takes her place at the court as a man, while her brother Wakagimi, brought up as a girl, enters court as a lady. It is through forms of rigorous self-fashioning, that is to say, through the cultivation of particular emotional dispositions and forms of bodily comportment appropriate to their respective genders, that Himegimi and Wakagimi are able to transform themselves such that they can successfully take on their new gendered roles, regardless of their sexual attributes. As Gregory Plugfelder observes, "Words designating 'man' or 'woman' often appear with verbs that imply the mutability or superficiality of that very status—'becoming' (*naru, arisomu*), 'changing into' (*kawaru, kau*), 'making someone into' (*nasu, torinasu*), 'imitating' (*manebu*), 'behaving as' (*motenasu*), 'spending time as' (*tsugu*), 'getting used to being' (*narau, narasu, tsukainarasu, arinaru*), 'reverting to' (*narikaeru, kaeriaratamu*), and so on." See Gregory Plugfelder, "Strange Fates: Sex, Gender, and Sexuality in Torikaebaya Monogatari," *Monumenta Nipponica* 47:3 (Autumn 1992): 355.

8. I am drawing here on the work of Judith Butler who argues that "gender is the repeated stylization of the body, a set of repeated acts within a highly rigid regulatory frame that congeal over time to produce the appearance of substance, of a natural sort of being" and that this leaves open the possibility of a subversive performance that disrupts the apparent naturalization of gender identity. See Judith Butler, *Gender Trouble: Feminism and the Subversion of Identity* (London: Routledge, 1990), 33.

9. *GM*, vol. 1, 385; Tyler, *Tale of Genji*, 216.

10. Genji has been drinking wine, which is why Seidensticker translates the lines in question as "A slight flush from drink made Genji even handsomer than usual. His skin glowed through his light summer robes." See Edward G. Seidensticker, trans., *The Tale of Genji*, (London: Penguin Books, 1976), 210. The word *midare* also lends itself to the interpretation I have suggested.

11. By contrast, Kojima Naoko reads the use of the term in this scene as being particularly significant because its transposition onto a male character draws attention to Genji's androgynous body, which transcends both sexes, and "to a kind of bisexual beauty which arises *through the erotic nature of his body*" (emphasis added). See Kojima Naoko, "Hikaru Genji no shintai to sei: Ōchō monogatarishi kara," in Kojima Naoko, ed., *Ōchō no sei to shintai: itsudatsu suru monogatari* (Tokyo: Shinwasha, 1996), 53–54.

12. *GM*, vol. 1, 38; Tyler, *Tale of Genji*, 24. There is debate about whether Genji's friends see him as a woman or whether they wish they themselves were women. See *GM*, vol. 1, footnote 7, 38.

13. Tyler, *Tale of Genji*, footnote 14, 24.

14. See Chapter 2 of this volume for poems about *Shitahimo*.

15. *GM*, vol. 1, 318; Tyler, *Tale of Genji*, 180–181. In another memorable scene in the "Beneath the Autumn Leaves" chapter, both Genji and Prince Hyōbu, brother of Fujitsubo and father of Murasaki, find themselves gazing amorously at one another, each thinking how pleasurable it would be if the other were a woman. It is Hyōbu's elegance and languorously sexy appearance (*iromekashu nayobitamaeru*) that trigger Genji's interest. Hyōbu too, finding himself in this relaxed and intimate setting with Genji, is stirred into an amorous mood (*iromekitaru onkokoro*). Tyler translates *iromekashū nayobitamaeru* as "romantically languorous" and *iromekitaru onkokoro* as "roving fancy." *GM*, vol. 1, 245–246; Tyler, *Tale of Genji*, 138.

16. See Kawazoe Fusae, "Hikaru Genji no shintai to yosōi o megutte," *Murasaki* 34:12 (1997): 18–20.

17. Royall Tyler has argued that since women in the *Genji* were not permitted to express their own desire for Genji, it was through the eroticized male gaze that female audiences of the time, who had the text read out to them or who were themselves readers of the text, indulged in their own vicarious fantasies about Genji. See Royall Tyler, "Lady Murasaki's Erotic Entertainment: The Early Chapters of the *Tale of Genji*," *East Asian History* 12 (December 1996): 65–78. It is certainly the case that in amorous encounters, women of the upper rungs of the aristocracy were expected to perform in ways that would render any open acknowledgement of men's beauty indecorous. Ladies-in-waiting, on the other hand, were free to express their appreciation of men's appearances. In "The Green Branch" chapter, for example, it is the view of Genji in a relaxed state, with clothes loosened and in disarray due to the extreme heat, that Aoi's gentlewomen openly admire as well worth the sight. *GM*, vol. 1, 61; Tyler, *Tale of Genji*, 33.

18. See, for example, Kojima Naoko, "Hikaru Genji no shintai to sei," 53–54.

19. The new term *dōseiai*, same sex love, that came to be coined in the Meiji period to describe a perverse and abnormal identity and relationship had to be posited against its other, hence the need for a new normative category, designated *iseiai*, or heterosexual love. For one of the best accounts of the changing contours of erotic desires and practices from the Edo period to the postwar era, and of the realignment of categories that followed the emergence of sexuality as a discourse in Meiji Japan, see Gregory Plugfelder, *Cartographies of Desire: Male-Male Sexuality in Japanese Discourse 1600–1950* (Berkeley: University of California Press, 1999).

20. Takeda Sachiko focuses on the identical nature of men's and women's clothing to argue that there was little consciousness in premodern Japan of sexual difference articulated through a difference in attire. See "Ifuku de yominaosu nihonshi: dansō to ōken," in *Asahi Sensho 601* (Tokyo: Asahi Shimbunsha, 1998), 85.

21. Mark Morris, for example, engages with psychoanalytic theory to tease out some of the unrecognized presumptions about desire and the unconscious that underpin Norma Field's writings on the *Genji*. See his "Desire and the Prince: New Work on *Genji Monogatari*," *Journal of Asian Studies* 49:2 (1990): 298–301.

22. See Norma Field, *The Splendor of Longing in the Tale of Genji* (Princeton, N.J.: Princeton University Press, 1987), 251–256, 269–274; and Edith Sarra, *Fictions of Femininity: Literary Inventions of Gender in Japanese Court Women's Memoirs* (Stanford, Calif.: Stanford University Press, 1999). Joshua Mostow has written extensively on the subject of the gaze. See in particular his introduction in Joshua Mostow, Norman Bryson and Marybeth Graybill, eds., *Gender and Power in the Japanese Visual Field* (Honolulu: University of Hawai'i Press, 2003), 1–16.

23. *GM*, vol. 1, 86–87; Tyler, *Tale of Genji*, 48–49.

24. *GM*, vol. 1, 87; Tyler, *Tale of Genji*, 49.

25. There are only two instances when breasts are mentioned in the text. Murasaki, now in charge of the little Akashi princess, thinks of how the child's mother, the Akashi Lady, must long for her. It is in this context that the narrator observes, "The sight of her [Murasaki] playing with the child as she let her suck on her beautiful breasts had much to recommend it." *GM*, vol. 2, 225; Tyler, *Tale of Genji,* 352. In another scene, Kumoinokari tucking her hair behind her ears like a working woman exposes her plump, round, pretty breast and offers it to her baby, even though she has no milk. What is noteworthy in both instances is not the beauty of the breast as a sexual object. The fact that Murasaki has no child of her own and that the Akashi Lady, who does, has to be separated from it is captured through the poignant gesture of Murasaki letting the baby suck on her breast. In Kumoinokari's case, it is her unusual monogamous relationship with Yūgiri that renders her situation quite unlike that of other noblewomen. It is

the image of her as an ordinary wife, comforting her own baby rather than relying on the wet nurse, that the text draws our attention to through the scene where she exposes her breast. *GM*, vol. 4, 59; Tyler, *Tale of Genji*, 702. For a discussion of the political function of breasts in medieval Japanese texts, see Kimura Saeko, *Chibusa wa dare no mono ka: Chūsei monogatari ni miru sei to kenryoku* (Tokyo: Shinyōsha, 2009).

26. For a discussion of the different significations of the term *miru*, see Nakanishi Susumu, "Miru: kodai teki chikaku," *Bungaku* 43:4 (1975): 479–489. Recent debates have shifted to questions of focalization and of the multiple perspectives that complicate the simple binary of seeing and being seen. See, for example, Takahashi Tōru, *Monogatari to e no enkinhō* (Tokyo: Perikansha, 1991); Mitani Kuniaki, "Monogatari bungaku no 'shisen': miru koto no imi arui wa 'katari' no kyōen," in Monogatari kenkyūkai, ed., *Monogatari kenkyū tokushū: shisen* (Tokyo: Shinjidaisha, 1988), 89–108.

27. *GM*, vol. 1, 278; Tyler, *Tale of Genji*, 157.

28. *GM*, vol. 1, 284; Tyler, *Tale of Genji*, 161.

29. *GM*, vol. 1, 117.

30. *GM*, vol. 4, 375–376; Tyler, *Tale of Genji*, 866–867.

31. For an interesting discussion of how this scene presents not only the multiple perspectives of Kaoru, Nakanokimi, and her ladies-in-waiting but also that of a narrating figure who also watches and presents to the reader another point of focalization from which to view the scene, see Edith Sarra, *Fictions of Femininity*, 241–242.

32. *GM*, vol. 5, 98; Tyler, *Tale of Genji*, 962.

33. *GM*, vol. 5, 100–101; Tyler, *Tale of Genji*, 963.

34. *GM*, vol. 5, 107; Tyler, *Tale of Genji*, 966.

35. *GM*, vol. 5, 298; Tyler, *Tale of Genji*, 1063.

36. *GM*, vol. 5, 300–301; Tyler, *Tale of Genji*, 1064–1065.

37. *GM*, vol. 5, 312; Tyler, *Tale of Genji*, 1065.

38. *GM*, vol. 5, 180; Tyler, *Tale of Genji*, 1003.

39. *GM*, vol. 5, 182; Tyler, *Tale of Genji*, 1004. The reference to the vulgarity of rapid speech recalls the parodic figure of the Lady of Ōmi whose rusticity renders her politically useless to her father, Tō no Chūjō.

40. See *GM*, vol. 5, 307; Tyler, *Tale of Genji*, 1067–1068.

41. *GM*, vol. 5, 190; Tyler, *Tale of Genji*, 1009.

42. *GM*, vol. 5, 202–203; Tyler, *Tale of Genji*, 1015.

43. See Norma Field, *Splendor of Longing*, 276.

44. *GM*, vol. 5, 210; Tyler, *Tale of Genji*, 1019.

45. *GM*, vol. 5, 223–226; Tyler, *Tale of Genji*, 1026–1027.

46. Norma Field's nice translation of the phrase *asobi tawaburetsutsu*. *GM*, vol. 5, 226; Field, *Splendor of Longing*, 276.

47. *GM*, vol. 5, 164; Tyler, *Tale of Genji*, 994.

48. See Margaret Childs, "Value of Vulnerability," 1059–1079.

49. See, for example, H. Mack Horton, "They Also Serve: Ladies-in-waiting in *The Tale of Genji*," in Edward Kamens, ed., *Approaches to Teaching Murasaki Shikibu's The Tale of Genji* (New York: Modern Language Association of America, 1993), 95–107. For a discussion of the role of serving women as surrogates in the *Tale of Genji*, see Mitamura Masako, "*Genji monogatari* ni okeru katashiro no mondai: meshūdo o kiten ni shite," in *Heianchō bungaku kenkyū* 3, no. 7 (December 1970): 11–21.

50. *GM*, vol. 1, 217; Tyler, *Tale of Genji*, 120.

51. *GM*, vol. 1, 260; Tyler, *Tale of Genji*, 146.

52. *GM*, vol. 1, 291; Tyler, *Tale of Genji*, 165.

53. *GM*, vol. 1, 354; Tyler, *Tale of Genji*, 647.

54. *GM*, vol. 5, 359–360; Tyler, *Tale of Genji*, 1096–1097.

55. Jijū is a title. See William McCullough and Helen Craig McCullough, *A Tale of Flowering Fortunes*, vol. 2 (Stanford, Calif.: Stanford University Press, 1980), 818–822, for a description of the various ranks and functions of ladies-in-waiting at court.

56. *GM*, vol. 5, 225; Tyler, *Tale of Genji*, 1027; Taifu here refers to Tokikata.

57. *GM*, vol. 1, 205; Tyler, *Tale of Genji*, 113.

58. *GM*, vol. 1, 208; Tyler, *Tale of Genji*, 115.

59. *GM*, vol. 1, 211–212; Tyler, *Tale of Genji*, 117.

60. *GM*, vol. 1, 221; Tyler, *Tale of Genji*, 122.

61. As Mitani argues, the Gen no Naishi incident should be read not as an isolated episode but rather as one that functions as a central link to Genji's affairs with Fujitsubo and Oborozukiyo, replicating in comic form the sexual and political transgressions committed by Genji as *irogonomi*. See Mitani Kuniaki, "Gen no naishi no monogatari," in Akiyama Ken, Kimura Masanori, and Shimizu Yoshiko, eds., *Kōza Genji monogatari no sekai*, vol. 2 (Tokyo: Yūhikaku, 1980), 212–235.

62. *GM*, vol. 1, 259; Tyler, *Tale of Genji*, 145.

63. This is from a poem in *Kokinshū* (892).

64. *GM*, vol. 1, 263; Tyler, *Tale of Genji*, 148.

65. Meredith McKinney, trans., *The Pillow Book by Sei Shōnagon* (London: Penguin Classics, 2006), 22.

66. Fujioka Tadaharu et al., eds. *Murasaki Shikibu nikki, in Izumi Shikibu nikki, Murasaki Shikibu nikki, Sarashina nikki, Sanuki no suke no nikki*, Nihon koten bungaku zenshū, no. 18 (Tokyo: Shōgakukan, 1971), 149–150. See also Bowring, *Murasaki Shikibu*, 145.

67. The layered aster-colored robe comes close to capturing the color of the bluebell, which is in season.

68. *GM*, vol. 1, 109–110; Tyler, *Tale of Genji*, 60.

69. *GM*, vol. 5, 297; Tyler, *Tale of Genji*, 1062–1063.

70. *GM*, vol. 5, 204; Tyler, *Tale of Genji*, 1066.

Chapter 4. Woman, Love, Poetry, and Enlightenment

1. The theme of the cold night and empty bed without the presence of the lover, to take just one example, is a familiar trope of *waka* poetry, and appears in verses composed by male and female poets alike. Izumi Shikibu's poem on this subject, anthologized in *Izumi Shikibu shū*, bears a strong family resemblance to Ki no Tomonori's verse in *Kokinshū*. However, her poem, *unlike* his, becomes a piece of evidence that confirms her passionate involvement in many love affairs, followed by the sense of personal loneliness, occasioned by their failure. Ki no Tomonori's poem in *Kokinshū*, 563, composed in the early tenth century reads:

Sasa no ha ni	Sharper than the frost
Oku shimo yori mo	That forms on leaves of bamboo grass
Hitori nuru	These clear, crisp nights
Wa ga koromode zo	Is the cold that penetrates
Saemasarikeru	My sleeves when I sleep alone.

Izumi Shikibu's poem in *Izumi Shikibu shū*, 67, echoes a very similar sentiment when she writes:

Neya no ue ni	Over my chamber
Shimo ya okuramu	Frost must now be gathering
Katashikeru	For from underneath
Shita koso itaku	This robe spread out without a mate
Saenoboru nare	There mounts a penetrating cold.

Trans. in Edwin Cranston, "The Dark Path: Images of Longing in Japanese Love Poetry," *Harvard Journal of Asiatic Studies* 35 (1975): 83.

2. Many scholars of Japanese classical texts have pointed to the dangers of reading poems as if they were guides to mapping the poet's real life. Richard Bowring argues that the scholarship on Murasaki Shikibu's poetic memoirs (*kashū*) "is plagued by an insistence on interpreting and dating poems according to what Murasaki's life was like, notions which themselves stem from the conventions of the work itself and of others like it." See Bowring, *Murasaki Shikibu: Her Diary and Poetic Memoirs,* 210. Richard Okada explores the vexed question of the relationship between biography and *waka* discourse to argue, in the context of the poetry of Lady Ise, that "The real life figure of Ise the 'author' does not become the 'origin' or 'source' of texts bearing her name; rather the texts or textuality 'create' the life and figure of the author," and that the author becomes an "effect" of the texts. See Richard H. Okada, *Figures of Resistance: Language, Poetry and Narrating in The Tale of Genji and Other Mid-Heian Texts* (Durham, N.C.: Duke University Press, 1991), 119.

3. For a tendency to read Akazome Emon as the exemplar of good wife and wise mother, see, for example, Umeno Kimiko, "Akazome Emon: ryōsai kenbo no kagami," *Kokubungaku kaishaku to kanshō* 65:8 (2000): 116–124. See also Watanabe Takeshi's "Akazome Emon: her poetic voice and her persona," *Waka Workshop, 2013,* paper 13, http://elischolar.library.yale .edu/waka2013 (accessed 05/03/2014) for a discussion of Akazome's poems and an attempt to read her poems against her biography as well as her function as a professional poet at court.

4. For debates about the authorship of the work, see Edwin Cranston, *The Izumi Shikibu Diary, A Romance of the Heian Court* (Cambridge, Mass.: Harvard University Press, 1969), 44–52. Cranston makes a case for seeing the work as "essentially an *uta monogatari,* a treatment by an unknown author of an important turning point in the life of a famous poet, using materials at least some of which were actually written by its central figure," 125.

5. For an exploration of the power of rhetoric in the diary, see John Wallace, "Reading the Rhetoric of Seduction in *Izumi Shikibu nikki,*" *Harvard Journal of Asiatic Studies* 58:2 (1998): 481–512. See also Janet Walker, "Poetic Ideal and Fictional Reality in the *Izumi Shikibu Nikki,*" *Harvard Journal of Asiatic Studies* 37:1 (June 1977): 135–182, and in particular 137–152, for a discussion of how the diary follows in the tradition of the *Kokinshū*'s stylization of the experience of love.

6. As John Wallace argues, "*Lady Izumi's Story* is very much about the game of love and how that game is played with well-timed and minutely crafted poems." See John Wallace, *Objects of Discourse: Memoirs by Women of Heian Japan* (Ann Arbor: Center for Japanese Studies, University of Michigan, 2005), 121.

7. I am drawing here on the insights provided by Mark Morris almost thirty years ago in "Waka and Form: Waka and History," *Harvard Journal of Asiatic Studies* 46:2 (December 1986):

551–610. As Morris puts it, "However broken your heart or happy your mood, whatever the birds might sing or frogs croak, if you were a writer of *waka,* its traditions and poetic code preceded you, preparing the things you would feel or experience, then providing words and forms by which to confirm its wisdom," 600.

8. See Roland Barthes, *Image—Music—Text,* trans. Stephen Heath (London: Fontana, 1977), 146.

9. Mark Morris makes much the same point in speaking about Ono no Komachi when he says that she "has been for eleven hundred years an effect produced by a handful of ninth-century waka texts, mediated through later tales and plays." See Morris, "Waka and Form," 561.

10. If we are to read these texts historically, the only possible response to them becomes finger-wagging disapproval of their "inaccuracies." In his reading of *Koshikibu,* for example, Keller Kimbrough, *Preachers, Poets, Women, and the Way,* 16–17, warns us that we should not believe the text when it tells us that Murasaki, Izumi, and Koshikibu are related as mother, daughter, and grandchild. In his view, "the assertion is a flagrant misrepresentation of historical fact—comical in its ludicrousness—and in this sense typical of the many ostensibly biographical works of its genre."

11. Fukutō Sanae, for example, argues that Izumi's life came to be distorted in medieval *setsuwa* and that the misrepresentations of her were a product of a moralistic patriarchal system. She argues that in an age where we aim for gender equality, it is necessary to sweep away the patriarchal, moralistic view of women such as Izumi presented in *setsuwa* and to make an effort to produce a true picture of these women, based on sources. Sanae, *Heian ōchō shakai no gendaa* (Tokyo: Kōsō shobō, 2005), 313.

12. Masaharu et al., *Murasaki shikibu nikki,* 309.

13. Bowring's translation. See Bowring, *Murasaki Shikibu,* 131.

14. How this material, which was meant to be personal and private, came to circulate more widely, and how, and in what form, it found its way into the more public poetic anthologies are questions that are themselves the subjects of some speculation.

15. Matsumura Hiroji and Yamanaka Yutaka, eds., *Eiga monogatari,* Nihon koten bungaku taikei 75 (Tokyo: Iwanami shoten, 1964), 136; Matsumura Hiroji, ed., *Ōkagami,* Nihon koten bungaku taikei 21 (Tokyo: Iwanami Shoten, 1960), 173; Helen Craig McCullough, trans., *Ōkagami, The Great Mirror: Fujiwara Michinaga (966–1027) and His Times* (Princeton, N.J.: Princeton University Press, 1980), 165–66.

16. I do not attempt here to cover the large corpus of literature that was generated in Izumi's name. Keller Kimbrough, *Preachers, Poets, Women, and the Way* has to date provided the most extensive discussion in English of the many stories that were created around Izumi Shikibu in the medieval period and their possible connections with temples and proselytizers. I am more interested in reading narratives about Izumi as "texts," and in this my approach is significantly different from the one he takes.

17. Many reasons have been offered for this change in the way *waka* came to be practiced. A nobility that had once possessed considerable political, social, and financial power, and that had taken its engagement with refined aesthetic pursuits for granted, now began to grow more sharply aware and self-conscious of its culture and sought to carve out for itself an exclusive domain in the areas of scholarship, literary writing, and the arts in general. The defense of *their* culture proved to be one effective way in which aristocrats maintained their superiority over the emergent warrior clans who had divested them of real power.

18. For a study and translations of *shakkyōka* in *Goshūishū*, see Robert E. Morrell, "The Buddhist Poetry of *Goshūishū*," *Monumenta Nipponica* 28:1 (1973): 87–100.

19. Konishi Jin'ichi, *Michi: chūsei no rinen, Nihon no koten* 3 (Tokyo: Kōdansha, 1975).

20. In her *Hosshin wakashū*, the Kamo priestess Senshi anticipated many of the debates that became de rigueur among *waka* theorists of the Kamakura period. As Edward Kamens puts it, "She may still be recognized as one of the important antecedents of those who argued that a capacity for composing waka is identical with the capacity for attaining enlightenment, that the 'way of Japanese poetry' and the 'way of the Buddha' are one and the same." Kamens, *The Buddhist Poetry of the Great Kamo Priestess: Daisaiin Senshi and "Hosshinwakashū"* (Ann Arbor: Center of Japanese Studies, University of Michigan, 1990), 74.

21. For a detailed account of the justification of poetry in Buddhist terms, see Rajyashree Pandey, *Writing and Renunciation in Medieval Japan*, 37–45.

22. Hisamatsu Sen'ichi, ed., *Korai fūteishō*, in *Karonshū, Chūsei no bungaku*, vol. 1 (Tokyo: Miai shoten, 1971), 119–120.

23. In the Kennin 1 (1201) section of his diary *Ienaga nikki*, Minamoto Ienaga (1170?–1234) records that the Cloistered Emperor Go-Toba lamented the fact that once the elderly women poets passed away there would be no one to take their place, and that it was for this reason that he invited young women poets such as Kunaikyō and the Daughter of Shunzei to participate in poetry events held at court. See *Minamoto Ienaga nikki*, in Ishida Yoshisada, ed., *Koten bunko*, 141 (Tokyo: Koten bunko, 1959), 90–94.

24. Minamoto no Toshiyori (1055–1129), known for his unconventional compositions, was the compiler of the fifth imperial anthology *Kin'yōshū* (1127). However, it required several amendments before being accepted by his patron, the ex-Emperor Shirakawa.

25. The poem Kintō refers to is:

tsu no kuni no	she should have beckoned him
koya to mo hito o	to her hut
iubeki ni	in the province of Tsu
hima koso nakere	but the thatched roof of reeds
ashi no yaebuki	left no crack from which to call

26.

kuraki yori	from darkness
kuraki michi ni zo	into the path of greater darkness
irinubeki	must I enter:
haruka ni terase	shine upon me from afar
yama no ha no tsuki	o moon above the mountain crest

This is Izumi's famous poem, which alludes to a passage in the *Lotus Sutra*: "Living beings undergo constant suffering and anguish / benighted, without teacher or guide / not realizing there is a way to end suffering, / not knowing how to seek emancipation. / Through the long night increasingly they follow evil paths, / reducing the multitude of heavenly beings; / from darkness they enter into darkness, / to the end never hearing the Buddha's name." Translated by Burton Watson, *The Lotus Sutra* (New York: Columbia University Press, 1993), 121. The poem, anthologized in *Shūishū* (A Collection of Gleanings, ca. 1005), was supposedly composed by Izumi on her deathbed, and sent to Priest Shōkū. Some scholars have argued, however, that since she is identified as Shikibu, daughter of Masamune, it is more likely that it was composed when she was only sixteen or seventeen years of age, before her marriage to Michisada. On this point, see Susan Klein, *Allegories of Desire* (Cambridge, Mass.: Harvard University Press, 2002), 31–33.

27. Hashimoto Fumio et al., eds., *Shunrai zuinō* in *Karonshū,* Nihon koten bungaku zenshū 86 (Tokyo: Shōgakukan, 2001), 237–238.

28. Sasaki Nobutsuna, ed., *Fukurozōshi,* in Nihon kagaku taikei, vol. 1 (Tokyo: Kazama shobō, 1956), 37. For a discussion of how female poets in *Fukurozōshi* become an ambivalent site for working out the relations between poetic authority and gender, see Rosalind Bundy, "Gendering the Court Woman Poet: Pedigree and Portrayal in *Fukurozōshi,*" *Monumenta Nipponica* 67:2 (2012): 201–238.

29. Hisamatsu Sen'ichi et al., eds., *Mumyōshō,* in Nihon koten bungaku taikei 65 (Tokyo: Iwanami shoten, 1961), 79–80.

30. Tayū, a poet of the late twelfth century, was lady-in-waiting to Impu Mon'in (1147–1216), eldest daughter of the Go-Shirakawa emperor, and is credited with a private collection of her own poems, *Impumon'in no Tayū shū* (ca. 1186–1187).

31. Kojijū, a contemporary of Tayū, was lady-in-waiting to Empress Fujiwara Tako. She had a private collection of poems, *Kojijū shū,* to her name.

32. Fujiwara no Toshinari no musume (Shunzei-kyō no musume), (ca. 1171–1254) or "Daughter of Toshinari" was in fact Toshinari's granddaughter, and a well-known poet of her times.

33. Kunaikyō (ca. 1185–1204), also called Wakakusa no Kunaikyō, was the daughter of Minamoto Moromitsu. Such was her devotion to poetry that she worked at it day and night; her early death was attributed to her obsessive focus on poetry composition.

34. Sen'ichi et al., *Mumyōshō,* 76–77.

35. For a detailed study of one famous medieval poet, the nun Abutsu, and of the centrality of poetry in the lives of Kamakura women, see Christina Laffin, *Rewriting Medieval Japanese Women.*

36. I am grateful to Robert Morrell for pointing out the centrality of the concept of *shiki* to Buddhist thought, and to the broader significations of the term that go beyond its association with "carnal love."

37. A collection of *setsuwa* authored by the priest Mujū Ichien (1226–1312). For a study of his life and a partial translation of the text, see Robert E. Morrell, *Sand and Pebbles (Shasekishū): The Tales of Mujū Ichien, A Voice for Pluralism in Kamakura Japan* (New York: State University of New York Press, 1985).

38. Watanabe Tsunaya, ed., *Shasekishū,* in Nihon koten bungaku taikei 85 (Tokyo: Iwanami shoten, 1976 [11th imprint]), 222–223. See also Yamada Shōzen, "Chūsei kōki ni okeru waka soku darani no jissen," *Indogaku bukkyōgaku kenkyū* 16:1 (December 1967): 290–292.

39. *Shasekishū,* 222–223.

40. A *chigo* was a youth between the ages of seven and fourteen who often resided in a temple and was in the service of a monk, who served as his mentor. In the brief period before he entered adulthood he could become the object of his master's affections, and the two often established sexual ties with one another. For a discussion of *chigo* in medieval narratives, see Margaret Childs, "*Chigo monogatari:* Love Stories or Buddhist Sermons?" *Monumenta Nipponica*

35:2 (1980): 127–151. See also Kimura Saeko, *Koi suru monogatari no homosekushuarite: Kyūtei shakai to kenryoku* (Tokyo: Seidosha, 2008), 149–181.

41. The poem the boy recites is:

te ni musubu	the moon's reflection
mizu ni yadoreru	resting in the water
tsuki kage wa	which I hold in my hand—
aru ka naki ka no	such is the world we live in
yo ni mo sumu ka na	for we know not if it is real

This is a poem that appears with minor variations in *Shūishū* and is attributed to Ki no Tsurayuki. It is of no consequence that the boy recites a poem that is not his own. Poems formed part of a shared cultural repertoire, and the ability to use them in appropriate contexts, rather than the expression of an authentic or original voice, was what was most valued.

42. Washio Junkei, ed., *Togano o Myōe shōnin denki*, in *Tōhō bukkyō sōsho*, vol. 5 (Tokyo: Tōhō bukkyō sōsho kankōkai, 1925), 287.

43. *Shasekishū*, 251.

44. Ibid., 233–234.

45. Ibid., 230–231.

46. Ibid., 234.

47. Kojima Noriyuki, *Kokinshū*, 4.

48. Nagasumi Yasuaki and Shimada Isao, eds., *Kokonchomonjū*, in Nihon koten bungaku taikei 84 (Tokyo: Iwanami shoten, 1966), 177–178.

49. Ibid., 177–178.

50. *Shasekishū*, 446.

51. Donald Philippi, trans. *Kojiki (Record of Ancient Matters)* (Tokyo: Tokyo University Press, 1968), 84.

52. W. G Aston, trans. *Nihongi: Chronicles of Japan from the Earliest Times to A.D. 697* (London: Allen and Unwin, 1957), 77.

53. Anne Allison, "Cutting the fringes: pubic hair at the margins of Japanese censorship laws," in Alf Hitebeitel and Barbara Miller, eds., *Hair: Its Power and Meaning in Asian Cultures* (New York: SUNY Press, 1998), 214.

54. Fukutō Sanae, *Heian chō no onna to otoko*, 88–92.

55. *Shasekishū*, 493.

56. *Shasekishū*, 493–494.

57. See *Shinsarugakuki* in Yamagishi Tokuhei, Takeura Rizō, Ienaga Saburō, and Ōsone Shōsuke, eds., *Kodai seiji shakai shisō*, Nihon shisō taikei, 8 (Tokyo: Iwanami shoten, 1979), 135–136.

58. *Shasekishū*, 445–446.

59. Ibid., 446–447.

60. For example, Mujū narrates the story of a young *chigo* who, resentful of his master, decides to attach himself to another temple. The master, discovering that the boy has forgotten his copy of *Shikashū* (Collection of Flowers of Words), returns the anthology to the boy together with the following poem:

ika ni shite	how is it that
kotoba no hana o	these flowers of words

<table>
<tr><td>nokoriken</td><td>remain</td></tr>
<tr><td>utsuroihateshi</td><td>in the heart of one</td></tr>
<tr><td>hito no kokoro ni</td><td>for whom the hues of love have faded?</td></tr>
</table>

The *chigo* is so moved and impressed by the poem that he returns to his former master. See *Shasekishū*, 230.

61. Fujii Takashi, *Jippon Ōgi* in *Chūsei koten no shoshi-gakuteki kenkyū: otogizōshi hen* (Osaka: Izumi Shoin, 1996, first published 1972), 325–340.

62. She uses the phrase *hito mo oto sezu* (no human voice sounds), which appears in the "Teacher of the Law" chapter of the *Lotus Sutra* in the following stanza: "If those who expound the Law / are alone in an empty and silent place / and in that stillness where no human voice sounds / they read and recite this sutra / at that time I will manifest / My pure and radiant body for them." Translated by Burton Watson, *Lotus Sutra*, 168.

63. *Shasekishū*, 488.

64. Ibid.

65. Kimbrough, *Preachers, Poets, Women, and the Way*, 44.

66. Ibid.

67. Shiba Kayono, "Chūsei setsuwashū ni egakareta Izumi Shikibu," *Kokubungaku kaishaku to kanshō* 60:8 (1995): 106–111, argues that Izumi and Dōmyō came to be associated with one another because of their connection with the *Lotus Sutra*.

68. Watanabe Tsunaya and Nishio Kōichi, eds., *Uji shūi monogatari*, Nihon koten bungaku taikei 27 (Tokyo: Iwanami shoten, 1977 [9th imprint]), 53–54.

69. See Kojima Yoshiyuki, "Izanagi, Izanami no kon'in," *Shūkyō kenkyū* 35:4 (1962): 15; translated in Hank Glassman, *The Face of Jizō: Image and Cult in Medieval Japanese Buddhism* (Honolulu: University of Hawai'i Press, 2012), 167. As Glassman argues, Buddhism "always remained deeply tied to the autochthonous, to old customs and beliefs anchored in particular to old places," and the bodhisattva Jizō became "a pivotal figure in this process of the incorporation of Buddhism into local cults," 167.

70. For a discussion of the gods of love, see Abe Yasurō, "Irogonomi no kami: Sae no Kami to Aihōshin," in Yamaori Tetsuo, ed., *Nihon no kami: Kami no shigen*, vol. 1 (Tokyo: Heibonsha, 1995), 132–172.

71. Kimbrough, *Preachers, Poets, Women, and the Way*, 89.

72. See *Izumi Shikibu* in Ōshima Takehiko, ed., *Otogizōshi shū*, Nihon koten bungaku zenshū 36 (Tokyo: Shōgakukan, 1974), 385–393.

73. Koizumi et al., eds., *Hōbutsushū, Kankyo no tomo, Hirazan kojin reitaku*, Shin nihon koten bungaku taikei 40 (Tokyo: Iwanami Shoten, 1993), 211–212.

74. The English renditions "courtesan," "geisha," "singing girl," "woman of pleasure," or "prostitute" do not adequately capture the many inflections of the term and its trajectory through Japanese history. The problem lies not simply with finding the mot juste. The English terms have their own genealogies and are embedded in the particular meanings that have come to be assigned to sexual activity within their own histories. The terms *asobi*, *asobime*, and *ukareme* were often used interchangeably with the word *yūjo*. I use the term *yūjo* to designate a professional class of women entertainers who excelled in artistic accomplishments, particularly in music, poetry, dancing, and the performance of sex.

75. Hitomi Tonomura, "Re-envisioning women in the Kamakura age," in Jeffrey P. Mass, ed., *The Origins of Japan's Medieval World: Courtiers, Clerics, Warriors, and Peasants in the Fourteenth Century* (Stanford, Calif.: Stanford University Press, 1997), 160.

76. Gotō Norihiko, "Yūjo to chōtei, kizoku: chūsei zenki no yūjotachi," in *Nihon no rekishi* 3: *Chūsei*, 1, *Shūkan asahi hyakka* (Tokyo: Asahi shinbunsha, 1985), 4–74.

77. To mention just a few: Amino Yoshihiko, *Chūsei no hinin to yūjo* (Tokyo: Akashi shoten, 1998); Fukutō Sanae, "Ukareme kara asobi e," in Joseishi sōgō kenkyūkai, ed., *Nihon josei seikatsushi, Genshi, kodai*, vol.1 (Tokyo: Tokyo daigaku shuppankai, 1990); Gorai Shigeru, "Chūsei josei no shūkyōsei to seikatsu," in Joseishi sōgō kenkyūkai, ed., *Nihon joseishi, Chūsei*, vol. 2 (Tokyo: Tokyo daigaku shuppankai), 1982; Saeki Junko, *Yūjo no bunkashi: Hare no onnatachi* (Tokyo: Chūō kōronsha, 1987); and Wakita Haruko, *Nihon chūsei joseishi no kenkyū: seibetsu yakuwari buntan to bosei, kasei, seiai* (Tokyo: Tokyo daigaku shuppankai, 2001).

78. Jacqueline Pigeot, *Femmes galantes, femmes artistes dans le Japan ancien, XIc—XIIIc siècle* (Paris: Editions Gallimard, 2003); Terry Kawashima, *Writing Margins;* Janet Goodwin, *Selling Songs and Smiles;* Michele Marra, "The Buddhist Mythmaking of Defilement: Sacred Courtesans of Medieval Japan"; Yung-hee Kim Kwon, "The Female Entertainment Tradition in Medieval Japan: The Case of *Asobi*," in *Performing Feminisms: Feminist Critical Theory and Theatre*, ed. Sue-Ellen Case (Baltimore, Md.: Johns Hopkins University Press, 1990); and Rajyashree Pandey, "Poetry, Sex, and Salvation."

79. Koizumi et al., *Hōbutsushū, Kankyo no tomo, Hirazan kojin reitaku*, 345–346.

80. Terry Kawashima, *Writing Margins*, 115, makes the same point when she argues that within the didactic framework of the text, "Tonekuro's story serves as evidence to support a teaching of the Daihōshaku Sutra," and that "[t]o emphasize the omnipotence of this teaching, it was convenient to stress her 'sinful habits' (especially from a Buddhist perspective), so that the message that even one who is as 'lowly' as this woman can be saved comes forth clearly."

81. Koizumi et al., *Hōbutsushū, Kankyo no tomo, Hirazan kojin reitaku*, 346.

82. *Kojidan*, 303–304. For a translation and detailed analysis of this story, see Kawashima, *Writing Margins*, 51–57. For a discussion of the different ways in which this narrative has been read, see Janet Goodwin's account in *Selling Songs and Smiles*, 112–115.

83. The Ten Worlds are the worlds of hell, of the hungry ghosts, of animals, of *asuras*, of humans, of celestial beings, of arhats, of the self-enlightened, of the bodhisattvas, and of the buddhas. Each of the ten worlds was seen as having an independent existence: an inhabitant of the human world, for example, might be reborn after death in the world of hell or the world of the celestial beings, depending on his past karma. Thus the human world was separate from the nine worlds. However, Tendai doctrine also conceived of each world as simultaneously containing within itself the other nine worlds. Thus one world was the ten worlds and the ten worlds were the hundred worlds.

84. See James Sanford, "The Abominable Tachikawa Skull Ritual," *Monumenta Nipponica* 46:1 (1991): 1–20; and Sasama Yoshihiko, *Sei no shūkyō: Shingon Tachikawaryū to wa nani ka* (Tokyo: Daiichi shobō, 1988).

85. My discussion of these medieval commentaries draws heavily on Susan Klein, *Allegories of Desire* (Cambridge, Mass.: Harvard University Press, 2002).

86. Klein, *Allegories of Desire*, 153.

87. Ibid., 154.

88. Ibid., 153–154.

89. Ibid., 157.

90. Ibid.

91. Ōshima Takehiko, ed., *Otogizōshi shū*, Nihon koten bungaku zenshū 36 (Tokyo: Shōgakukan, 1974), 127.

92. Ishikawa Tōru, "Muromachi jidai ni okeru Ise monogatari kyōju," in Tokue Gensei, ed., *Ise mongatari chū, Muromachi bungaku sanshū* (Tokyo: Miai shoten, 1987), 169–222.

93. Yokoyama Shigeru and Matsumoto Ryūshin, eds., *Jōruri monogatari,* in *Muromachi jidai monogatari, Koten bunko* 6 (Tokyo: Koten bunko, 1964), 292–333.

94. For a study of these narratives, see Ohnuma Reiko, *Head, Eyes, Flesh and Blood: Giving Away the Body in Indian Buddhist Literature* (New York: Columbia University Press, 2007).

95. Ruch, *Engendering Faith,* 194–195.

96. Keller Kimbrough, *Preachers, Poets, Women, and the Way,* 227.

97. Michele Marra, "The Buddhist Mythmaking of Defilement," 283.

98. Michele Marra, *Representations of Power: The Literary Politics of Medieval Japan* (Honolulu: University of Hawai'i Press, 1993), 99.

Chapter 5. "Meditating on the Impure Body"

1. For an incisive account of the inextricable links between figurative speech and the materiality of the body in Buddhist textual culture, see Charlotte Eubanks, *Miracles of Book and Body: Buddhist Textual Culture and Medieval Japan* (Berkeley and Los Angeles: University of California Press, 2011).

2. *Hosshinshū* is a collection of exemplary tales about monks and wandering holy men (*hijiri*) who reject Buddhist institutions as well as the secular world to follow their own eccentric course to enlightenment. Through these tales, Chōmei examines the conditions that are conducive to awakening the bodhi-mind (*hosshin*), which is the basis for enlightenment and for birth in the Pure Land. The text that forms the basis of this study is Miki Sumito, ed., *Hosshinshū* in *Hōjōki, Hosshinshū,* Shinchō nihon koten shūsei (Tokyo: Shinchōsha, 1976).

3. *Kankyo no tomo* is a text attributed to the Priest Keisei, who is said to have written the work for the edification of a noblewoman who commissioned the text. In the colophon to the text he addresses the work's intended reader as someone who "sits behind brocaded curtains." Written not long after the compilation of *Hosshinshū, Kankyo no tomo* is directly influenced by Chōmei's text. The text I have used here is Koizumi Hiroshi et al., eds., *Hōbutsushū, Kankyo no tomo, Hirasan kojin reitaku,* Shin nihon koten bungaku taikei 40 (Tokyo: Iwanami shoten, 1993). For a study of the connections between *Hosshinshū* and *Kankyo no tomo* in their treatment of *fujōkan,* with a particular focus on how these texts were shaped by the lives of Chōmei and Keisei, respectively, see Fujimoto Tokumei, "Aiyoku to fujōkan: *Hosshinshū* to *Kankyo no tomo* no hikaku," in *Chūsei setsuwa,* vol. 1, Nihon bungaku kenkyū taisei (Tokyo: Kokusho kankōkai, 1992), 71–81.

4. One of the four Āgama sutras (*Agongyō*) translated from Sanskrit into Chinese and which correspond to the Pali Nikāyas.

5. Liz Wilson, *Charming Cadavers: Horrific Figurations of the Feminine in Indian Buddhist Hagiographical Literature* (Chicago: University of Chicago Press, 1996), 50–51.

6. Ibid., 55. *Mahāprajnāparāmitopadesa,* a commentary on the Mahāprajnāpāramitā sutra, is attributed to Nagārjuna and was translated into Chinese by Kumārajiva.

7. Edward Conze, *Buddhist Meditation* (London: Allen and Unwin, 1956), 104–105.

8. Ibid., 104.

9. Ibid., 101.

10. Ibid., 96–100.

11. Ibid., 106.

12. Kathryn Blackstone, *Women in the Footsteps of the Buddha: Struggle for Liberation in the Therigāthā* (Richmond, Surrey, U.K.: Curzon Press, 1998), 63.

13. I.B. Horner, trans. *The Book of Discipline,* vol. 1 (London: Luzac and Co. Ltd, 1970), 36–37.

14. Ishida Mizumaro, ed., *Ōjōyōshū,* vol. 1 (Tokyo: Iwanami shoten, 1992), 55–62.

15. A *bhiksu* or monk who meditated on the impurity of the body and was so profoundly repelled by his own body that he hired the brahmin Mrgalandika to kill him.

16. Mizumaro, *Ōjōyōshū,* 62.

17. For a detailed study of the different pictorial traditions that grew around the theme of bodily decay, see Kanda Fusae, "Behind the Sensationalism: Images of a Decaying Corpse in Japanese Buddhist Art," *Art Bulletin* 87:1 (March 2005): 24–49.

18. For a study of *Kusōshi,* see James Sanford, "The Nine Faces of Death: Su Tung-po's *Kuzō-shi,*" *Eastern Buddhist* 21:2 (1988): 54–77. As Sanford points out, the Chinese poems came to be accompanied by *waka* poems, which captured in a different generic idiom the themes of the Chinese verses by Su Tung-po.

19. Kanda, "Behind the Sensationalism," 32.

20. Translated in Sanford, "Nine Faces of Death," 63. As Sanford points out, this text presents a sharp distinction between the Chinese poems, which betray a fascination with the more grotesque aspects of the *kusō* theme, and the *waka,* which "manage to intermix equal amounts of proper Buddhist sorrow for things passing in general and a more romantic and courtly sorrow for a particular, recently lost loved one."

21. Kanda points out that while the theme of evanescence stems from Buddhism, the sutras that talk about *fujōkan* do not link it with the theme of transience. See "Behind the Sensationalism," 33.

22. As Edgar Allan Poe once famously observed, "the death of a beautiful woman is unquestionably, the most poetical topic in the world." See "The Philosophy of Composition," in Gary Richard Thompson, ed., *Essays and Reviews* (New York: Literary Classics of the United States, 1984), 19.

23. Shirane, *Bridge of Dreams,* 70.

24. *GM,* vol. 3, 377.

25. *GM,* vol. 4, 457.

26. Jacqueline Stone, "Death," in Donald S. Lopez, ed., *Critical Terms for the Study of Buddhism* (Chicago: University of Chicago Press, 2005), 57.

27. Ibid., 71.

28. Field, *Splendor of Longing in the Tale of Genji,* 251; *GM,* vol. 4, 174.

29. Murasaki's death also resonates with a theme common to Japanese folktales, that of the "heavenly maiden," for like the heroine of *Taketori monogatari,* she is a beautiful woman who belongs to another realm, who descends on earth temporarily, brings joy to a young man, and then leaves the world to return to her spiritual home. Shirane, *Bridge of Dreams,* 128.

30. *GM,* vol. 4, 457.

31. Ibid., 23.

32. For a discussion of the use of the term *sarabou* in the *Genji,* see Matsui Kenji, "Kashiwagi no juku to shintai: Fukumari yuku mi, mi no fukami e," *Genji kenkyū* 2 (1997): 67–69.

33. Field, *Splendor of Longing in the Tale of Genji,* 257.

34. Aileen Gatten, "Death and Salvation in *Genji Monogatari,*" in Aileen Gatten and Anthony Hood Chambers, eds., *New Leaves: Studies and Translations of Japanese Literature in*

Honor of Edward Seidensticker (Ann Arbor: Center for Japanese Studies, University of Michigan, 1993), 20–24.

35. *GM,* vol. 2, 141.

36. Ibid., 142.

37. Mitamura Masako, "Genji monogatari no jendaa: nani gokoro nashi, uranashi no risoku," *Kokubungaku kaishaku to kanshō* 65:12 (2000): 119–126.

38. Royall Tyler describes it as a "violent fit of retching." Tyler, *Tale of Genji,* 176.

39. *GM,* vol. 1, 311.

40. Ibid., 312.

41. Ibid., 125.

42. Ibid., 126.

43. Ibid., 133.

44. For a detailed account of the influence of religious texts on Chōmei and Keisei's understanding of *fujōkan,* see Hirota Tetsumichi, "Fujōkan setsuwa no haikei," *Joshidai bungaku kokubun hen* (March 1983): 58–76.

45. *Kankyo no tomo,* 403–407. Translated in Rajyashree Pandey, "Desire and Disgust: Meditations on the Impure Body in Medieval Japanese Narratives," *Monumenta Nipponica* 60:2 (2005): 220–222.

46. *Shidai zenmon* is one of the abbreviated names for *Shazen haramitsu shidai hōmon,* composed by the Chinese T'ien-t'ai master Chih-i.

47. The sources for these two quotes are not known.

48. *Hosshinshū,* 328.

49. This description of the body draws on *Ōjōyōshū.*

50. *Hosshinshū,* 181–182.

51. Ibid., 205.

52. Ibid., 204–208. Translated in Rajyashree Pandey, "Suki and Religious Awakening: Kamo no Chōmei's Hosshinshū," *Monumenta Nipponica* 47:3 (Autumn, 1993): 306–308.

53. For a discussion and translation of tales of enlightenment connected to artistic practices, see Pandey, "Suki and Religious Awakening," 299–323.

54. This episode appears in *Ise monogatari.* When a man gives a poem to a certain lady in whom he has lost interest she responds with the following verse:

no to naraba	if it be a wild field
uzura to narite	then I shall be a quail
nakioran	calling plaintively—
kari ni dani ya wa	and surely you will at least
kimi wa kozaramu	come briefly for a hunt.

The man, we are told, is so deeply moved by the poem that he decides not to leave her. Watanabe Minoru, ed., *Ise Monogatari,* Shinchō nihon koten shūsei (Tokyo: Shinchōsha, 1976), 134–135.

55. A reference to Empress Teishi, daughter of Fujiwara Michitaka and wife of Emperor Ichijō; she died at the age of twenty-four. The poem, with the headnote explaining that she composed it and left it behind for Ichijō, appears in *Goshūishū* (536):

yomosugara	if you have not forgotten
chigiri shi koto o	the pledge we made

wasurezu ba	through the night,
koinu namida no	eager am I to see
iro zo yukashiki	the color of the tears of love

The story of their love is found in works such as *Hosshinshū, Eiga Monogatari, Hōbutsushū,* and *Jikkinshō.*

56. An anonymous poem found in the lamentations section of *Kokinshū* (858):

koe o dani	it grieves my spirit
kikade wakaruru	to take leave without hearing
tama yori mo	the sound of your voice;
naki toko ni nemu	even sadder am I to think of you sleeping alone
kimi zo kanashiki	in the bed you once shared with me

57. The fire and smoke that rose from Mt. Fuji were popular symbols of the ardor and passion of a person in love.

58. The tears that drench the sleeves of lovers are compared to the waves at Kiyomi Barrier. Kiyomigaseki was a common *utamakura,* or pillow word for Suruga province.

59. The area at the foot of Higashiyama in Kyoto where, from Heian times, the dead were cremated.

60. A commonly used metaphor for a cremation ground.

61. Prince Atsuyoshi, son of Emperor Uda, died at the age of forty-four in 930.

62. The poem appears in *Kokinshū* (857), but in this version it is the Fifth Imperial Princess who dies rather than Atsuyoshi. The mountain mist is a metaphor here for the smoke that rises from the funeral pyre.

63. This sentence bears a close resemblance to the opening lines of *Makura no sōshi.*

64. *Kankyo no tomo,* 416–418. Translated in Pandey, "Women, Sexuality, and Enlightenment," 335–337.

65. Paula Richman, "Gender and Persuasion: The Portrayal of Beauty, Anguish, and Nurturance in an Account of a Tamil Nun," in Ignacio Cabezon, ed., *Buddhism, Sexuality, and Gender* (New York: New York University Press, 1992), 119.

66. Ibid., 118.

67. See Wilson, *Charming Cadavers,* 163; also Daniel H. Ingalls, trans., *An Anthology of Sanskrit Poetry* (Cambridge, Mass.: Harvard University Press, 1965), 164.

68. Lee Siegel, *Fires of Love, Waters of Peace: Passion and Renunciation in Indian Culture* (Honolulu: University of Hawai'i Press, 1983), 104.

69. *GM,* vol. 5, 378.

70. LaMarre, *Uncovering Heian Japan,* 166.

71. This practice served to signal a range of feelings and intentions—granting permission, warning or advising someone, expressing joy or repentance, and so on.

72. *Hosshinshū,* 179–182. Translated in Pandey, "Desire and Disgust," 227–229.

73. Based on a passage from *Ōjōyōshū.*

74. Sadamoto reached the fifth rank, lower grade, and was appointed governor of Mikawa. In 986 he became a disciple of Jakushin (the famous scholar of Chinese Yoshishige no Yasutane) and took the religious name Jakushō. He also received religious instruction from Genshin. He travelled to China, where he stayed for thirty-two years, dying there in 1034.

75. *Hosshinshū,* 98–99. Translated in Pandey, "Desire and Disgust," 230–231.

76. See Yamada Yoshio et al., eds., *Konjaku monogatari shū*, vol. 4, 19:10, 86–87. Versions of this story also appear in *Uji shūi monogatari* and *Ima kagami*.

77. In another tale in Yamada Yoshio et al., eds., *Konjaku monogatari shū*, vol. 4, 19:2, 57–60, for example, a young man who loses his wife keeps her body for ten days and is gripped by such unbearable longing for her that he opens up her coffin and peeps in only to discover that:

> Her long hair had fallen out and lay scattered about on the pillow; her adorable eyes were empty sockets like the joints of a branch that had been broken off from the tree; her body had acquired a blackish yellow color and was frightening to behold; the bridge of her nose had collapsed and the nostrils were wide open; her lips had become like thin paper and had shrunk so that her white teeth looked as if the upper and lower teeth had become enmeshed. The stench from her body penetrated his mouth and nose and it was so unspeakably foul that he felt as if he might choke and suffocate.

We are told that the repulsive sight of the disintegration of his wife's body, and the foul odor it emitted, led Munemasa to take the tonsure and to retreat to Tōnomine to become the disciple of the holy man Zōga.

78. *Kankyo no tomo*, 403–407. For a complete translation of this story, see Pandey, "Desire and Disgust," 229–230.

79. Another possible explanation for the more "diluted" rendering of *fujōkan* in Japanese narratives, and one that I do not explore here, might be that these texts reflect Mahāyāna devotional practices that promised eternal bliss in one of the Buddha's paradises rather than the more austere emphasis on *annita*, or nonself, and the goal of nirvana, or complete cessation, as theorized in Theravāda texts.

80. Kumārajīva (350–409) was a member of the Indian aristocracy. He took the tonsure together with his mother at the age of seven. He translated many Buddhist scriptures, most famously the *Lotus Sutra*, into Chinese.

81. This statement, attributed to Kūkai, the founder of the esoteric Shingon sect at Mount Koya, is a quotation from *Kusōshi*.

82. *Kankyo no tomo*, 411.

83. Ibid., 412.

84. In my analysis of such tales, I have focused on how generic conventions travel, and how these narratives are part of intra- and intertextual conversations across genres. For another approach, which convincingly argues that narratives on *fujōkan* are to be understood not purely at the discursive level but as producing material effects, transforming and reconfiguring the body through a correlation between text and flesh, see Eubanks, *Miracles of Body and Book*, 97–133.

85. *Hosshinshū*, 199–204. For a translation of this tale, see Pandey, "Suki and Religious Awakening," 304–306.

86. It is striking that in the two illustrations of hell, one Japanese and the other Thai, the Japanese image of the hell into which men with sensual desires fall is markedly different from its Thai counterpart in that the lady who is the object of the lustful male gaze is fully clothed in many-layered robes. She exudes courtly grace, beauty, and refinement, which are in no way connected to her corporeality. This is in sharp contrast with the figures of the Thai couple who fall into hell due to their uncontrollable sexual desires: here, both the man and woman are naked, reaching out for each other's bodies. See Barbara Ruch, *Mō hitotsu no chūseizō: bikuni, otogizōshi, raise* (Tokyo: Shibunkaku shuppan, 1991), 1.

Epilogue

1. Vanita Seth, "Difference with a Difference," 83.

2. Yamada Yoshio et al., eds., *Konjaku monogatari shū*, vol. 5, 29:39, 205–207.

3. Ibid., 29:40, 207–208.

4. Michelle Osterfeld Li, *Ambiguous Bodies: Reading the Grotesque in Japanese Setsuwa Tales* (Stanford, Calif.: Stanford University Press, 2009), 110.

5. Ibid., 114.

6. For a discussion of the term *totsugu* and for alternate readings of some of the tales I have considered, see Hitomi Tonomura, "Black Hair and Red Trousers: Gendering the Flesh in Medieval Japan," *American Historical Review* 99:1 (February 1994): 129–154.

7. Yamada Yoshio et al., eds., *Konjaku monogatari shū*, vol. 5, 24:9, 205–207.

8. Yamada Yoshio et al., eds., *Konjaku monogatari shū*, vol. 4, 26:2, 410–412.

9. Ashis Nandy, "A Report on the Present State of Health of the Gods and Goddesses in South Asia," *Postcolonial Studies* 4:2 (July 2001): 126.

10. Jacqueline Stone, *Original Enlightenment,* 179.

11. See Komatsu Shigemi, ed., *Gaki zōshi, Jigoku zōshi, Yamai zōshi,Kusō shi emaki,* in Nihon no emaki 7 (Tokyo: Chūō kōronsha, 1994), 2–37.

12. For a discussion of *gaki,* see Barbara Ruch, "Coping with Death: Paradigms of Heaven and Hell and the Six Realms in Early Literature and Painting," in James Sanford, William LaFleur, and Masatoshi Nagatomi, eds., *Flowing Traces: Buddhism in the Literary and Buddhist Arts of Japan* (Princeton, N.J.: Princeton University Press, 1992), 124–127.

13. Yamada Yoshio et al., eds., *Konjaku monogatari shū*, vol. 5, 28:25, 93.

14. Ibid., 28:26, 93–94.

15. Ibid., 28:43, 126–129.

16. *Kamuri* was a formal hat worn while in attendance at the imperial court.

17. *Eboshi* was a form of headgear worn by aristocratic men as daily wear.

Bibliography

Abe Yasurō. "Irogonomi no kami: Sae no kami to aihōshin." In *Nihon no kami 1, Kami no shigen,* edited by Yamaori Tetsuo. Tokyo: Heibonsha, 1995.

Ali, Daud. *Courtly Culture and Political Life in Early Medieval India.* Cambridge: Cambridge University Press, 2004.

Allison, Anne. "Cutting the fringes: pubic hair at the margins of Japanese censorship laws." In *Hair: Its Power and Meaning in Asian Cultures,* edited by Alf Hitebeitel and Barbara Miller. New York: SUNY Press, 1998.

Ames, Roger. "The Meaning of the Body in Classical Chinese Philosophy." In *Self as Body in Asian Theory and Practice,* edited by Thomas P. Kasulis, Roger Ames, and Wimal Dissanayake. New York: SUNY Press, 1993.

Amino Yoshihiko. *Chūsei no hinin to yūjo.* Tokyo: Akashi shoten, 1998.

Aston, W. G., trans. *Nihongi: Chronicles of Japan from the Earliest Times to A.D 697.* London: Allen and Unwin, 1957.

Barcan, Ruth. *Nudity: A Cultural Anatomy.* Oxford: Berg, 2004.

Barlow, Tani. "Theorizing Women: Funü, Guoja, Jiating." In *Body, Subject and Power in China,* edited by Angela Zito and Toni Barlow. Chicago: University of Chicago Press, 1994.

Barthes, Roland. *Image—Music—Text,* translated by Stephen Heath. London: Fontana, 1977.

Berger, John. *Ways of Seeing.* London: Penguin Books, 1972.

Blackstone, Kathryn. *Women in the Footsteps of the Buddha: Struggle for Liberation in the Therigāthā.* Richmond, Surrey, U.K.: Curzon Press, 1998.

Bonfante, Larissa. "Nudity as Costume in Classical Art." *American Journal of Archaeology* 93, no. 4 (1989).

Bordo, Susan. *The Flight to Objectivity: Essays on Cartesianism and Culture.* New York: SUNY Press, 1987.

Bowring, Richard. *Murasaki Shikibu: Her Diary and Poetic Memoirs.* Princeton, N.J.: Princeton University Press, 1982.

Brower, Robert, and Earl Miner. *Japanese Court Poetry.* Stanford, Calif.: Stanford University Press, 1961.

Bundy, Rosalind. "Gendering the Court Woman Poet: Pedigree and Portrayal in *Fukurozōshi.*" *Monumenta Nipponica* 67, no. 2 (2012).

Butler, Judith. *Bodies that Matter: On the Discursive Limits of 'Sex.'* New York: Routledge, 1993.

———. *Gender Trouble: Feminism and the Subversion of Identity.* London: Routledge, 1990.

Bynum, Caroline. "The Body of Christ in the Later Middle Ages: A Reply to Leo Steinberg." *Renaissance Quarterly* 39, no. 3 (1986).

———. "The Female Body and Religious Practice in the Later Middle Ages." In *Fragments for a History of the Human Body,* pt. 1, edited by Michael Feher, with Ramona Naddaff and Nadia Tazi. New York: Zone Books, 1989.

———. "Why all the Fuss about the Body? A Medievalist's Perspective." In *Beyond the Cultural Turn: New Directions in the Study of Society and Culture,* edited by Victoria Bonnell and Lynn Hunt. Berkeley: University of California Press, 1999.

Cavanaugh, Carol. "Text and Textile: Unweaving the Female Subject in Heian Writing." *Positions* 3, no. 6 (1996).

Chakrabarty, Dipesh. *Provincializing Europe: Postcolonial Thought and Historical Difference.* Princeton, N.J.: Princeton University Press, 2000.

Childs, Margaret. "*Chigo monogatari:* Love Stories or Buddhist Sermons?" *Monumenta Nipponica* 35, no. 2 (1980).

———. "The Value of Vulnerability: Sexual Coercion and the Nature of Love in Japanese Court Literature." *Journal of Asian Studies* 58, no. 4 (November 1999).

Chino Kaori. "Chōshō suru kaiga: Obusumasaburō emaki ni miru jendaa to kurasu." In *Onna to otoko no jikū: Nihon josei shi saikō,* edited by Ito Seiko and Kōno Nobuko, vol. 2. Tokyo: Fujiwara shoten, 1996.

Clark, Kenneth. *The Nude: A Study in Ideal Form.* Bollingen Series. New York: Pantheon Books, 1956.

Conze, Edward. *Buddhist Meditation.* London: Allen and Unwin, 1956.

Cranston, Edwin, trans. "The Dark Path: Images of Longing in Japanese Love Poetry." *Harvard Journal of Asiatic Studies* 35 (1975).

———. *The Izumi Shikibu Diary, A Romance of the Heian Court.* Cambridge, Mass.: Harvard University Press, 1969.

———, trans. *A Waka Anthology: Grasses of Remembrance,* vol. 2, pt. B. Stanford, Calif.: Stanford University Press, 2006.

Cryle, Peter. *The Telling of the Act: Sexuality as Narrative in 18th and 19th Century France.* Newark: University of Delaware Press, 2001.

Ebersole, Gary. "Long black hair like a seat cushion: Hair symbolism in Japanese popular religion." In *Hair: Its Power and Meaning in Asian Cultures,* edited by Alf Hiltebeitel and Barbara Miller. Albany, N.Y.: SUNY Press, 1998.

Eubanks, Charlotte. *Miracles of Book and Body: Buddhist Textual Culture and Medieval Japan.* Berkeley and Los Angeles: University of California Press, 2011.

Eustace, Nicole, Eugine Lean, Julian Livingstone, Jan Plamper, William Reddy, and Barbara Rosenwein. "AHR Conversation: The Historical Study of Emotions." *American Historical Review* 117, no. 5 (December 2012).

Faure, Bernard. *The Power of Denial: Buddhism, Purity, and Gender.* Princeton, N.J.: Princeton University Press, 2003.

Featherstone, Michael, Mike Hepworth, and Bryan S. Turner, eds. *The Body: Social Process and Cultural Theory.* London: Sage, 1991.

Field, Norma. *The Splendor of Longing in the Tale of Genji*. Princeton, N.J.: Princeton University Press, 1987.

Foucault, Michel. "Nietzsche, Genealogy, History." In *Language, Counter-Memory, Practice: Selected Essays and Interviews by Michel Foucault*, edited by Sherry Simon and Donald F. Bouchard, translated by Donald F. Bouchard. Ithaca, N.Y.: Cornell University Press, 1977.

————. *Power/Knowledge: Selected Interviews and Other Writings 1972-1977*, edited by Colin Gordon. New York: Pantheon Books, 1972.

————. *The Will to Knowledge: History of Sexuality*, vol. 1, translated by Robert Hurley. London: Penguin Books, 1998. First published in French in 1976.

Fujii Takashi. *Jippon Ōgi* in *Chūsei koten no shoshigakuteki kenkyū: otogizōshi hen*. Osaka: Izumi shoin, reprinted 1996.

Fujimoto Tokumei. "Aiyoku to fujōkan: *Hosshinshū* to *Kankyo no tomo* no hikaku." In *Chūsei setsuwa*, vol. 1, Nihon bungaku kenkyū taisei. Tokyo: Kokusho kankōkai, 1992.

Fujioka Tadaharu, Nakano Kōichi, Inukai Kiyoshi, and Ishii Fumio, eds. *Murasaki Shikibu nikki, in Izumi Shikibu nikki, Murasaki Shikibu nikki, Sarashina nikki, Sanuki no suke no nikki*. Nihon koten bungaku zenshū 18. Tokyo: Shōgakukan, 1971.

Fukutō Sanae. *Heian chō no onna to otoko*. Tokyo: Chūō kōronsha, 1995.

————. "Ukareme kara asobi e." In *Nihon josei seikatsushi*, vol. 1, *Genshi, kodai*, edited by Joseishi sōgō kenkyūkai. Tokyo: Tokyo daigaku shuppankai, 1990.

Furth, Charlotte. *A Flourishing Yin: Gender in China's Medical History, 960-1665*. Berkeley and Los Angeles: University of California Press, 1999.

Gatten, Aileen. "Death and Salvation in *Genji Monogatari*." In *New Leaves: Studies and Translations of Japanese Literature in Honor of Edward Seidensticker*, edited by Aileen Gatten and Anthony Hood Chambers. Ann Arbor: Center for Japanese Studies, University of Michigan, 1993.

Glassman, Hank. *The Face of Jizō: Image and Cult in Medieval Japanese Buddhism*. Honolulu: University of Hawai'i Press, 2012.

GM. See Yanai Shigeshi, Murofushi Shinsuke, Ōasa Yūji, Suzuki Hideo, Fujii Sadakazu, and Imanishi Yūichirō, eds., *Genji monogatari*.

Goodwin, Janet. *Selling Songs and Smiles: The Sex Trade in Heian and Kamakura Japan*. Honolulu: University of Hawai'i Press, 2007.

Gorai Shigeru. "Chūsei josei no shūkyōsei to seikatsu." In *Nihon joseishi*, edited by Joseishi sōgō kenkyūkai, vol. 2, *Chūsei*. Tokyo: Tokyo daigaku shuppankai, 1982.

Gotō Norihiko. "Yūjo to chōtei, kizoku: chūsei zenki no yūjotachi." In special issue *Nihon no rekishi 3, Chūsei 1-3, Asobi, kugutsu, shirabyōshi*. Shūkan asahi hyakka. Tokyo: Asahi shinbunsha, 1985.

Gross, Rita. *Buddhism after Patriarchy: A Feminist History, Analysis and Reconstruction of Buddhism*. New York: SUNY Press, 1993.

Grosz, Elizabeth. *Volatile Bodies: Toward a Corporeal Feminism*. Bloomington: Indiana University Press, 1994.

Hasegawa Masaharu and Imanishi Yūichi, eds. *Murasaki Shikibu nikki*. In *Tosa nikki, Kagerō nikki, Izumi shikibu nikki, Sarashina nikki*. Shin nihon koten bungaku taikei 24. Tokyo: Iwanami shoten, 1989.

Hashimoto Fumio, Ariyoshi Tamotsu, and Fujiwara Haruo, eds. *Shunrai zuinō.* In Nihon koten bungaku zenshū 87, *Karonshū.* Tokyo: Shōgakukan, 2001.

Hay, John. "Is the Body Invisible in Chinese Art?" In *Body, Subject, and Power in China,* edited by Angela Zito and Tani Barlow. Chicago: University of Chicago Press, 1994.

Hirota Tetsumichi. "Fujōkan setsuwa no haikei." *Joshidai bungaku kokubun hen,* March 1983.

Hisamatsu Sen'ichi, ed. *Korai fūteishō.* In *Karonshū, Chūsei no bungaku,* vol. 1. Tokyo: Miai shoten, 1971.

Hisamatsu Sen'ichi and Nishio Minoru, eds. *Mumyōshō.* In Nihon koten bungaku taikei 65. Tokyo: Iwanami shoten, 1961.

Hollander, Ann. *Seeing Through Clothes.* Berkeley: University of California Press, 1993.

Horner, I. B., trans. *The Book of Discipline,* vol. 1. London: Luzac and Co. Ltd., 1970.

Horton, H. Mack. "They Also Serve: Ladies-in-waiting in *The Tale of Genji.*" In *Approaches to Teaching Murasaki Shikibu's The Tale of Genji,* edited by Edward Kamens. New York: Modern Language Association of America, 1993.

Horton, Sarah. *Living Buddhist Statues in Early Medieval and Modern Japan.* New York: Macmillan, 2007.

Hosokawa Ryōichi. "Sairinji sōji to ama." In *Shirīzu josei to Bukkyō, Sukui to oshie* 4, edited by Ōsumi Kazuo and Nishiguchi Junko. Tokyo: Heibonsha, 1989.

Hurvitz, Leon, trans. *Scripture of the Lotus Blossom of the Fine Dharma (The Lotus Sutra).* New York: Columbia University Press, 1976.

Ikeda Shinobu. "The Image of Women in Battle Scenes: 'Sexually' Imprinted Bodies." In *Gender and Power in the Japanese Visual Field,* edited by Joshua Mostow, Norman Bryson, and Maribeth Graybill. Honolulu: University of Hawai'i Press, 2003.

Ingalls, Daniel H., trans. *An Anthology of Sanskrit Poetry.* Cambridge, Mass.: Harvard University Press, 1965.

Inukai Wataru. "Genji monogatari no utsukushi to rōtashi." *Heian bungaku kenkyū* 11, no. 1 (1953).

Ishida Mizumaro. "Bikuni kaidan: ama no tokui na seikaku." In *Musashino joshi daigaku kiyō* 18 (1978).

———, ed. *Ōjōyōshū,* vol. 1. Tokyo: Iwanami shoten, 1992.

Ishida Yoshimisa, ed. *Minamoto Ienaga nikki.* In *Koten bunko* 141. Tokyo: Koten bunko, 1959.

Ishikawa Tōru. "Muromachi jidai ni okeru Ise Monogatari kyōju." In *Ise mongatari chū, Muromachi bungaku sanshū,* edited by Tokue Gensei. Tokyo: Miai shoten, 1987.

Johnson, Walter. "On Agency." *Journal of Social History* 37, no. 1 (2003).

Jullien, François. *The Impossible Nude: Chinese Art and Western Aesthetics.* Translated by Maey de la Cuardia. Chicago: University of Chicago Press, 2007.

———. *The Propensity of Things: Towards a History of Efficacy in China.* Translated by Janet Lloyd. New York: Zone Books, 1995.

Kamens, Edward. *The Buddhist Poetry of the Great Kamo Priestess: Daisaiin Senshi and "Hosshinwakashū,"* Ann Arbor: Center of Japanese Studies, University of Michigan, 1990.

———. "Dragon-Girl, Maidenflower, Buddha: The Transformation of a Waka Topos, 'The Five Obstructions.'" *Harvard Journal of Asiatic Studies* 53, no. 2 (1993).

Kanda Fusae. "Behind the Sensationalism: Images of a Decaying Corpse in Japanese Buddhist Art." *Art Bulletin* 87, no. 1 (March 2005).

Kasulis, Thomas P. "The Body—Japanese Style." In *Self as Body in Asian Theory and Practice,* edited by Thomas P. Kasulis, Roger Ames, and Wimal Dissanayake. New York: SUNY Press, 1993.

Katsuura Noriko. "Tonsure Forms for Nuns: Classification of Nuns according to Hairstyles." In *Engendering Faith: Women and Buddhism in Premodern Japan*, edited by Barbara Ruch. Ann Arbor: Center for Japanese Studies, University of Michigan, 2002.

Kawashima, Terry. *Writing Margins: The Textual Construction of Gender in Heian and Kamakura Japan.* Cambridge, Mass., and London: Harvard University Press, 2001.

Kawazoe Fusae. "Hikaru Genji no shintai to yosōi o megutte." *Murasaki* 34, no. 12 (1997).

———. *Sei to Bunka no Genji monogatari: Kaku onna no tanjō.* 2nd ed. Tokyo: Tsukuma shobō, 1999.

Kim Kwon, Yung-hee. "The Female Entertainment Tradition in Medieval Japan: The Case of *Asobi.*" In *Performing Feminisms: Feminist Critical Theory and Theatre*, edited by Sue-Ellen Case. Baltimore, Md.: Johns Hopkins University Press, 1990.

Kimbrough, Keller. *Preachers, Poets, Women, and the Way: Izumi Shikibu and the Buddhist Literature of Medieval Japan.* Ann Arbor: Center for Japanese Studies, University of Michigan, 2008.

Kimura Saeko. *Chibusa wa dare no mono ka: Chūsei monogatari ni miru sei to kenryoku.* Tokyo: Shinyōsha, 2009.

———. "Genji monogatari to feminizumu." *Kokubungaku kaishaku to kanshō* 73, no. 5 (2008).

———. *Koi suru monogatari no homosekushuarite: Kyūtei shakai to kenryoku.* Tokyo: Seidosha, 2008.

Klein, Susan. *Allegories of Desire.* Cambridge, Mass.: Harvard University Press, 2002.

Koizumi Hiroshi, Yamada Shōzen, Kojima Takayuki, and Kinoshita Motoichi, eds. *Hōbutsushū, Kankyo no tomo, Hirazan kojin reitaku.* Shin nihon koten bungaku taikei 40. Tokyo: Iwanami shoten, 1993.

Kojima Naoko. "Hikaru Genji no shintai to sei: Ōchō monogatarishi kara." In *Ōchō no sei to shintai: itsudatsu suru monogatari,* edited by Kojima Naoko. Tokyo: Shinwasha, 1996.

Kojima Noriyuki, ed. *Kokin wakashū.* Shin nihon koten bungaku taikei 5. Tokyo: Iwanami shoten, 1989.

Kojima Yoshiyuki. "Izanagi, Izanami no kon'in." *Shūkyō kenkyū* 35, no. 4 (1962).

Komashaku Kimi. *Murasaki no messēji.* Asahi Sensho 422. Tokyo: Asahi shuppan, 1991.

Komatsu Shigemi, ed. *Gaki zōshi, Jigoku zōshi, Yamai zōshi, Kusō shi emaki.* Nihon emaki taisei 7. Tokyo: Chūō kōronsha, 1994.

Konishi Jin'ichi. *A History of Japanese Literature, The Archaic and Ancient Ages,* vol. 1. Translated by Aileen Gatten and Nicolas Teele. Princeton, N.J.: Princeton University Press, 1984.

———. *Michi: chūsei no rinen, Nihon no koten* 3. Tokyo: Kodansha, 1975.

Kristof, Nicholas D. "Kyoto Journal; The Nun's Best Seller: 1,000-Year-Old Love Story." *New York Times,* May 28, 1999.

Kuriyama Shigehisa. "The imagination of the body and the history of embodied experience: the case of Chinese views of the viscera." In *The Imagination of the Body and the History of Bodily Experience.* Kyoto: International Research Center for Japanese Studies, 2001.

Laffin, Christina. *Rewriting Medieval Japanese Women: Politics, Personality, and Literary Production in the Life of Nun Abutsu.* Honolulu: University of Hawai'i Press, 2013.

LaFleur, William. *The Karma of Words: Buddhism and the Literary Arts in Medieval Japan.* Berkeley: University of California Press, 1983.

LaMarre, Thomas. *Uncovering Heian Japan: An Archaeology of Sensation and Inscription.* Durham, N.C.: Duke University Press, 2000.

Laqueur, Thomas. *Making Sex: Body and Gender from the Greeks to Freud.* Cambridge, Mass.: Harvard University Press, 1990.

Li, Michelle Osterfeld. *Ambiguous Bodies: Reading the Grotesque in Japanese Setsuwa.* Stanford, Calif.: Stanford University Press, 2009.

Mahmood, Saba. "Feminist Theory, Embodiment, and the Docile Agent: Some Reflections on the Egyptian Islamic Revival." *Cultural Anthropology* 16, no. 2 (May 2001).

Malik, Kenan. *The Meaning of Race: Race, History and Culture in Western Society.* New York: New York University Press, 1996.

Marra, Michele. *The Aesthetics of Discontent: Politics and Reclusion in Medieval Japanese Literature.* Honolulu: University of Hawai'i Press, 1991.

———. "The Buddhist Mythmaking of Defilement: Sacred Courtesans of Medieval Japan." *Journal of Asian Studies* 52, no. 1 (1993).

———. *Representations of Power: The Literary Politics of Medieval Japan.* Honolulu: University of Hawai'i Press, 1993.

Massumi, Brian. *Parables for the Virtual: Movement, Affect, Sensation.* Durham, N.C.: Duke University Press, 2002.

Matsui Kenji. "Kashiwagi no juku to shintai: Fukumari yuku mi, mi no fukami e." *Genji kenkyū* 2 (1997).

Matsumura Hiroji, ed. *Ōkagami.* Nihon koten bungaku taikei 21. Tokyo: Iwanami shoten, 1960.

Matsumura Hiroji and Yamanaka Yutaka, eds., *Eiga monogatari.* Nihon koten bungaku taikei 75. Tokyo: Iwanami shoten, 1964.

Matsumura Seichi. "Genji monogatari no rōtashi." *Kokugo to kokubun* 42, no. 6 (1965).

McCullough, Helen Craig, trans. *Kokin Wakashū: The First Imperial Anthology of Japanese Poetry.* Stanford, Calif.: Stanford University Press, 1985.

———, trans. *Ōkagami, The Great Mirror: Fujiwara Michinaga (966–1027) and His Times.* Princeton Library of Asian Translations. Princeton, N.J.: Princeton University Press, 1980.

McCullough, William, and Helen Craig McCullough. *A Tale of Flowering Fortunes.* 2 vols. Stanford, Calif.: Stanford University Press, 1980.

Meeks, Lori. "Buddhist Renunciation and the Female Life Cycle: Understanding Nunhood in Heian and Kamakura Japan." *Harvard Journal of Asiatic Studies* 70, no. 1 (2010).

Miki Sumito, ed. *Hosshinshū* in *Hōjōki, Hosshinshū*. Tokyo: Shinchōsha, 1983 [6th reprint].

Miles, Margaret. *Carnal Knowing: Female Nakedness and Religious Meaning in the Christian West*. Boston: Beacon Press, 1989.

Mitamura Masako. "*Genji monogatari* ni okeru katashiro no mondai: meshūdo o kiten ni shite," *Heianchō bungaku kenkyū* 3, no. 7 (December 1970).

———. "*Genji monogatari* no jendaa: nani gokoro nashi, uranashi no risoku." *Kokubungaku kaishaku to kanshō* 65, no. 12 (2000).

———. "Kurokami no *Genji monogatari*: manazashi to tezawari kara." *Genji kenkyū* 1 (April 1996).

———. "Yūgiri monogatari no jendaa kisei: osanasa, wakawakashisa to iu hihan kara." *Kokubungaku kaishaku to kanshō* 69, no. 8 (2004).

Mitamura Masako, Kawazoe Fusae, and Matsui Kenji, eds. *Genji kenkyū*. 10 vols. Tokyo: Kanrin shobō, 1996–2005.

Mitani Kuniaki. "Gen no naishi no monogatari." In *Kōza Genji monogatari no sekai*, vol. 2. Edited by Akiyama Ken, Kimura Masanori, and Shimizu Yoshiko. Tokyo: Yūhikaku, 1980.

———. "Monogatari bungaku no 'shisen': miru koto no imi arui wa 'katari' no kyōen." In *Monogatari kenkyū tokushū: shisen*, edited by Monogatari kenkyūkai. Tokyo: Shinjidaisha, 1988.

Miyake, Lynne. "The Tosa Diary: In the Interstices of Gender and Criticism." In *The Woman's Hand: Gender and Theory in Japanese Women's Writing*, edited by Paul Schalow and Janet Hunter. Stanford, Calif.: Stanford University Press, 1996.

Morrell, Robert E. "The Buddhist Poetry of *Goshūishū*." *Monumenta Nipponica* 28, no. 1 (1973).

———. *Sand and Pebbles (Shasekishū): The Tales of Mujū Ichien, A Voice for Pluralism in Kamakura Japan*. New York: State University of New York Press, 1985.

Morris, Ivan. *The World of the Shining Prince: Court Life in Ancient Japan*. Oxford: Oxford University Press, 1964.

Morris, Mark. "Desire and the Prince: New Work on *Genji Monogatari*." *Journal of Asian Studies* 49, vol. 2 (1990).

———. "Waka as Form: Waka as History." *Harvard Journal of Asiatic Studies* 46, no. 2 (1986).

Mostow, Joshua. "National Erotics, Gender and Representations of Sexuality in Heian Japan." Unpublished paper.

Mostow, Joshua, Norman Bryson, and Marybeth Graybill, eds. *Gender and Power in the Japanese Visual Field*. Honolulu: University of Hawai'i Press, 2003.

Nagasumi Yasuaki and Shimada Isao, eds. *Kokonchomonju*. Nihon koten bungaku taikei 84. Tokyo: Iwanami shoten, 1966.

Nakanishi Susumu. "Miru: kodai teki chikaku." *Bungaku* 43, no. 4 (1975).

Nandy, Ashis. "A Report on the Present State of Health of the Gods and Goddesses in South Asia." *Postcolonial Studies* 4, no. 2 (July 2001).

Nead, Lynda. *The Female Nude: Art, Obscenity, and Sexuality*. London and New York: Routledge, 1992.

Nietzsche, Friedrich. *The Will to Power*. Translated by W. Kaufmann. New York: Random House, 1968.

Ohnuma Reiko. *Head, Eyes, Flesh, and Blood: Giving Away the Body in Indian Buddhist Literature*. New York: Columbia University Press, 2007.

Okada, Richard H. *Figures of Resistance: Language, Poetry and Narrating in The Tale of Genji and Other Mid-Heian Texts*. Durham, N.C.: Duke University Press, 1991.

Ōshima Takehiko, ed. *Izumi Shikibu*. In *Otogizōshi shū*. Nihon koten bungaku zenshū 36. Tokyo: Shōgakukan, 1974.

———, ed. *Otogizōshi shū, Nihon koten bungaku zenshū*, vol. 36. Tokyo: Shōgakukan, 1974.

Pandey, Rajyashree. "Desire and Disgust: Meditations on the Impure Body in Medieval Japanese Narratives." *Monumenta Nipponica* 60, no. 2 (Summer 2005).

———. "Poetry, Sex and Salvation: The 'Courtesan' and the Noblewoman in Medieval Japanese Narrative." *Japanese Studies* 24, no. 1 (May 2004).

———. "Suki and Religious Awakening: Kamo no Chōmei's *Hosshinshū*." *Monumenta Nipponica* 47, no. 3 (Autumn 1993).

———. "Women, Sexuality and Enlightenment: *Kankyo no tomo*." *Monumenta Nipponica* 50, no. 3 (Autumn 1995).

———. *Writing and Renunciation in Medieval Japan: The Works of the Poet-Priest Kamo no Chōmei*. Ann Arbor: Center for Japanese Studies, University of Michigan, 1998.

Perniola, Mario. "Between Clothing and Nudity." In *Fragments for a History of the Human Body*, pt. 4, edited by Michael Feher, with Ramona Naddaff and Nadia Tazi. New York: Zone Books, 1989.

Philippi, Donald, trans. *Kojiki (Record of Ancient Matters)*. Tokyo: Tokyo University Press, 1968.

Phillips, Kim. *Medieval Maidens: Young Women and Gender in England 1270–1540*. Manchester: Manchester University Press, 2003.

Pigeot, Jacqueline. *Femmes galantes, femmes artistes dans le Japan ancien, XIc—XIIIc siècle*. Paris: Editions Gallimard, 2003.

Plugfelder, Gregory. *Cartographies of Desire: Male-Male Sexuality in Japanese Discourse 1600–1950*. Berkeley: University of California Press, 1999.

———. "Strange Fates, Sex, Gender, and Sexuality in *Torikaebaya Monogatari*." *Monumenta Nipponica* 47, no. 3 (Autumn 1992).

Poe, Edgar Allan. "The Philosophy of Composition." In *Essays and Reviews*, edited by Gary Richard Thompson. New York: Literary Classics of the United States, 1984.

Richman, Paula. "Gender and Persuasion: The Portrayal of Beauty, Anguish, and Nurturance in an Account of a Tamil Nun." In *Buddhism, Sexuality, and Gender*, edited by Ignacio Cabezon. New York: New York University Press, 1992.

Riley, Denise. *'Am I that Name?': Feminism and the Category of 'Women' in History*. Minneapolis: University of Minnesota Press, 1988.

Rosenfeld, John. *Portraits of Chōgen: The Transformation of Buddhist Art in Early Medieval Japan*. Leiden: Brill, 2011.

Ruch, Barbara. "Coping with Death: Paradigms of Heaven and Hell and the Six Realms in Early Literature and Painting," in *Flowing Traces: Buddhism in the Literary and*

Visual Arts of Japan, edited by James Sanford, William LaFleur, and Masatoshi Nagatomi. Princeton, N.J.: Princeton University Press, 1992.

———, ed. *Engendering Faith: Women and Buddhism in Premodern Japan.* Ann Arbor: Center for Japanese Studies, University of Michigan, 2002.

———. *Mō hitotsu no chūseizō: bikuni, otogizōshi, raise.* Tokyo: Shibunkaku shuppan, 1991.

———. "The Other Side of Culture." In *The Cambridge History of Japan,* vol. 3, edited by Kozo Yamamura. Cambridge: Cambridge University Press, 1990.

Saeki Junko. *Yūjo no bunkashi: Hare no onnatachi.* Tokyo: Chūō kōronsha, 1987.

Sanford, James. "The Abominable Tachikawa Skull Ritual." *Monumenta Nipponica* 46, no. 1 (1991).

———. "The Nine Faces of Death: Su Tung-po's *Kuzō-shi.*" *Eastern Buddhist* 21, no. 2 (1988).

Santangelo, Paolo. "The language of body as repulsive/seductive language: the case of the literati in late Imperial China." In *The Imagination of the Body and the History of Bodily Experience,* edited by Kuriyama Shigehisa. Kyoto: International Research Center of Japanese Studies, 2001.

Sarra, Edith. *Fictions of Femininity: Literary Inventions of Gender in Japanese Court Women's Memoirs.* Stanford, Calif.: Stanford University Press, 1999.

Sasaki Nobutsuna, ed. *Fukurozōshi.* Nihon kagaku taikei 1. Tokyo: Kazama shobō, 1956.

Sasama Yoshihiko. *Sei no shūkyō: Shingon Tachikawa ryū to wa nani ka.* Tokyo: Daiichi shobō, 1988.

Sawday, Jonathan. *The Body Emblazoned: Dissection and the Human Body in Renaissance Culture.* London and New York: Routledge, 1995.

Schultz, James. *Courtly Love, the Love of Courtliness, and the History of Sexuality.* Chicago: University of Chicago Press, 2006.

Scott, Joan Wallach. "The Evidence of Experience." In *Practicing History: New Directions in Historical Writing after the Linguistic Turn,* edited by Gabrielle Spiegel. New York: Routledge, 2005.

———. "'Gender' A Useful Category of Historical Analysis." In *Feminism and History, Oxford Readings in Feminism,* edited by Joan Wallach Scott. Oxford: Oxford University Press, 1996.

Seidensticker, Edward G., trans. *The Tale of Genji.* London: Penguin Books, 1976.

Seldon, Mark. "Tales of Shen and Xin: Body-Person and Heart-Mind in China during the last 150 Years." In *Fragments for a History of the Human Body,* pt. 4, edited by Michael Feher, with Ramona Naddaff and Nadia Tazi. New York: Zone Books, 1989.

Seth, Sanjay. "Reason or Reasoning? Clio or Siva?" *Social Text* 78 (2004).

Seth, Vanita. "Difference with a Difference: Wild Men, Gods and Other Protagonists." *Parallax* 9, no. 4 (2003).

Shiba Kayono. "Chūsei setsuwashū ni egakareta Izumi Shikibu." *Kokubungaku kaishaku to kanshō* 60, no. 8 (1995).

Shilling, Chris. *The Body and Social Theory.* 2nd ed. London: Sage, 2003.

———. *The Body in Culture, Technology and Society.* London: Sage, 2004.

Shirane Haruno. *The Bridge of Dreams: A Poetics of The Tale of Genji.* Stanford, Calif.: Stanford University Press, 1987.

———. ed. *Envisioning the Tale of Genji: Media, Gender, and Cultural Production*. New York: Columbia University Press, 2008.

———. *Japan and the Culture of the Four Seasons: Nature, Literature, and the Arts*. New York: Columbia University Press, 2012.

Siegel, Lee. *Fires of Love, Waters of Peace: Passion and Renunciation in Indian Culture*. Honolulu: University of Hawai'i Press, 1983.

Stone, Jacqueline. "Death." In *Critical Terms for the Study of Buddhism*, edited by Donald S. Lopez. Chicago: University of Chicago Press, 2005.

Takahashi Tōru. *Monogatari to e no enkinhō*. Tokyo: Perikansha, 1991.

Takeda Sachiko. "Ifuku de yominaosu nihonshi: dansō to ōken."*Asahi Sensho* 601. Tokyo: Asahi shinbunsha, 1998.

Tanabe, Willa Jane. "The Persistence of Self as Body and Personality in Japanese Buddhist Art." In *Self as Image in Asian Theory and Practice*, edited by Roger Ames, Wimal Dissanayake, and Thomas P. Kasulis. New York: SUNY Press, 1994.

Thurman, Robert A. F., trans. *The Holy Teaching of Vimalakīrti: A Mahāyāna Scripture*. University Park and London: Pennsylvania State University Press, 1976.

Toda Akiyoshi. "Izumi Shikibu zō no henyō: setsuwa kara no manazashi." *Hikakubunka* 11 (2003).

Tonomura Hitomi. "Black Hair and Red Trousers: Gendering the Flesh in Medieval Japan." *American Historical Review* 99, no. 1 (February 1994).

———. "Coercive Sex in the Medieval Japanese Court: Lady Nijō's Memoir." *Monumenta Nipponica* 61, no. 3 (Autumn 2006).

———. "Re-envisioning women in the Kamakura age." In *The Origins of Japan's Medieval World: Courtiers, Clerics, Warriors, and Peasants in the Fourteenth Century*, edited by Jeffrey P. Mass. Stanford, Calif.: Stanford University Press, 1997.

Turner, Bryan. *The Body and Society*. Blackwell: Oxford University Press, 1984.

Tyler, Royall. "Lady Murasaki's Erotic Entertainment: The Early Chapters of the Tale of Genji." *East Asian History* 12 (December 1996).

———. "Marriage, Rank and Rape in *The Tale of Genji*." *Intersections: Gender, History and Culture in the Asian Context* 7 (March 2000).

———, trans. *The Tale of Genji*. New York: Viking Press, 2001.

Umeno Kimiko. "Akazome Emon: ryōsai kenbo no kagami." *Kokubungaku kaishaku to kanshō* 65, no. 8 (2000).

Vieillard-Baron, Michel. "Male? Female? Gender confusion in classical poetry (waka)." *Cipango-French Journal of Japanese Studies* 2 (2013).

Wakita Haruko. *Nihon chūsei joseishi no kenkyū: seibetsu yakuwari buntan to bosei, kasei, seiai*. Tokyo: Tokyo daigaku shuppankai, 2001.

Wakita Haruko, Ryūichi Narita, Anne Walthall, and Hitomi Tonomura. "Appendix: Past Developments and Future Issues in the Study of Women's History in Japan: A Bibliographical Essay." In *Women and Class in Japanese History*, edited by Hitomi Tonomura, Anne Walthall, and Wakita Haruko. Ann Arbor: Center for Japanese Studies, University of Michigan, 1999.

Walker, Janet. "Poetic Ideal and Fictional Reality in the *Izumi Shikibu Nikki*." *Harvard Journal of Asiatic Studies* 37, no. 1 (1977).

Wallace, John. *Objects of Discourse: Memoirs by Women of Heian Japan.* Ann Arbor: Center for Japanese Studies, University of Michigan, 2005.

———. "Reading the Rhetoric of Seduction in *Izumi Shikibu nikki.*" *Harvard Journal of Asiatic Studies* 58, no. 2 (1998).

Washio Junkei, ed. *Togano o Myōe shōnin denki,* in *Tōhō bukkyō sōsho,* vol. 5. Tokyo: Tōhō bukkyō sōsho kankōkai, 1925.

Watanabe Minoru, ed. *Ise Monogatari.* Tokyo: Shinchōsha, 1976.

Watanabe Takeshi. "Akazome Emon: her Poetic Voice and her Persona." *EliScholar—A Digital Platform for Scholarly Publishing at Yale,* 2013. Text is available online: http://elischolar.library.yale.edu/waka2013 (accessed 5/03/2014).

Watanabe Tsunaya, ed. *Shasekishū.* Nihon koten bungaku taikei 85. 11th imprint. Tokyo: Iwanami shoten, 1976.

Watanabe Tsunaya and Nishio Kōichi, eds. *Uji shūi monogatari.* Nihon koten bungaku taikei 27. 9th imprint. Tokyo: Iwanami shoten, 1977.

Watson, Barton, trans. *The Lotus Sutra.* New York: Columbia University Press, 1993.

Wilson, Liz. *Charming Cadavers: Horrific Figurations of the Feminine in Indian Buddhist Hagiographical Literature.* Chicago: University of Chicago Press, 1996.

Yamada Shōzen. "Chūsei kōki ni okeru waka soku darani no jissen." *Indogaku bukkyōgaku kenkyū* 16, no. 1 (December 1967).

Yamada Yoshio, Yamada Tadao, Yamada Hideo, and Yamada Toshio, eds. *Konjaku monogatari shū.* Nihon koten bungaku taikei 5. Tokyo: Iwanami shoten, 1979–1980.

Yamagishi Tokuhei, Takeura Rizō, Ienaga Saburō, and Ōsone Shōsuke, eds. *Shinsarugakuki* in *Kodai seiji shakai shisō.* Nihon shisō taikei 8. Tokyo: Iwanami shoten, 1979.

Yanai Shigeshi, Murofushi Shinsuke, Ōasa Yūji, Suzuki Hideo, Fujii Sadakazu, and Imanishi Yūichirō, eds. *Genji monogatari.* Shin koten bungaku taikei, vols. 1–5. 4th ed. Tokyo: Iwanami shoten, 2001.

Yoda, Tomiko. *Gender and National Literature: Heian Texts in the Construction of Japanese Modernity.* Durham, N.C.: Duke University Press, 2004.

Yokoyama Shigeru and Matsumoto Ryūshin, eds. *Jōruri monogatari,* in *Muromachi Jidai Monogatari, Koten bunko 6.* Tokyo: Koten bunko, 1964.

Yoshida Kazuhiko. "The Enlightenment of the Dragon King's Daughter in the Lotus Sutra." In *Engendering Faith: Women and Buddhism in Premodern Japan,* edited by Barbara Ruch. Ann Arbor: Center for Japanese Studies, University of Michigan, 2002.

Yuhara Miyoko. *Ōchō monogatari bungaku in okeru yoshibi no kenkyū.* Tokyo: Yūseido, 1988.

Index

Page numbers in boldface type refer to illustrations.

Abutsu, 164n.57

aesthetics interpretation, 55–57, 169n.3

Aesthetics of Discontent (Marra), 169n.3

agency: in Buddhism, 24, 26–30, 150; identity and, 24, 56, 164n.58; scholarship on, 163n.48; tonsure and, 27. *See also* subjection

aging: as decaying of beauty, 136–137; of Gen no Naishi, 76–77; hair and, 45, 47, 49, 54; in *Hosshinshū,* 132–133; *irogonomi* and, 77, 101–102; status and, 53–54. *See also* death and dying; youth

aiyoku, 150. *See also* desire

Akashi Lady, 41–43, 53

Akazome Emon, 82–83, 90–91

Akazome Emon shū, 82–83

Ali, Daud, 165n.2

Amaru, 137, 138

amasogi, 48, 168n.52. *See also* hair

Amaterasu Ōmikami, 99

Ame no Uzume, 99

Ames, Roger, 159n.11

Amida Buddha, 49, 108, 110–111, 115, 143

amorous relationships. *See* relationships

angry spirit. *See ikiryō*

Anguttara Nikāya, 120, 122

animals, 21–22, 149–156

Aoi, 40, 45, 129, 141

aristocratic body in *Genji,* 13–14, 32

Ariwara no Narihira, 107, 113, 114

Ashuku Buddha, 116

asobi, 110–111, 179n.74. *See also yūjo*

Atsumichi, Prince, 83, 86

Atsuyoshi, Prince, 134, 184n.61

attachment, 52, 146, 150–151. *See also aiyoku;* desire; love and religious awakening

attraction, 2–3. *See also* beauty

awakening. *See* love and religious awakening

Ban Dainagon emaki, 13–14, **15**

Barcan, Ruth, 34

Barlow, Tani, 162n.39

Barthes, Roland, 84

beauty: bodhisattvas and, 24; of Genji, 37, 40–41, 57–58; of nuns, 136–137; robes and the body, 42–45; transparent robes and, 58, 59, 61, 66–67, 70; *vs.* ugliness, 43, 167n.37. *See also* body

Berger, John, 165n.7

bestiality, 150. *See also* human/animal sexuality

biblical references to the body, 34, 165n.7

biographical textuality, 82–84, 173n.1, 174n.2, 175nn.9–11

biological category of woman: body discourse and, 10–11, 12, 14–15, 18–19, 158n.4; in Buddhism, 22–23; in *waka,* 162n.42. *See also* woman/women

bisexuality, 59–60, 171n.17, 171n.19. *See also* gender; sexuality

bleedings, 160n.23

bodhisattvas, 24, 113–114, 115

About the Author

Rajyashree Pandey is Reader in Asian Studies at the Politics department of Goldsmiths, University of London. She received her education in India, the United Kingdom, the United States, and Australia and has taught in many academic institutions across the world. She is the author of *Writing and Renunciation in Medieval Japan: The Works of the Poet-Priest Kamo no Chōmei* (1998). She has also published articles in a wide range of journals from *Monumenta Nipponica* to *Postcolonial Studies* on medieval Japanese literature and Buddhism as well as on sexuality and Japanese popular culture.